LINDSAY WINCHERAUK is an author, journalist, and one-time bartender; he loves writing about the world as he sees it. He was a contributing writer to 24 Hours Vancouver. He co-authored a book titled: SEED'S SKETCHY RELATIONSHIP THEORIES – A GUIDE TO THE PERILS OF DATING (HOW NOT TO BECOME A BAR REGULAR) (2004).

FUN FACTS: Lindsay quarterbacked high school, junior, and university football teams, winning city, provincial, and national championships. He holds the record for the longest touchdown pass in Canadian junior football league history, 108 yards. Amazingly, he's blind in one eye.

www.lindsaywincherauk.com

COVER DESIGN BY: Joyce InHwa Seo

Fit into the picture @ #ibelong

→ → →

Luc—
Enjoy the trip into my life!

Lindsy

Dedication: Part 1

I dedicate this book to **THE NEW ME**—the one I discovered while writing the book. Not that there was anything wrong with the old me. I think he was a pretty good guy. You will get to know him as you flip through the pages. I hope you like him, at least cheer for him.

I've just been informed: "You are not supposed to dedicate your book to yourself."

I will take heed of my new found wisdom.

In the spirit of thankfulness, I'd like to dedicate this book to anyone, and everyone, who helped pick me up, dust me off and encouraged me to never give up during this exhilarating ride through my life (I mention many of you in the acknowledgements). Without this collection of wonderful characters in my life, well, I don't know where I'd be today.

THANK YOU!
Together we can make the world a kinder place!

Before you flip the page and dive into my life, let me take you off-tangent for a moment:

At work one day, an employee, JR, came up to me and asked, "Lindsay, have you ever noticed how many white guys are dating Asians?"

To which I replied, "No, I haven't JR, but have you ever noticed how many white guys are dating Germans?"

He stared back at me, blankly.

Lindsay Wincherauk

DRIVING IN REVERSE

THE LIFE I ALMOST MISSED

AUSTIN MACAULEY PUBLISHERS™

LONDON • CAMBRIDGE • NEW YORK • SHARJAH

A CIP catalogue record for this title is available from the British Library.

ISBN 9781786935113 (Paperback)
ISBN 9781786935120 (E-Book)
www.austinmacauley.com

First Published (2017)
Austin Macauley Publishers Ltd.
25 Canada Square
Canary Wharf
London
E14 5LQ

CONTENTS

	PREFACE	9
1		13
	LETTERS TO ED	13
2		31
	FOUNDATION	31
3		49
	THE BIG C	49
4		63
	GOING THROUGH	63
5		69
	THE WORLD OF V*I*CE	69
6		81
	LOVE *&* A TROPICAL BEACH	81
7		95
	SUPPORT NETWORK	95
8		121
	↑D*R*UGS↑	121
9		127
	~~TRASH~~ TRISH	127
10		141
	FREE FALL	141
11		151
	COLLAPSE	151
12		165
	TRANSITION	165
~~13 14~~ 15		173
	ESCAPE	173
16		215
	REBIRTH	215
17		253
	THE TRUTH WILL SET YOU FREE	253
18		277
	HOME	277
19		305
	WHAT MATTERS	305

PREFACE

What happens when you learn that your life was never your own?
- Seed

Welcome to the story of my life.

I penned my story in two months in one-take, commencing in April 2006, after a publisher at a "Sell Your Story Forum" in Vancouver requested to see my book. My dear friend Wes persuaded me to pitch my life story at the event. I was astonished to attract the attention of the panel of critics and the audience. I must admit, my presentation was outstanding: "How often does a man discover, sixteen years after putting both his parents to rest in their graves, that they weren't his parents after all!"

And that wasn't even the most shocking part of my story.

My manuscript notes at the time consisted of 160 words scribbled in a travel diary my good friend Dave had given me before we headed on an EPIC 31 DAY *ESCAPE* to Europe in 2003. The year my world was rocked when I discovered the truth about my identity.

I wrote the story in a fever of excitement, letting bits and pieces fly from keyboard onto the screen. Skits from bar scenes, hotels, and wild characters we met during our travels got mixed in with the story about my "dark family secret." I titled my book ***RUSSIANS CLOWNS & DRAG QUEENS - SEED'S IDENTITY TOUR.*** I thought this title, like the trip, was EPIC! I printed a copy of my manuscript, put it in an envelope and placed it in the mail. I became overwhelmed with a sense of great accomplishment. The publisher returned a polite rejection.

The rejection stung. I lost sight of the fact my memoir had been REQUESTED by a publisher, a word every author longs to hear. So instead of reworking my one-take-manuscript, I did what many an author drowning in insecurity would do: I decided to write a different book.

I needed a concept. For some unknown reason, the name Ed sprang to mind and gave me a wild idea for a book. My idea was to mail a series of bizarre, mostly comedic, letters, to a roster of randomly chosen people in North America, all named Ed: seven Ed's and one Ellen, Ellen DeGeneres.

In the letters, I would ask their help with solving trivial or absurd problems, like how to fix the weather. Writing these letters to Ed gave me a way to avoid the risk of opening myself to judgement by revealing the truth about my life. I figured: twenty or so odd letters could turn into a cutting-edge, chortle-worthy, deliciously-original: book.

Over the next few days, I cranked out the first batch of letters and sent them to my roster of Ed's. I signed the letters with the name "Seed," a nickname my friends had given me. I sent the letters without a return address. The letter to Ellen probably died in her gatekeeper's trash bin.

On the day I started typing the next round of letters to Ed, everything suddenly changed. That dreary Monday morning, I had watched a man die in a car accident on my way to work. Part of my job involved driving construction workers to job sites for a labour agency. On my first drive of the day, I transported a suicidal tool-belt-equipped carpenter to his job. He frightened me by confessing his plan to commit suicide if his life didn't magically turn around by his birthday, a mere few weeks away.

I tried to help him get to the root of his problems, but to no avail. This man's downward spiral blasted a light on in my mind. Hearing his story made me realise I desperately needed to tell my own story. I knew it was crucial to return to my jettisoned manuscript and delve into my past to piece together the missing parts of myself. My early family life haunted me now more than ever.

That night, I began revising my original manuscript. Much like my life, my book was chaotic – totally out of order. Writing down random memories enabled me to do exactly, what I needed to do to survive! After my foundation had collapsed, I needed to find a way to express my emotions. Most important: I needed to redefine who I was by looking at what I once thought to be true and making sense of what it had become.

While I was working on my memoir, my life didn't stop. Every day new discoveries lay around each corner, discoveries that needed a place in the manuscript. So, the story of my past and present life—blended together. Ed took on a new role as my friend and confidant. I began to write to Ed about what was going on in my life while sorting through the pieces of my manuscript. The letters found their way into my book in CHAPTER 1. I also pasted family letters, comic skits, and opinion editorials into my story as I struggled to make sense of it all. Clipping together these pieces of my life allowed the manuscript to morph into a book that was still scattered but more cohesive.

I began shopping my manuscript to agents and publishers, only to have it rejected...and rejected...and rejected. I set my book aside. Months later, I picked it up and revised it again. The process followed a pattern: revise, set it aside; months later, pick it up again, revise, set it aside.

The years drifted by, but I never gave up on my book. In 2014, I was invited to attend a publisher's workshop in Vancouver with six other authors. When I presented my story, the group was riveted. The consensus: "powerful voice" and "an important story to share".

After the workshop, I was ready to put the final polish on my story—or so I thought. Regardless of the compelling content of my story, everyone who read my manuscript said it lacked focus. In my defence: I was fond of quoting a line from Senior Edward Bloom (in the movie *Big Fish*):

Most men, they'll tell you a story straight through. It won't be complicated, but it won't be interesting either.

My memoir was without question interesting—but too chaotic.

I was referred to the editor Kendra Langeteig, based in Bellingham, Washington, just a short hop from Vancouver. I was lucky to find an editor who appreciated what I was trying to do by writing my memoir in such an unconventional way. When I began to write my memoir I wasn't aiming for a traditional narrative. My life was far from traditional.

Still in the midst of reading your book, finding it provocative and playful, edgy, disturbing and disruptive—

"Disruptive"—the word delighted me! Kendra understood why I didn't want to tell my story straight, but "with a twist."

With Kendra's help and encouragement, another light went on. I found a way to play with my timeline and splice together scenes from different parts of my life. I also wanted my readers to be involved in the process of constructing my story. Ed plays that role in my "Letters to Ed." After serving as my confidant in CHAPTER 1, he drifts away and morphs into Every Reader. When you enter CHAPTER 2, "Foundation," Ed essentially becomes YOU: the reader!

The wild and crazy story I tell in this book – *The truth that set me free* – is more than the story of my own life. It is LARGER than me. It will resonate with every reader who has ever faced a life-altering identity challenge. As much as this story is about me, it is also about EVERYONE. My story is about surviving as the underdog. It's about being dealt cards filled with trauma. It is about falling to the depths of despair when discovering a life-shattering truth about yourself, and climbing out of the gutter like a new person, cleansed and stronger than ever before.

I believe: with every step in life we arrive at two doors. The door on the left leads to misery. The door on the right leads to happiness. Maybe we are destined to pick the doors we pick. My life lessons have taught me I have a choice. I could have chosen to continue spiralling downward, losing myself in misery, dragging everyone down with me. But instead, I selected the door on the right.

We all have the choice as to the path we decide to take. The way I see things now, I was extremely-lucky—I got a chance to find out the truth about who I am and make a fresh start in life, a second chance.

To live a life that's true to who you are takes courage.

I hope my story shines a light on your own life. We are all dealt strikingly different life cards, but by sharing the stories we collect while travelling down life's highways, we see that underneath it all, we share a common bond.

NONE OF US IS EVER TRULY ALONE!

Lindsay Wincherauk
Vancouver, B.C.

1

LETTERS TO ED

My role, at least on the acquaintance front, is to be happy, gregarious, and a tad out there!
-   Seed

A meta-memoir

FREE TICKETS

Dear Ed

How are you doing?

I hope this letter finds you well. I owe you a huge thank you. You saved me from ME.

THANK YOU

You're probably wondering how you could have helped when we haven't even met.

Just knowing you're out there reading these letters is enough. Writing to you is helping me immensely. I'd like to ask you to come along with me for a while. Who knows, perhaps you can help me change the course of my life?

Since I started writing newspaper articles last June, I usually carry a notebook with me wherever I go to capture life unfolding in front of me in real time. Lately, I've been jotting down the random thoughts entering my mind to add to the memoir I'm writing – more on that later. Now that I write letters to you, Ed, I feel like you are a newfound friend to share thoughts with, and I feel less alone. That means a lot to me.

Before we get to what grinds my gears, I'd like to crack open a small window into my life to help you understand who I am. I will start with today's events.

Work sucks. The only good part about it is I don't have to pretend to like it. The job description doesn't include faking enthusiasm. You see, I work at a labour agency. Part of my job is to drive construction workers to job sites. Sometimes they stink. Sometimes they're still drunk from the night before. Anyway, it just is what it is, as they say.

Today at work I was offered a pair of tickets to an NHL hockey game; the Vancouver Canucks versus the Los Angeles Kings. Immediately after accepting, I realised I royally screwed up. It was Monday night, the night reserved for facing the tube and watching "The Donald" on "The Apprentice". I debated whether or not to go to the game before reluctantly accepting. I asked Jeff, a colleague, to go with me.

So, this Monday night was fated to be Trumpless. Jeff and I had arrived at the arena fifteen minutes before the game started.

I'm sitting in Row 6; within spitting distance of the Home Team's bench. GM Place is packed and roaring with a near-playoff-intensity—with the fans hoping our fanatically worshipped local heroes crank out a 110% effort. Strangely, I'm pissed—

I'd much rather be sitting on my sofa, sipping cola; watching Trump's hair bounce from side-to-side. Instead, I'm pretending to be interested while also scribbling these notes I'll type up later for you to read. Please bear with me. If I seem distracted, it's because every now-and-then—I may take a peek at the action on the ice.

SHOOT!

With LA in town, I just flashed back to a jaunt I made down the Interstate 5 to Portland Oregon in 1992. Why did LA stir up memories of a trip to Portland, you might ask?

I'm not entirely sure.

I just checked a map. Los Angeles is on Interstate 5. Could it be that simple?

After all, both Portland and Vancouver are on Interstate 5 as well.

In any case, I was playing pool and imbibing on a pre-Trump Monday, before Trump had made his way to the small screen, when I suggested to four friends we blast down to Portland after the bar.

Yes! They said in unison.

My friends bailed on me. Undeterred – I set off alone.

After four hours of roaring down the I5 blacktop, sleep was calling. I pulled off the Interstate into the parking lot of a Holiday Inn for much-needed downtime. At 8 AM the light from the VACANCY sign pulsed and pierced through the windshield, wakening me.

What was I thinking?

Bed – reclining car seat – bed – reclining car seat – the car seat won.

C'MON REF, OPEN YOUR EYES! *Jeff shouted.*

Besides the VACANCY sign waking me, the only other obstacle I faced during the trip to Portland was a brief visit with a State Trooper to discuss horsepower when I was pulled over for speeding on the outskirts of Portland.

Just a second Ed, the period ended. Jeff and I have to fill out loan applications for beer.

Welcome to Portland!

Big city with an enticing small city vibe—immensly cool!

Come along with me on a Portland walking tour. I visited the Trail Blazer Store, followed by Powell's Bookstore—one of the oldest and largest book emporiums in the west. They carry my first book:

SEED'S SKETCHY RELATIONSHIP THEORIES
A GUIDE TO THE PERILS OF DATING
(HOW NOT TO BECOME A BAR REGULAR)

I gazed out the windows at the back of the store to find a delightful vision luring me away from perusing the aisles: Henry Weinhard's Brewery. A BEER TOUR was next on the docket.

After quaffing several ales, I was magically transported from the brewery to a stool at Jakes Famous Crawfish Restaurant; a Portland institution. I injected myself into the conversation of the occupants of neighbouring bar stools, showering them with small talk. A crew of Portlanders took a shine to me. I remember them as Guy, Girl, Girl and somewhat Skanky Girl.

We flirted our way to another bar. I played darts with Guy. The trio of Girls chatted with each other off to the side.

Guy bought the first round for the two of us.

Round two was my shout. *I'll have two draughts, please!*

That'll be 50 cents said the bartender.

I returned to the table with 24 beers.

At pint fest's end, I discovered "pickled" was quickly leading to slurring.

We departed company making plans to hook up later.

It was time to find a place to stay. It was also time to find sustenance.

I began to *CHASE NEON.* A flickering HOTEL sign drew me in.

Checked in, showered and shaved, it was time to eat!

I stopped at a nightclub. With beverage in hand, I queried the crowd for dining suggestions. Near the club's entrance sat two dudes, chilling. They were draped in bling, wearing tracksuits. They happened to be counting heaps of cash.

Must be the bar managers, I thought.

I left without asking their dining suggestions.

Great Jeff! Our beer applications: STAMPED APPROVED. Who needs food?

Out on the street, I walked in circles for twenty minutes. When I finished circling, I looked up to find the two managers standing next to me.

They asked me if I was a cop—dropping the question on me in an echoing loop, five-times.

Each time I volleyed back: *NO.*

They pressed me to be truthful.

I'm telling the truth, I slurred back.

Once convinced, they asked if I wanted to buy drugs.

Hey, they're not, bar managers, crossed my mind.

They said if I'm ever in San Diego, I should look them up.

As I relive this story, I can't help but wonder: *WHAT THE FUCK,* how will I find them? Do they have a billboard in San Diego? If I find them, will they let me sleep on their sofa-bed?

We parted company.

I'm sloshed, in a big, unfamiliar city, which without question, screams: SMART!

From across the street, sultry, soulful voices were calling. I glided toward them. I found two gorgeous African-American damsels sitting in what I made out to be either an AMC Gremlin or a hearse.

They asked me to get in.

I got in and sat between them in the front seat.

Strangely, like the bar managers, they asked me five times: if I was a cop.

I replied, *NO*, each time.

I showed them my driver's license.

They believed me.

They began to caress my body, brushing over my—they asked me if I'd like to party.

A dim light gleamed, hookers?

I slithered away from the Gremlin. I found a take-out restaurant. When I went to pay I discovered my pockets were empty—and $60 was missing.

I learned a valuable lesson on that tipsy evening: Sitting between hookers in Portland costs $60.

I ran into Guy, Girl, Girl, and somewhat Skanky Girl on the street; we *CHASED NEON* searching for drinks.

The next morning I awoke naked in a bathtub, a cool antique bathtub—I was sporting several pairs of underwear on my head. Skanky wore mine on hers.

I managed to escape Portland unscathed, with a scintilla of dignity after being festooned in lingerie.

Wow, Jeff, 6 to 3 for our beloved Canucks! I missed the game—next time, I'll try to watch.

Ed, I really should've been focusing my attention on the ice; screw that, I'd rather be writing this letter to you.

As for the game: I used to love the game. I used to live and die by sporting events. I used to follow my favourite teams. I knew the numbers of every player. Then, one day, athletes started raking in fistfuls of dough. And, many of these athletes seem to have forgotten, most of us mere mortals who are just trying to get by, don't.

What's my point?

Before Jeff and I went to the game, I went for a long stroll.

The day was brilliantly sunny. When I left my place, three police cars and two ambulances were in front of my apartment building—an older gentleman lay on the road. My spirit sank as I watched an ambulance attendant pound on the man's chest. The attendant's expression showed defeat.

I walked away, deep in thought. One hour later I returned. The emergency vehicle's lights were no longer flashing. Off to the side, the emergency responders quietly conversed. A white sheet was covering the man. His hands peeked out from the edge of the sheet.

Ed, at the sight of this man, I was at a loss for words. I began to sink into a dark pit. Fortunately, the game allowed me to focus on what's right in front of me.

Lately, I've been in a state of flux, shifting in and out of the past and present. I'm trying to find sanity after a period of terrible uncertainty. I've been trying to avoid thinking about my past. This man's tragic ending began to pull my mind toward darkness. Writing this letter helped me to avoid the descent. It also helped me to lighten things up—except for the past few paragraphs, of course.

Anyway, it's time to put the **FINAL PERIOD** on this letter.

Gotta' run, the games over, a 7 to 4 – VICTORY for the Home Team.

Regards,
Seed

P.S. Unlike Trump's gorgeous locks, my hair is tragic. I've been shaving it off for about five years. Today I'm sporting two weeks' growth. I don't think I have the patience to let it grow past the awkward stage (ten or eleven months). Ed, do you happen to know of a good barber?

→→→

FARMER'S HEAD

Dear Ed

Our ~~beloved~~ Canucks missed the playoffs. I guess 100% wasn't good enough. Don't let the strike-through in the previous sentence fool you; I don't hate the Canucks—I matter-of-factly don't care about the games anymore.

Anyway, this week I'm facing one humdinger of a decision.

Would you like fries or salad?

I'll have a side salad with Italian dressing, please.

Sorry about that, I'm ordering lunch.

The decision I'm facing is life changing. I'm about to flip the decision-making coin. Let's hope the coin comes up heads.

Or maybe you could help me decide what to do? It's about my hair.

FLASHBACK: FALL OF 1981

I remember it as if it was yesterday...

I was the quarterback of the University of Saskatchewan Huskies Football Team. One day, George V, a teammate, came up to me in the lower quad of campus and said: *Seed, I can see your scalp. Are you going bald?*

His query shot fear into my soul. I was terrified baldness would end my popularity. I was positive I would never get laid again.

The lower quad was buzzing with students scurrying to class on this fateful morning. I was with a small selection of teammates and friends.

I gazed into my hands, hoping they would not be my only source of pleasure from this day forward. I looked to the ~~skies~~ roof above and screamed. *Why me; I have a lifetime of conquests to fulfil. I don't want it to be just me, my ten-digits, twenty, if you count my toes. Bald isn't beautiful. Bald is alone.*

When I stopped screaming in this fantasy, I returned to reality. I was alone in the lower quad.

My friend George was a bit of a *dick* that day. A glance to the right →→ and you will see I wasn't going bald; however, George's words scared me nonetheless.

I decided: just in case George was right, I was going to fight for my hair. I didn't want life to lead me to a dimly lit bachelor pad with just my hands, potato chips, and porn. I'm not sure I even like porn.

But—we'll swallow.

Shut up hands. Don't make me put on gloves.

An epic struggle lay ahead. I frantically flipped through magazines searching for cures for baldness. Beer helped me with my search efforts. Finally, a solution jumped off the glossy pages of a fashion magazine: BRAZILIAN FROG EJACULATE & GINGER (BFEG). The advertisement claimed: *Clinical studies showed in 92% of cases, test subject; experienced – new hair growth.*

I placed my order.

Two weeks passed. With each passing day, I was more certain I'd soon be bald.

I pondered long and hard: *Would pet stores carry Brazilian frogs? What type of porn would they like? Would I get warts?*

My order arrived, saving me from finding out.

With BFEG firmly in hand, I rushed to my bathroom. I rubbed the goo all over my scalp. It dripped onto my face. It clumped. I looked into my mirror full of anticipation. What I discovered looking back at me was a head with no **new found fullness** and no receding hair line. My skin never felt so smooth. My frown lines were disappearing right before my eyes.

I don't want to be hairless. I don't want to be hairless. I don't want to be hairless.

What are hardwood floors?

Bob said I might like them.

FLASH FORWARD: SPRING 2001

Twenty years later, my hair, *sans* goo, was still the same. I lost a bet with a friend. I can't recall what the bet was about, or my friend's name—I just know the loser had to shave his head. I was the loser. I became bald of my own accord.

Self-consciously, I *headed* out for a night on the town. My hairless globe was a hit. Co-eds approached, caressed, and fondled, my head. One fine young lady while stroking my dome stated: *You have a spectacular looking head— keep it shaved, ewe—why is your belt undone?*

My ego was so gratified by this flattery that I've shaved my dome ever since.

I'm still terrified of becoming bald. Once a month, I let my hair grow out for about eight days. When it reaches a length that allays my fear of going bald—I shave it off once more.

If I ever detected any sign of baldness, I'd start flipping through the pages… no… I'd *surf* the web in search of a magic ointment. I heard PREGNANT MARE URINE & RHUBARB (PMUR) is all the rage these days.

Happily, baldness doesn't appear to be on the horizon. I choose to be bald. Luckily, I have an enticing head shape, or so women say. If you don't believe me, ask my hands!

Would you like a rub, Ed?

Maybe later – Right now I need your wisdom. Recently, an acquaintance saw a picture of me with hair. Excitedly she said: *Wow, you were hot! If you want a shot at this*—while licking her lips, staring at me with bedroom eyes, bosoms heaving—*I suggest growing your hair back.*

Her words confused me. Maybe I am hotter with hair. Maybe hair will increase my belt notch count. She couldn't be right, could she?

Maybe I'll have soup for lunch tomorrow?

I've let my hair grow for fifteen days—twenty by the time you receive this letter. I like stroking it.

Now, that I have been religiously shaving my head every eight days or so, the prospect of growing my hair back is scary. From this day, until ten or eleven months from now, it will look tragic. Growing my hair back could potentially end my popularity, and perhaps lead me to the land of celibacy?

Barring an unforeseen tragedy that leaves me in a comatose state, baldness by choice was going to be my destiny. Until one fateful day when the heaving bosoms and words of one woman: *If you want a shot at this*—made me question if I do look better with hair?

Ed, you may be wondering: *What's the big deal, its only hair?*

Well, summer is coming, and I only have a week or two to make up my mind. Because, once the sun kicks up the UV-alphabet (of vitamins), it will be too late. I can't risk FARMER'S HEAD

So, my friend, I need your help with this decision.

- Say shave: I'll shave.
- Say flow: I'll let it flow.

What's it going to be?

I'll eagerly await your reply.

Seed

P.S. I have drafted a document for my loved ones to follow if I'm ever in a comatose state:

DO NOT ALLOW ANY MEDICAL PROFESSIONAL TO ORDER MY HAIR CUT WHILE I RECOVER
FOR ANY REASON
DNAAMPTOMHCWIR-FAR
IT HAS BEEN NOTARIZED

I Drove a Dead Man to Work

DATELINE: 7 May 2006: Vancouver, British Columbia

Dear Ed

FYI: I've kept my cranium clean-shaven since our last correspondence. Life keeps ticking along. I'm ridiculously busy trying to earn enough money to survive by working two jobs:

JOB 1: Trades Labour Corporation (TLC) – Driver – Driving construction workers to job sites.

JOB 2: Chintz & Company (high-end furniture store) – Shipper/Receiver - Working in the warehouse.

Bartending would have been my job of choice. I was damn good at it. The bar provided me with a stage. I loved the performance. I loved bringing people together. Now in my 40s, I guess the age factor erased that option. Oh well, I can still drink in bars!

Driving for TLC requires me to wake each morning before 5 AM. Waking before 5 AM sucks, it is nearly impossible to get used to rising at that ungodly hour. It leaves me out of sync with the rest of society. I have dinner at 4 PM. I'm drunk by 5:30. I hit the sack by 9, my midnight. At least being out-of-sync, showers me in individuality. I often walk alone.

Monday's are the worst. This Monday was to be unavoidably calamitous.

I rounded the second last corner before the office. Emergency vehicles were racing toward me. A car similar to my non-descript beige Toyota Corolla had been t-boned by a large truck and spun through the intersection of Quebec Street and National Avenue; finally coming to rest one-hundred feet from the point of impact.

I was first on the scene. I stopped twelve feet from the mangled wreckage. I looked to my left to see a middle-aged man slumping over the steering wheel of the Corolla. I could see his neck pulse faintly. His eyes went blank. They became vacant. He died.

Tears rolled over my cheeks, breaking at my chin, dripping onto my lap.

Soon, I would be driving a dead man to work.

My first run of the day was four workers to two different construction sites. I had never met them before. We engaged in *lightly-flavoured* small talk about the never-ending rain and teleportation.

The conversation u-turned from *light* when one of the workers expressed he was in a rut. He said if his life didn't turn around by the seventeenth – his birthday; he was going to go to the highest point on a bridge, and jump. He shared his upsetting story before he even shared his name. His name was Ken.

Struggling for words I asked if he could do it during *off-hours* to avoid screwing up traffic. My attempt at adding levity failed miserably.

I desperately tried to treat his words as if they belonged in a normal conversation. I asked him what was stewing in the rut that was destroying him.

What's so tragic that you want to end your life? I asked.

My job has deposited me in a place where such conversations are commonplace. Many of the workers I transport have been marginalised and struggle for survival.

Ken told me his debilitating mental state was a product of the death of his parents, his wife leaving him; and arriving at midlife, alone.

If you listen carefully, you can almost hear self-righteous people yelling: *Take responsibility for your life!*

I've come to understand for some people—it's not that easy.

I could tell by the calm resignation in his voice and the emptiness in his eyes, he was serious.

He experimented with crazy drug concoctions.

Sprinkle CRACK and DOWN into the rut, and stir vigorously.

His voice began to tremor when he added: *Down is heroin.*

His desperation caused me to consider whether I could ever pull the proverbial trigger. Ed, I'd like to say the answer to the question was an emphatic *NO*.

Unfortunately, I think most of us, when life brings us darkness, are capable of doing unthinkable measures; like suicide.

I tried once. Fortunately, I failed miserably.

Let's hop into the WAYBACK MACHINE and travel back to that tragic moment.

WAYBACK: JULY 1991: VANCOUVER, BRITISH COLUMBIA

The love of my life dumped me. How often have you heard *'love of my life'* and *'dumped'* in the same sentence? Ed, why do we punish ourselves by holding onto a love that is no longer there?

Is being friends with someone who doesn't want you an accomplishment?

We've been through so much together. Oh, you've replaced me. Tell me all about your new...oh, please.

After my breakup, I sank deeper and deeper into misery. I believed I couldn't go on. The weight of my anguish was crushing me. I needed to end the pain. I phoned a Crisis Hotline for help and then refused to accept the advice.

I decided to take the misery into my own hands. I filled my bathtub with tepid water and climbed in. My left hand pushed the back of my head under the water. *I gasped.* Before I surrendered, my right hand came to the rescue.

I stepped out of the tub and collapsed onto the floor in laughter.

The healing process began at that precise moment and this time: I won.

If I had succeeded with my selfishness, you wouldn't have read the last line.

DATELINE: MARCH – OCTOBER 2003: VANCOUVER, BRITISH COLUMBIA

In March 2003, a series of traumatic events knocked at my door and entered my life, each one pushing me closer to an emotional breaking point. Each trauma introduced a new low point.

Ed, I badly needed to escape. I decided to travel to Europe with my buddy David. In October we embarked on a 31-day trip. I needed to find my happiness.

DAY 15: 22 OCTOBER 2003: MUNICH, GERMANY

On Day 15, I hit an all-time low. I became privy to a dark family secret, one my entire family cloaked in secrecy, even the family pets. It seemed horrific they were all complicit in a lie.

Since July, I had been struggling with a revelation about my parents, placing my very identity in question. It was consuming every ounce of my spirit. On this crisp fall day in Munich, my foundation was shaken more when my dear friend Wayne called from Vancouver. He read the contents of a letter revealing a secret about my family. I was now being challenged to change the course of my life. I needed my family more than ever before; I just didn't know how to tell them I knew they had participated in a lie?

I believed I had sunk as far as I could, that all changed on DAY 19 in Nice.

DAY 19: 26 OCTOBER 2003: NICE, FRANCE

Sunday morning in Nice brought with it a warm, overcast haze. I crawled out of bed at 6 AM, sleepless from the night before. Sleep had become torturous because my past kept swirling in my head.

I walked to an internet café with my head and spirit slumping.

When I opened my mailbox, one email greeted me. It was from my ex-girlfriend, Trish.

Dear Asshole. I hate everything about you. You suck. I love my new man more. He's far better than you—blah, blah, fucking blah.

Trish twisted the dagger by finishing with—*I hate you.*

I left the café in tears.

My life up to now had been a rollercoaster ride of extreme highs and lows, but I had always managed to mask my pain with humour.

For the first time in my life, I couldn't find a comedic way to cope with the pain I was feeling.

PAIN + PAIN + MORE PAIN + TIME = COMEDY/ (PAIN (CUBED)) = DESPAIR.

My next comedic performance: CANCELLED, maybe forever.

WAYBACK: 17 FEBRUARY 1981 – SASKATOON, SASKATCHEWAN – ST PAUL'S HOSPITAL

Three days after reconstructive knee surgery, I was pleasantly hallucinating on a morphine drip. My nurse came in and upped my dosage. Fifteen minutes later she returned to remove a drain inserted on the outside of my left knee. She tugged vigorously on the drain. It wouldn't budge. She tugged again. When the hardware finally came out, it felt like a wire brush was tearing my veins to shreds. I screamed **FUCK** so loudly it ricocheted throughout the hospital— sparking coma patients awake.

The pain I was experiencing on this day in Nice was far more agonising than knee surgery. My life was spinning out of control.

I walked away from the internet café, stumbling with every few steps. A brick appeared out of thin air and landed on the pavement in front of me. Brick after brick were stacked upon each other by invisible hands in rapid succession until an impossibly high wall was built.

I sank further into depression. I needed to find the strength to climb over the wall. I needed desperately to move forward, but how?

With this new revelation disrupting my life, life had become: STRANGER THAN FICTION.

Tears continued spilling from my eyes as I staggered down Nice's promenade. I wondered if I'd be better off dead. *That would teach them*, I thought. I was facing two ethereal doors:

DOOR 1: Life and all of its struggles, good and bad.

DOOR 2: DEATH.

I sat down on a bench and looked out at the Mediterranean, tears pouring from my eyes.

My mind flashed to an episode of "The Simpsons": Moe's college professor asks Moe if he has a cure for cancer. He then walks into a lake, taking his own life.

Moe watches from the shore and says: *Professor, don't you want to take off your shoes? Oh... Oh... oh.*

I contemplated doing the same – and having my bloated corpse spat out of the Mediterranean days later.

I wanted to go home. I just wasn't sure where my home was, anymore. Home had always meant the place where I grew up; however, with the truth about my family—was that place ever truly my home?

The previous night; NIGHT 18 of the trip, was blissful. Dave and I met Steph & Arno. They used to be a couple. They speak French.

I sheepishly tried to break down language barriers by speaking the only French I knew. *Bon retour guimauves*, I said.

Guimauves means "marshmallows". I'm not entirely sure why I know that?

Anyway, this rendezvous with Steph and Arno led to the night stopping just shy of casual sex. I'll spare the details. I believed: casual…would have spoiled the moment.

Instead, I bid them adieu and hopped back on the despair train.

I had cried every day for more than four months.

I decided to return to the hotel to wake Dave. It was now 9 AM.

Two blocks away from the hotel, I came across a well-dressed man wearing a driving cap. He was standing in front of a taxi. My eyes were nearly swollen shut. I peered at him through droplets of tears.

Time stood still.

I glanced over my left shoulder. The man was crouching beside the taxi. My vision was blurry from crying, like a drinking & driving advertisement where you look through a series of empty beer glasses lined up in a row. My crying marathon continued.

The Academy Award for entering an Emotional Wasteland goes to—

And then, SMASH.

The man smashed out the passenger window of the car directly in front of the taxi. He looked at me, pressing his index finger against his lips, and shushed. He started running. He was clutching a purse.

I chased after him. I shouted at him in French. Since I don't speak French, I was only making loud, incoherent sounds in a non-existent language.

When he rounded the corner and saw me running after him, he realised: I was about to catch him, so, he threw the purse into the air. I caught it. He scurried away like a rat.

I dropped to the ground, panting; I was now clutching the purse.

I strolled back toward the car.

Poulet vous policia, cell phone—I called out to the people on the promenade.

Eventually, I found someone who cared. I spoke loud and clear to make my English understandable.

Two more good Samaritans joined us. They called the police. By this time my tears had slowed to a trickle.

We're supposed to take care of each other; aren't we?

A tall, handsome middle-aged woman approached us, with her husband (?) in tow. Her voice broke with emotion as she listed the items in her purse. She told us they were flying home in less than two hours.

Her purse contained: passports, cash, and credit cards.

Everything is okay. I have your clutch. I chased after the man who stole it from you—

As I uttered the last word, my eyes began to well up with tears again.

Gratefulness beamed on the handsome woman's face. She thanked me. I handed her the purse and ambled away.

I need to find out how to be happy. When I arrived back at the hotel, I shared the story with the desk clerk. He didn't care.

I shared it again with Dave. I told him about the *'you suck'* message.

He suggested: I stop sucking.

I'm a good, kind man. This day confirmed that truth.

I must find a way to come to terms with my family members who kept the dark family secret from me. I might have to let them go. I need my pain to stop. I don't know how to cast them aside. Maybe it's not my decision?

DAY 19 in Nice—taught me I'm capable of things far greater than I ever imagined.

Don't worry about me too much, Ed. I am going to be okay. I'm not sure when the clouds will part. But my gut tells me, one day, they will.

Did I think about ending my life that beautiful misty day?

Sure. It would have been easy to end it all, just swig down some pills. But I didn't have the strength – No, I guess what happened is that a stronger sense of purpose came over me. And besides, I'm not sure taking the easy way out is what any of us are supposed to do – isn't the easy way just wasting valuable lessons about life?

Ed, I'm getting closer to blasting the door open to my past and revealing the dark secrets I've been hiding from you. Be patient with me. The truth shook my foundation to the core. Before I get into the story about Europe and the rest of the trip, I want to tell you more about my drive with the dead man.

My Drive With a Dead Man Continued

DATELINE: 7 May 2006: Vancouver, British Columbia

Hey Ed, now, where was I?

Would I be upset if Ken took his life?

He shared his life views with me; some trivial, others deeper.

When I rounded the corner onto Trafalgar Street, a homeless (?) man riding a bike rode past us. He was towing a shopping cart while talking on a cell phone. We agreed it was hilarious.

Ken is teetering on the verge of homelessness himself.

May 17 – his birthday was on the horizon. His self-imposed deadline to his life—was looming ahead.

Thinking inside the box: The frailty of living

Life is a fragile experiment. We take turns being the TEST SUBJECT. For some, their number comes up more often than others, and TEST SUBJECT gets to be part of the life plotline: TWISTS & TURNS – POKES & PRODS leave them scrambling to find meaning.

After dropping off the first three workers, I was alone with Ken, trapped into listening to his heartache. When he finished talking, I asked permission to offer insight.

Fuck, Ken, life can be tough. Your wife left you years ago. Your wife didn't want you for whatever reason. You weren't responsible for your parents' deaths. Death won't fix your problems. Did your parents love you?

Yes, he said.

Then why would you destroy their memory by being a selfish shit-head? Get help with your addictions. Stop whining about what you don't have. I've already seen one man die today; I don't want to hear about number two, later.

A news story came on the radio: If the Avian flu mutates, the death toll around the world could be massive.

Ken smiled. He declared that five-billion people dying would be a great thing.

I was dumbfounded. I began lecturing Ken, trying to convey how horrific that would be.

Ken chose to disgust me.

Yeah, the only problem would be the survivors. They'd probably be chinks and niggers—the cockroaches of society.

He expressed his hatred calmly.

I sat in disbelief. Confronting Ken or trying to change his attitude was my other options. I quickly determined they would be to no avail – and may put me in a dangerous situation. He had potential weapons and a hatred for life at his disposal. I only had air freshening spray, and my wit and charm.

I drove to a bridge. Stopping mid-span across, I reached over Ken's large, gruff body and opened his door.

Final destination, have a great flight!

Certainly, my second drive of the day would be better?

26

JOHNNY FOX

MY SECOND DRIVE OF THE DAY
7 MAY 2006 - 7:47 AM

Sitting in the passenger seat of my car was a man I had never seen before. He introduced himself. His name was Johnny Fox.

Johnny was eager to tell me about his life. He calmly stated he had done hard-time in prison.

Why were you incarcerated, I asked.

He told me he made some mistakes. He said he didn't regret what he had done.

I came home from work and headed up to my room on the third floor. I laid out my goods: a bag a blow to the right, next to the blow, my rigs. On the left, five beautiful joints lined up in perfect order: cigarettes; cold ones in the fridge. I wanted to go up.

I made a right-hand turn. I looked at Johnny, riveted by with his tale.

I popped the cap off a beer, tilted back, and took a swig. I puffed on a cigarette, drawing in the flavour-infused death of nicotine. I toked. I slammed a rig into my veins. Instantaneously a warm rush of cocaine entered my veins. I began to climb.

Johnny's eyes sparkled as he relived his story.

I never missed work. I was a functioning addict. In my life, I host a roster of demons. I took another toke and looked down to the street below. I saw a white van parked on the corner, engine idling. Two cretins were standing beside it—one large, balding, gruff—the other skinny, slimy, both lowlifes. They were forcing two girls into the van. The girls were resisting. I slammed another rig into my veins, continued my climb, took another swig—and started my descent to the street below.

He took a deep breath and continued.

The slimy one passed me on my way out the door. He entered my building leaving the big guy by himself. I turned around the back of the van and put my boots so far up his ass they came out his mouth. I went into a fit of blind rage and didn't stop beating him until his movement ceased. The girls thanked me and ran away. I back stepped into my building. The other scumbag was in the communal washroom on my floor. I confronted him and did what needed to be done. He paid for his vile indiscretions.

What did you do to him? I asked.

I can't recall. I blanked out as I shot for the stars above. I took another smack, toke of a joint and a shot of liquid—and headed down to the Sunrise Pub. At the pub I sat at the bar, blood staining my shirt and knuckles. I shot back scotch and swigged beers. The police arrived. They chanted my name.

Johnny Fox. Are you Johnny Fox?

They took me outside, asked me where I lived—then escorted me to my home. The haze was beginning to lift. We climbed the stairs as I dropped from the sky. The slimy punk was a bloody mess—out cold—lying on the floor of my room—a butcher knife lay next to his scalp. My room was dripping in blood. I took control of the situation—doing what needed to be done—I have no regrets. You don't fuck with women.

Did the man die? I asked.

Johnny paused, opened the car door, and stepped out onto the sidewalk. Johnny looked back at me, the devil was in his eyes, and said: *Unfortunately, no.*

27

GOD'S NEW RECRUIT

After dropping off Johnny, I arrived at Chintz & Company at 9:30 AM.

I shared the stories of my two drives with co-workers. They didn't care.

You seem down. Is something wrong?

I was assigned to work with Shaun. Shaun, a fresh recruit, had recently turned to the Lord for salvation.

He offered me God's perspective on my morning's upset. I never asked him for it.

He persisted in focusing on my first drive with Ken. He strongly suggested I could have helped him more, that Ken was a child of God. He said I did the wrong thing by kicking him out of my car.

I would offer Ken love and support. I would try to get to the root of his hatred. Your problem, Seed, is that you judge. He said.

I suggested: he was fucking stupid.

Would you also offer Saddam and Hitler love? I asked sternly.

Yes was his answer; *God is in charge of judgement.*

After slightly puking in my mouth, I strongly suggested: *God needs to learn how to judge faster. Allowing six-million people to die in the Holocaust was a disgusting lesson about (?)—the gavel could have slammed down sooner.*

An ex-Chintz salesman named Derrick entered the store. Shaun threw his arms around him.

Hours later Shaun pressed me for my opinions on life.

You do know Derrick is gay, don't you? Your greeting reeked of insincerity. I bet you don't know his partner's name?

Skirting the question, he asked my views on life. I took a deep breath and shared:

I think we're supposed to love, support, encourage, and nurture our families and friends. Treat every other person on the planet with kindness. Avoid confrontation whenever possible. We're supposed to try to leave the world better than we found it. And, I believe: if we make mistakes, we're not to be too hard on ourselves—we're simply supposed to do our best to learn from them.

He looked at me and smirked.

Am I missing something? I wondered.

Shaun has never asked about my religious beliefs.

His smirk prompted me to end our conversation.

What happens if I don't believe in your God in the same manner as you? I asked.

You'll burn in Hell, he said.

I suggested he *fuck off* and no longer speak to me. Sorry, I forgot to avoid.

At times my anger with God spills out of my soul, I don't understand why there needs to be so much agony and despair in the world. It seems like we're pawns. If we get with the program and worship, we go to Heaven; if not: Burn baby, burn.

I don't understand Shaun's God.

"GOODBYE" SHAUN

Two weeks later Shaun left Chintz & Co. He planned his own going away party. Nobody went.

During his last day, he approached a salesman named Duane. Duane is gay. Shaun expressed how he believed Duane's next life would be stupendous. *Things will be better for you*, he said.

You know I suck cock, right—Duane replied.

Another gay sales associate named Calvin approached.

He glared into Shaun's eyes and asked: *Do you receive a free toaster for each conversion you make?*

2

FOUNDATION

BIRTH + MEMORIES + PUPPY LOVE + DRIVING IN REVERSE

A meta-memoir

LUCKY NUMBER 7

Y ou want to know more, I'm guessing. Thank you for sticking around. For us to become bona fide friends, I must start letting you into my family life. Family life is vital to our well-being. Our formative years have a lot to do with shaping who we eventually become.

Remember suicidal Ken?

His family life crumbled, and so did he. I haven't seen him since I left him mid-span across the bridge. Today is his birthday: Happy Birthday?

This morning I ventured to a pharmacy and purchased a five-blade razor. Once home, armed with the sleek device I *headed* to the shower; quickly undressed, slathered my dome, I then swathed my skull with the razor back to front. Clumps of hair peeled off my scalp. Blood began to pool at my feet.

When I completed scraping, I folded toilet paper into twenty mini-sheets, attached them to my wounds, and smiled. In eight days I will follow these steps again; unless—

What does Seed look like, you ask?

I have sparkling, soulful, brown eyes.

I smiled when I typed that.

I've been told I look like—I'll close my right eye and let my Alter-Ego BLIND ME, answer the question.

Seed is devilishly handsome. He's sexy and virile. He's a combination of Charlton Heston, George Clooney; Tom Cruise before he went nuts on Oprah's couch, Mark Harmon, the Domino Pizza Noid; and, the dog from Scooby Doo.

He has a wonderfully dry sardonic wit. When people get him, it's glorious. When they don't, it's even better!

I'll take the keyboard from here, Alter-Ego.

Am I good enough?

Life has put me in a place where I struggle with self-worth. I'm terrified to write the story of my life because it opens me to judgement. What will people say when they read the dirt about me?

By exposing our truths, we risk vulnerability. But I know I must tell my story. I have a gut feeling it may help others with their own lives. Maybe it will help you somehow.

With each page I type, I find myself coming closer to a place—a place where it's okay to embrace who I am.

I'm about to introduce you to my family. If you happened to grow up in a loving, stable family, consider yourself lucky. The Wincherauk family was anything but—

One of the biggest challenges of telling the story of your life is—it's incredibly hard for a writer to make strangers feel things about the events and people in their lives readers have no reason to care about—that brings me to the question:

Am I a good enough writer?

After countless hours of reflection, I feel confident: I am. I do know without hesitation our lives are meant to be shared—that's the main reason for living. Our stories share lessons capable of making someone's day a little brighter. They connect us. Where to start? I guess the best place would be DAY 1.

ANNOUNCEMENT OF BIRTH

DATELINE: 16 JULY 1960 – EDMONTON, ALBERTA

FOR IMMEDIATE RELEASE

A beautiful baby boy named Lindsay was born to proud parents Nicholas and Rebekah.

Lindsay weighed a whopping - Sorry, don't know his birth weight—the scale went missing last week.

His length was; don't know that either; the tape measure seems to be missing too.

Time of birth: We've scored a hat trick. The clock batteries were dead at the time. It was sunny outside – it was before lunch.

The name Lindsay is of Scottish origin and means: from the island of the lime tree.

It is also a unisex name. Significance: Who knows?

OTHER NOTABLES BORN ON THIS DAY—OR TO BE BORN IN THE FUTURE ON THIS DAY!

- Will Ferrell - Actor: Stranger than Fiction +++
- St. Claire – Religion: founder of Franciscan Nuns
- Shoeless Joe Jackson: Athlete - *say it ain't so, Joe*
- Ginger Rogers - Actor: The Gay Divorcee
- Barry Sanders – Running Back – Detroit Lions

LOVING SIBLINGS

- Bernice - Sister – 23 years of age.
- Sadie - Sister – 21 years of age.
- Beverly - Sister – 16 years of age.
- James - Brother – 12 years of age.
- Donald - Brother – 8 years of age.
- Brian - Brother - 4 years of age.

Lindsay's parents are 56 and 46 respectively.

Lindsay truly is LUCKY NUMBER 7.

I'm exhausted, stated an exhausted, ecstatic mother. *I never planned on having another child at this age. I love him dearly! Lucky for me since he was NUMBER 7, he, sort-of; fell out.*

Get me a scotch and a cigar, shouted Nicholas. *I'm 56, virile, and I have a seventh child. That'll show the guys down at the shop who's the man.*

TO VIEW THE NEWBORN

Nick and Rebekah invite you to drop by Rebekah's mum & dad's home to partake in food, cigars, beverages, and the celebration of new life!

The home is festive with balloons and tables piled with a fantastic variety of food the women lovingly prepared for the occasion. Just follow the scents wafting from the house throughout the neighbourhood!

They've even booked a band to help celebrate the festivities on this glorious day.

Remember to stop by soon, as Nick & Rebekah, James, Donald, Brian, and Beverley will be returning home to Saskatoon soon, once Rebekah feels up to it.

Lindsay would like to thank his grandma & grandpa, aunts & uncles, brothers & sisters, cousins, and friends, for their love and support on this day and the days to come.

He'd especially like to thank his sisters Bernice and Sadie for rushing up from Picture Butte to make it in time for his birth.

BABY REVIEWS HAVE BEEN GREAT THUS FAR:

- *He sure is cute*. - Aunt Rosemary.
- *He seems to sleep a lot.* – Rebekah's mum's next door neighbour, Tom.
- *I'll make you pay.* An unidentified sibling.

Thanks again!

Lindsay looks forward to the unending supply of love and support from all of you. He already knows he is lucky to have such a large extended family. Seven is a lucky number. Without question, Lindsay is in store for a remarkable life.

Thank you for sharing Lindsay's birth with us. We appreciate your support and look forward to many marvellous years ahead with each of you!

Visit anytime!

Love,

Nicholas & Rebekah

Proud parents

The Real Truth, starting to Unfold

Read on. The truth is about to set me free—I know; cliché?

SEVENTH BORN = BLESSED-LIFE, FILLED WITH LOVE AND NURTURING.

FAMILY SNAPSHOT
THE WINCHERAUK FAMILY

	FATHER	MOTHER	
	NICHOLAS	REBEKAH	
	BORN 1904	BORN 1914	

NUMBER 1	NUMBER 2	NUMBER 3	NUMBER 4	NUMBER 5	NUMBER 6	NUMBER 7
BERNICE	SADIE	BEVERLY	JAMES	DONALD	BRIAN	LINDSAY
BORN 1937	BORN 1939	BORN 1944	BORN 1948	BORN 1952	BORN 1956	BORN 1960

PORTRAIT OF DAD

I'd like to think my dad's heart was full of love and support.

I'd like to remember him teaching me how to ride a bike and throw a ball.

I'd like to remember an incredibly close father-son bond.

I can't.

What I do recall: he was a proud, strong, brooding man who was stubborn to a fault.

He taught me mediocrity.

He failed at expressing love. I don't think he knew how to show it.

I remember him at times becoming so enraged while fighting with my mother he would repeatedly slam his fists into his head.

Dad was a hard-living, scotch-drinking, chain-smoking man.

My father was a broken, deteriorating old man, forced to spend his golden years struggling to support his family. A seventh child was a curse to him.

He wore the anguish openly.

He never minced words when it came to the financial burden associated with raising another child.

PORTRAIT OF MUM

My mother Rebekah was the rock in our family foundation.

Mum was 46 when I was born. Dad was 56. Most of my friends' parents were at least twenty years younger than mine.

Rebekah's walk through life appeared challenging to me. Dad was angry, his fuse short; Mum took the brunt of his temper.

Regardless of the struggle, she was proud, loving and took great pride in caring for the family. Her expressions of love came more from what she did than in the form of outward expression. She worked herself to exhaustion. She was a champion of care.

My mother often sacrificed her happiness to care for our family. Maybe caring was her happiness?

I would need my mother's love the most when THE BIG C arrived at our door, looking to take my father away. *THE BIG C* was sent to tear our foundation apart.

I loved my mother. Every Saturday after her sixth day work day of the week, I'd have alone time with her grocery shopping. I made her go down every aisle in the store to maximise our time together.

My mother could never find the words to express her love—she let her actions speak on her behalf.

She kept me warm.

POLAR OPPOSITES & WILD BILL HICKOK

Mum was nurturing. Dad was a rough, hard man. Their connection seemed odd to most outsiders.

My dad's side of the family was hard-living and cold—at least that was my projection—I can't recall meeting any of them.

Mum's side was tight-knit and extremely religious. Their religious proclivities lay with Protestant.

My maternal grandfather was a pastor in the Wild West during the times of Wild Bill Hickok and Buffalo Bill Cody. A fact confirmed in a book entitled: *Cherished Memories*.

Somehow, Dad swept Mum away despite the polar opposite nature of their families.

Religion dropped judgement into the dynamic. Mum's family tried to pry Mum and Dad apart. The attempt failed.

My mother quickly became the black sheep of the family. Or so I was told.

If they had succeeded, in prying them apart that is; I wouldn't be sharing this story with you.

THE GIRLS

BERNICE

Born 1937

Bernice was born in the middle of the Great Depression in a rural town in the prairies, on New Year's Day. She was the first born.

One might think with her being the first and me being seventh we'd share a strong bond. You'd think she'd look out for me. Protect me from my older brothers. For the most part, she was absent from my life, except when we visited her on family vacations and when she'd return to the family nest a couple of times every year for the holidays.

We were never close—she had left the family home years before I was born. She hung in the background of my life, filling the air with a biting, running commentary, each time she visited: *Lindsay, you will never amount to anything. You will never be as good as your older brothers.*

Bernice's words were laced with hatred (?)—never love. I wish I could say I was lying—or stretching the truth. Her words stung. I thought she was a bitch.

Like our father, she was a chain-smoker. She gallivanted around the world with my second oldest sister Sadie (NUMBER 2). Both of them were attractive in a flight attendant sort of way.

SADIE

Born 1939

Sadie is two years younger than Bernice. Like Bernice, she too had left home years before I was born.

Sadie and Bernice have lived their entire lives together. They still do to this day.

Bernice's words directed toward me were full of judgment and what seemed to be misguided anger. Sadie, on the other hand, was reserved. Her quiet nature helped to balance, only slightly, the angry verbal assaults coming out of Bernice's mouth.

They moved to Alberta together working as operators for the Government Telephone Company (AGT). Eventually, they landed in the heart of Calgary, living in a twenty-nine storey apartment building.

We visited them once per year.

Lindsay, you'll never—

When we visited, I was allowed to roam the streets of Calgary alone—I was 12. When I type this fact now, it strikes me as neglect. Calgary, much like any big city, is no place for a twelve-year-old to be roaming alone.

Sadie was timid and shy; whereas, Bernice was loud, opinionated and bullying. Sadie seemed defeated, often taking the backseat to Bernice's verbose demeanour.

BEVERLY

Born 1944

Beverly, the youngest daughter; NUMBER 3 in the family pecking order; answered the door one day and was crusaded into the Jehovah's Witnesses—where meadows of happiness and eternal salvation were to become her destiny.

In reality: She met Garth. Garth's family were devout churchgoers. The concept of living clean and giving 10% of their earnings to a higher power somehow enticed her.

Garth neglected to tell her he wasn't a fan of clean living. He drank; smoked, avoided the collection plate, uttered profanities—and occasionally, he'd remove his glass eye and slip it into drinks at bars, deriving pleasure from the reactions of the hapless victims drinking the drinks.

Garth treated me special. I think he may have had a fondness for me because we both had one blind eye.

Beverly, like my other sisters, had left home before my arrival date; though, she remained in Saskatoon with Garth.

I was the ring-bearer at their wedding. Garth and Bev told me I looked incredibly cute.

Garth worked as a cobbler. Beverly—I can't recall what she did for work.

They eventually relocated to Calgary. They have two daughters: Shannon and Aimee.

THE BOYS

JAMES

Born 1948

James was the fourth child and the first born son, revered by our father. He was a star athlete until he suffered a career-ending leg injury—*or so I was told*—I never did see a trophy or photo to confirm the truth of this.

During my early years, he was only present part of the time.

I vaguely remember his presence in the early childhood memories I will soon describe. Vaguely, because as I relive my past; I remember him as a caring man.

Maybe my young mind used creative license when it unblocked my memory. You'll see what I'm talking about in the next few pages.

James looked out for me. He cheered for me. He lifted me up when my other siblings knocked me down.

I looked up to Jim. He was cool. He rode a motorcycle. He had friends with cool names such as Grog.

James built a career working for the Alberta Government as an auditing officer for the Department of Indian and Northern Affairs.

Eventually, he married a woman named Charlotte and moved to Edmonton. They have two kids: Robyn and Allison.

DONALD

Born 1952

Donald, the fifth born child, was also a star athlete. Unlike James, he had the trophies and newspaper clippings to prove it. He was the top high school quarterback in Saskatoon. Dad gushed with pride every time the local media ran a story on Don's athletic accomplishments.

Being a star quarterback, needless to say, Don was on a pedestal—loved by teammates, adored by the fairer sex. He was a trendsetter, the first football player in Saskatoon to wear white cleats, ala Broadway Joe Namath of the New York Jets.

Eventually, Don took his talents to junior, and then, university football.

Once his playing days ended, he went on to receive a Master's Degree in Public Administration from Queen's University.

He's now married. His wife's name is Naomi. They live in Regina with their son Matthew.

Oh yeah, he has managed to cultivate a lengthy career with the Government of Saskatchewan working as a civil servant. One of his lofty positions was Deputy Minister of the Department of Highways.

I wanted to be just like Don.

BRIAN

Born 1956

Brian was the third-born son.

A daunting slot in the family pecking order, sixth-born,

Mum was 42 and Dad 52 at the time of his birth. He had the unenviable role of following the revered first two sons. Like me, Brian witnessed the nightly fights about money (more on them later). Without jumping into much description of Brian, I'd like to say: he's a good man.

He looked out for Mum; often deflecting Dad's wrath. He was good to me.

I can't say the same for myself; when I became strong enough, I was a bit of a *dick* to him.

I can't recall our father treating him well—I remember him being looked down upon—he wasn't a star athlete. He wasn't outspoken. He was somewhat timid.

He was, without question, our mother's somewhat fragile rock.

LUCKY NUMBER 7
ME
BORN 1960

→ → →

CHILDHOOD MEMORIES

DATELINE: 22 SEPTEMBER 1965: SASKATOON, SASKATCHEWAN

Let me paint you a picture of the place where I grew up.

We lived on the highway in a house in back of a Texaco Gas Station on Idylwyd Diner. My mother managed the diner. My father ran the gas station. He was a mechanic. Our home was meagre, a small bungalow with three bedrooms. With my sisters long gone, Don, Brian, and I shared a room. James had his own.

Our home was located four miles from the heart of Saskatoon on a highway stretching out of town.

Northbound on the highway—a mile away from our home, you come to a fork in the road. If you veer left onto the Yellowhead Highway, the next big city, three-hundred-twenty-five miles away, is Edmonton, the place of my birth.

If you continued right, you'd head straight north ninety miles to Prince Albert; with each mile closer to Prince Albert the Northern Lights glow brighter and dance gleefully in all of their glory on clear nights.

The gas station and diner faced the highway. The gas pumps were located thirty feet directly in front of their entrances, and another thirty feet from the roadway's blacktop. Sweeping around the right side of the garage was a line of tractors; occasionally we would find one of our missing pets dead inside the workings of the machinery.

At the right side of the diner was the door of our home. About thirty feet from the door, a collection of dirt hills

in various sizes, made a mountainous playground for us kids to explore.

Just beyond the last hill, the horizon dropped sharply into the waters of a slough. I imagined purchasing a submarine like the one pictured on the back of a comic book and navigating its waterways.

I almost forgot, directly across the highway lay the runway of Saskatoon's Airport. Planes flew overhead on a regular basis, rattling the walls and windows of our home.

The garage and diner bustled during the day with farm families stopping by for a quick bite, or to fill up with gas on their way back to their homesteads after a day in the big city.

CLOSING TIME: 6 PM.

Within one hour of closing, the highway was empty except for an occasional vehicle.

Our closest neighbour lived at least three miles away.

FIRST MEMORY

The first five years of my life are a blank slate. It's as if everything before this chilly September night had been erased.

On this evening, around 6:30, when my parents left to enjoy a rare night on the town, I watched the tail-lights of the family Buick fade away as they drove down the highway toward Saskatoon. Clouds hung low over the Saskatoon skyline, the glow from the lights of the city reflected off the clouds, creating a brilliant city silhouette.

When the lights of the car disappeared from view, I turned around to go back indoors; I heard the loud click of our house door being locked—I ran to the door. I banged on it. I screamed as loudly as I could. *Let me in!*

I had been locked out of the house for about thirty minutes when the light from a light standard located at the left entrance of the gas station lot began to flicker, hissing and crackling as if it was about to expire—although, somehow, it never did. Insects buzzed around its dim glow. Except for the city lights off in the distance, this was the only light around.

With darkness, came cold. I began to shiver. Thirty minutes turned into what seemed like an eternity. Twilight fell fast.

A dog began to howl in the distance—or could it have been a hungry coyote?

I was terrified. I banged on the door once more with every ounce of my might.

When the darkness turned to pitch black, I heard the clack of the lock again. The door opened. I rushed inside—inside was draped in blackness. My shivers turned into trembling.

James, Donald and Brian began chanting together in a continuous loop.

Lindsay, we are going to get you. Lindsay, you are not one of us.

When my parents returned home, I was hiding under the couch shuddering and crying.

I rushed into my mother's arms.

I told her my brothers said *I'm not one of them.*

She assured me I was.

My brothers were 9, 13 and 17 at the time.

I was 5.

SECOND MEMORY

While I took a bath, Donald entered the bathroom carrying the family cat. He threw it into the bathtub.

THIRD MEMORY

My brother Brian smashed me in the back of the head with a brick when we were playing in the dirt hills in front of our home—blood poured from my wound—stitches were required.

FOURTH MEMORY

Donald and Brian tried to encourage me to stick my dinner knife into a wall socket.

That's enough reminiscing for now.

NO CURFEW

DATELINE: 1968: Saskatoon, Saskatchewan

When I was 8, my dad crushed his hand in an industrial accident. Poverty paid our family a visit. We were forced to move into a subsidised apartment complex called Sturby Place.

At least the move took us into the city. In Saskatoon, I made *real* friends. When we lived on the outskirts of town, all of my friends were imaginary. For sanity's sake, I created a fantasy world in a walk-in closet where I could hide from my siblings. It was either hide or risk physical and mental assaults.

In the city, I took it upon myself to rally the neighbourhood kids together by organising sporting events.

Being named Lindsay in the era of the Bionic Woman (actress Lindsay Wagner), posed a challenge, especially since I assumed the role of an anti-smoking advocate because of my disdain of my parents' smoking addiction. If I saw one of the neighbourhood kids lighting up, I'd try to talk him or her into quitting.

Hey, Billy, smoking is dumb. Do you want to die young?

Billy disagreed. He called me a *dick*. He then told me he was going to beat my ass while calling me Lindsay Wagner.

At least you won't be smoking while you're doing it—I said to him, my voice quavering.

Dad was required to enter into rehabilitation for his hand injury. Mum was forced to bring home the proverbial bacon; she took a job as the kitchen manager at the Coachman Restaurant in Market Mall. Mum was tired, beaten down. LUCKY NUMBER 7 made it necessary for her to continue working to provide for her family. *GUILT,* reminded me that if it weren't for me, she'd have an easier life.

Mum was on the verge of collapse. Dad was becoming an angry, bitter, and jaded. He eventually was able to return to work as a commissionaire at the airport, though his health, continued to decline.

To stay clear of the trouble at home, I organised football games for the kids in the neighbourhood. At night the porch lights would flash throughout our neighbourhood. The flashing lights signalled it was time for the kids to come home. I was always the last kid outside.

Our porch light never flashed.

SPAGHETTI

DATELINE: 18 January 1969: Saskatoon, Saskatchewan

The thermostat read -23.6 Fahrenheit. Dad and I were returning from lunch at an Italian restaurant where we feasted on spaghetti smothered in meat sauce.

Occasionally, I suffered from motion sickness when I rode in automobiles. On this freezing January day, that was to be the case.

We crossed the Broadway Bridge coming to the intersection of FIVE CORNERS. My stomach churned. I puked on the front floor mats of Dad's Buick Electra. Dad pulled over. He kicked me out of the car and sped away, forcing me to walk home. We lived three miles from FIVE CORNERS.

On that day, I developed an aversion to spaghetti.

42

MY FATHER'S FAMILY

DATELINE: JULY 1970: CALGARY, ALBERTA – FAMILY VACATION

Dad's family, for the most part, was invisible. We never visited them. Nor did they ever visit us. The only members of his family I remember were Mary and Bill Lupasko—an aunt and uncle. They lived in Calgary—close to Bernice and Sadie.

My parents told me the Lupasko bloodline traced back to the Royal Family in Romania. I boasted to my friends about having royal blood.

My bragging was often met with hostility from classmates because they didn't equate Sturby Place with Royal. *Guess what Ms Wagner? We're going to beat you senseless; Royal Family, what a joke.*

During our annual vacation to visit my sisters, we always made a point to visit the Lupasko's.

I despised Aunt Mary. Her voice was gravelly from years of inhaling Export A Cigarettes and the after-effects from the over consumption of gin. She donned winged glasses, resembling those of an evil librarian. Her eyes were a piercing black.

My anti-smoking campaign worked on my mother; however, when we visited Mary, my mother would always partake, chain-smoking right alongside her, tearing at my heart's fibres.

Aunt Mary insisted I stay a night or two at their house each visit. She gave me a place to sleep in the basement of her home, next to the furnace, water heater, pantry and cat litter box. The steps leading down into the dungeon were incredibly narrow and steep. When I climbed down or up, I needed to crawl on my belly or risk a painful fall. There was no railing.

Every time I stayed with them, Aunt Mary would send me downstairs to bring up veggies, soup and potatoes for dinner. It was perplexing because we always ate out when we visited the Lupasko's. When we'd eventually return to Aunt Mary's house, she'd bark at me to return the food to the basement.

NIGHTLY FIGHTS
PUPPY LOVE & CRYING FOR ATTENTION

6 PM SHARP – DAILY

DATELINE: August 1965 – Saskatoon, Saskatchewan

Five-fifty-nine and fifty-eight seconds, five-fifty-nine and fifty-nine seconds, click—

DAD: *Why isn't dinner ready? I work hard every damn day.*

MUM: *I slave away all day in the Diner. Give me a moment to unwind. I will have the family dinner ready soon.*

DAD: *Damn it! Is it too much to ask? I put the food on this table.*

MUM: *Why did you buy a new car? You know we can't afford it.*

DAD: *Don't talk about what I can and can't afford. I work hard. You don't do enough. I at least deserve food on the table when... Why are you crying? Stop it. Get back here. Damn kid.*

MUM: *Don't say that. Don't say things in front of—*

ME: *Mommy, don't cry. I'm sorry. See what you've done, Daddy, leave her be.*

Lindsay, Lindsay, you don't belong here. Lindsay, you're not one of us—

Surely, tomorrow will be better.

Five-fifty-nine and fifty-eight seconds, five-fifty-nine and fifty-nine seconds—

I was wrong.

Every single night, after my father walked the few yards from the garage to our home, the fighting would start all over again.

I retreated to the closet to hang out with my IMAGINATION.

I asked it if I was going to have a life filled with insecurity and dysfunction.

My IMAGINATION gave me a blank stare.

I asked friends at school if their parents fought every day. They told me it's embarrassing how much they're always touching and kissing.

I would then ask them how old their parents were. They told me their parents are only 25.

THEY CALL IT PUPPY LOVE

DATELINE: September 1971: Saskatoon, Saskatchewan – Sutherland Elementary School

In GRADE 7, I fell in love with Kim Benson—an older woman—by five months.

Although we never spoke I decided to try to win her heart. I bought her a gold-plated chain with Kim inscribed on it—and formulated a plan on how to give it to her.

I'd practice for hours in the front of the mirror, shaking during each rehearsal.

Hello um, Kim, pretty, hair. Like; do you, wash it?

It's shiny. Do you like doing stuff?

My dad watches Stampede Wrestling on Saturday's. He eats sardines.

I fetched you a present... pretty... hair... (I peed a little).

If we have a cat, we can name it Scooter. You love—

I ended up throwing the chain in a snow bank.

YEAR 7—FIGHTING ABOUT MONEY

DATELINE: 1972: Saskatoon, Saskatchewan

My parents' joint income allowed us to move from the subsidised housing to Sutherland, a lower-middle class neighbourhood two miles east of the University. They bought a three-bedroom bungalow for $14,000.

Sutherland was on the wrong side of the tracks. Ironic, when you consider we came from subsidised housing. Evan Hardy Collegiate, the high school I would eventually attend, was on the right side.

Life was teaching me valuable lessons: Climbing social classes is nearly impossible.

Dad loved scotch—and smoking.

I'd harp on him daily about his V*I*CES. Eventually, he quit smoking when one of his lungs collapsed. He was forced to choose: put down the smokes or die?

With Dad recovering from his lung ailment, Mum one again became the family's sole breadwinner. She was 59. My father was 69. I was now 12.

Little did we know his lung failure was the beginning of the end?

He was stubborn to a fault. He'd sneak smokes in the bathroom. I'd beg him to stop when the cigarette stench would drift out from under the bathroom door; he'd say he wasn't smoking, that I imagined things.

My heart broke every time he lied.

My father's inability to work didn't stop the fighting between my parents. The only difference was he'd have to wait for Mum to return from work for the heated battles to begin. The nightly fights were now entering their seventh year.

The fights were about everything to do with money. My father would fly into a blind rage and threaten violence. He'd smash himself repeatedly in the head with his clenched fists. The veins in his temple would pulse as if they were on the verge of exploding.

Brian and I were usually the only family members home to witness his rage. Mum would break—tears flowing from her eyes. Brian would comfort her. Nicholas would threaten to hit Brian. I'd scream at him to stop.

GUILT suggested my birth was responsible for the increased financial strains they were facing. Without me, *the burden would lift*.

On one occasion, when Don was at home, Dad threw a knife at him. It stuck into the wall behind his head.

COULD SOMEONE PLEASE PAY ATTENTION TO ME?

I needed to run as far away from my family as possible. I needed to avoid the fights. In the spring of 1972, sports became my escape. I wanted to live up to the standard Don had set. I wanted to be the golden child. But I knew in the eyes of my father, my quest was impossible.

I pursued baseball. I excelled. I was an All-Star Second Baseman on a city championship team. I would brim with joy when I returned home from games.

I always returned home alone.

High School + Driving & Gridiron Pursuits

Enter High School – The Right Side of the Tracks

DATELINE: September 1974: Saskatoon, Saskatchewan - Evan Hardy Collegiate

It was time for High School.

To avoid becoming a social outcast, I needed to find a place to fit in. The choices: Excel scholastically; be a stoner; be a rich kid; an option wrong side had eliminated, or sports?

Sports were to be my selection, specifically football. I wanted to be just like Don.

During my first gym class, Coach Knoll, who just so happened to be the head football coach, barked out my name during roll call, after my *"HERE,"* he asked: *Is Don Wincherauk your older brother?*

Yes.

Coach Knoll glanced at Coach Mooney, an assistant coach, and announced: *We have a star on our hands, coach.*

I was 14 years old, from the wrong side of the tracks, brother of a star athlete, son of a sick, aged father, and I shared my name with Lindsay Wagner, the Bionic Woman. There were no two ways about it; high school was going to be a bitch.

I feared not being able to live up to the expectations left behind by Donald's white cleats.

So, I played golf, tennis, and joined the track team instead. I succeeded at most of my sporting pursuits.

My family was glaringly absent from my many victories.

Driving Lessons

DATELINE: July 1976: A Farmer's Field – Outside of Saskatoon, Saskatchewan

I had just turned 16. It was time to learn how to drive. The open road was waiting. My father was to be my instructor.

My two automobile choices sat in the family car lot (a parking space in front of our house and a spot in the back yard): a 1963 Epic Envoy or an Oldsmobile 98. The Olds 98 was an incredibly large automobile—I had to struggle to see over the hood, made worse by my blind left eye. So, I chose the Epic for my driving lessons.

The Epic screamed babe magnet. It looked like a series of boxes stacked on top of each other. Wind tunnel tested? Not likely.

The farmer's field is where my father conducted the lessons. We'd hop into our un-sleek roadster, Dad behind the wheel. After he drove twenty miles out into the countryside, he'd turn off the highway onto a gravel road, drive a few more miles, make another turn, and manoeuvre his way between two fence posts wrapped in barbed wire, crows perching on top.

Dad would then navigate the beaten tracks formed by farm vehicles to the middle of the field, stop, and bark at me to get out of the car and get in the driver's seat.

It's your turn to drive, Son, he'd say.

Excitedly, I jumped in; stepped on the clutch and gas, gears grinding as I tried to find first. Dad yelled at me again: *Stop—reverse, you must learn how to drive in reverse.*

I stared at him blankly.

Son, my dad taught me how to drive in reverse. That is how you will learn unless of course, you want to go home.

I found reverse. During my forty-minute lessons, three times a week, he'd never allow me to go forward. Don't ask me why—there is no logic to it. Can you imagine riding in the back seat as I swathed my way around a wheat-maze; laughing inwardly with each grind of the gears?

At least my dad and I were spending time together. After two months, I was ready to take the test for my driver's license.

DRIVER'S TEST 1: FAILED. Being blind in one eye required the car to have two outside mirrors. The Epic only had one. The instructor never even let me get in the car.

DRIVER'S TEST 2: FAILED. I killed at parallel parking. However, for some reason, I struggled when looking through the front windshield.

DRIVER'S TEST 3: PASSED. I finally drove my way to licensed!

The Epic was going to provide me with FREEDOM.

The streets of Saskatoon were chanting my name; I managed to drive to Holiday Park Golf Course. With daily practice, within a year, I won my division in a junior tournament.

FOOTBALL

DATELINE: Aug – Nov 1978 – Saskatoon, Saskatchewan

It was time to find the courage to step out of the footprints left behind by Don's white cleats. I took to the gridiron and tried out for the football team: The Evan Hardy Souls. I was a senior.

I made the team.

I shared the quarterbacking duties with my best friend, Tony Gagnon. Tony was in Grade 10. He quickly became a star—on and off the field.

We both excelled, leading the Evan Hardy Souls to city and provincial championships.

FOOTBALL CAREER: 1979 – 1985 – SASKATOON – EDMONTON - SASKATOON

By the time Tony finished his high school career he had broken a few of my brother Don's long-standing city records. He continued to be a star with the local junior team, the Saskatoon Hilltops.

I also continued my football pursuits. I played with the Hilltops my first year after high school. We won the Canadian Championship. I went on to play for the Edmonton Wildcats (junior team), where I threw the longest touchdown pass in Canadian Junior Football League History (108-yards) to Gord Bolstad. And, I played for the University of Saskatchewan Huskies.

That's enough Al Bundy bravado; don't you think?

Longest Pass in Canadian Junior Football History:
Lindsay Wincherauk to Gord Bolstad – 108 Yards – A Touchdown!

3

THE BIG C

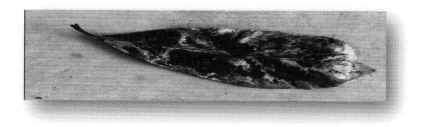

A meta-memoir

KNOCK – KNOCK – *(FUCKING)* KNOCK

DATELINE: March 1979: Saskatoon, Saskatchewan

One misty spring morning, I heard three knocks on the front door of our home. I cracked the door open ever so slightly to find a strange man standing on the other side. He looked ominous. The stranger said, in a grating voice, he was there for my father, Nicholas.

I asked him who he was. I told him my father wasn't interested in converting.

I tried to push him away from the door. I couldn't budge him.

He told me he was The *BIG C*.

He said my father's number had come up. He was going to inflict his wrath on our family.

I asked him what the *BIG C* was.

Cancer, he said, calling me naïve. He vanished into the shadows, but not before promising he would soon be back for my dad.

Cancer was about to take my father in its clutches. Nick's death march began when I was 19—he'd been battling illness since I was 15.

My classmate's parent's ages ranged between 40 and 50 – whereas, my father was 77.

My friend's dads taught their children life lessons, as well as how to throw a ball and ride a bike—whereas my father's path was to have us watch his illness destroy everything he once was.

I used to play catch alone. I'd throw a football in the air – sprint after it – and catch it.

To get away from my realities, I left home to pursue football in Edmonton. I made the Edmonton Wildcats—in an attempt to escape THE BIG C'S clutches.

I began to cry, profusely, as I prepared to drive away from home.

My plan was to stay with my aunt & uncle, Priscilla and Roy.

The moment before I drove away, my parents parting words to me were: *Don't be a burden on your aunt & uncle.*

Instead of staying with my aunt & uncle, I slept in the back of my car in Sherwood Park Mall's parking lot. After three days searching, Priscilla and Roy found me and took me into their home.

HELL'S INFERNO

DATELINE: 1980 -1985: Saskatoon, Saskatchewan

After my second season with the Edmonton Wildcats, I returned home. Dad's downfall was kicking into high gear.

GUILT took direct aim, laying it on heavy.

You had no business leaving your family. Your life isn't supposed to start until—

FIRST QUARTER

Football was once again to provide an escape. I enrolled in University; mostly to play football. Brother Don selected my courses – the same courses he had studied: PUBLIC ADMINISTRATION. I hated the program, but I made the team. I was going to be a University of Saskatchewan Huskie Quarterback!

TIME OUT

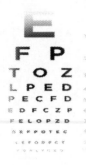

University Football = one-step below Professional. Quarterback = Leader of the Team. The Quarterback touches the ball on almost every offensive play. The fortunes of the team depend greatly on his skills. Quarterback is one of the most glorified and scrutinised positions in team sports. Skills a Quarterback needs to succeed: Arm strength, competitiveness, intelligence, mobility; and VISION + many others. VISION is required to scan the field to read the defence—and make the wisest decision.

Because I'm blind in my left eye, my peripheral vision is limited. I was playing one step below professional. My coaches—well—not a single one of them on my way up to University knew I was half-blind. Here's how I got away with it: I memorised the eye chart during preseason physicals!

SECOND QUARTER

During the summer of my second season, Coach Schneider called me into his office to discuss a campus scuffle I was involved in—and he cut me from the team.

Stunned, I asked why.

I don't want you to end up leaving the team the same way your brother Don did, he said.

Two days later he reinstated me on the team.

Occasionally at practice, Coach Schneider would scream at me, calling me Don, repeatedly.

Coach T, the offensive line coach, interjected each time: *Don was in the past*.

Don's white cleats were trampling me.

THIRD QUARTER

Football helped me to develop a strong dislike of the mass mentality. I loved team camaraderie; however, I preferred one-on-one interactions. As a pack, athletes can be, pardon the term, pig dogs.

FOURTH QUARTER WINDING DOWN—

My efforts to escape were futile; Dad was fighting for his life. He was running out of timeouts.

In late 1983 Dad was in-and-out of the hospital in fits and spurts: first, one week at a time, transitioning to monthly stays—and eventually, three months in, and one or two days out.

He'd forget my name.

He'd misplace my mother's name.

He'd forget where he was.

I used comedy to cope.

He'd ask one of my friends if he was his son Don.

He'd ask me if I was in Edmonton.

No Dad, are you?

He'd say he wished I would come home for dinner.

I'd sit in the chair next to his bed and wave my hands in the air trying to get his attention. At the very least, I hoped to get him to realise I was sitting in the chair right beside him.

For the first two years of *THE BIG C'S* mission, the doors between the hospital and our home perpetually revolved. I can't sufficiently describe the emotional pain Mum, Brian and me, were dealing with—my dad was dying. There was no escaping his fate.

Eventually, he required a colostomy bag.

One night, I watched helplessly as he made repeated trips to the bathroom. By night's end, he had used every towel in the house to attempt to hold onto a shred of dignity.

I retreated to my room and cried for hours.
GUILT didn't visit me that night.

LOVE INTERLUDE

CUPID'S ARROWS

With the heartache I experienced on a daily basis as my dad's cancer progressed, along with the pressure of my athletic pursuits and University classes, I needed to find a way to escape. More than anything, I needed to feel loved.

If I was to venture a guess as to how many times Cupid's arrows sent my heart fluttering blissfully into the insanity of love – let me think about it, I'll have to get back to you on that.

Once I discovered nudity – touching – kissing – leading to cleaning up – *usually with a towel* – I was on my way.

Athletic popularity presented me with opportunities for romance most weekends.

What do you mean: that's not love?

GUILT was back.

Buzz – Buzz - Buzz

Give me a minute. Stephanie's at the door. She's exceedingly hot. Did you see where I put the clean towels?

I'm back. I've been in love three, maybe four times: Kim Benson, Corrie, Gail, and Trish.

Corrie, Gail and Trish—are coming soon to this story—Corrie will grace the pages, a few lines from now.

As for Gail and Trish, well, they're in the future, you'll meet them in due time.

CORRIE

DATELINE: 9 September 1983: University of Saskatchewan

Twelve years later, I was finally over my first crush, Kim. I searched for the chain after the snow melted in the spring. I never found it.

While waiting for Cupid to reload his arrows, Stephanie, Kathy and Tara dropped by for a visit.

Don't forget, booze?

And, booze.

Corrie and I met at a University dance.

We were both drunk.

We kissed.

It was Corrie's first year of University. I was in my third.

~18 DAY BREAK~

DATELINE: 27 September 1983 – Slider's Nightclub – Saskatoon, Saskatchewan

You're just another pig dog, Corrie snapped at me

I'm sorry. I wanted to call you; I honestly did, I didn't know your last name.

Corrie was my first girlfriend. She had a younger brother named Wes. They were both adopted.

Wes was an attention whore, and reckless free spirit.

He crashed motorcycles—rode on the hoods of speeding cars—jumped off a ferry in Greece—and if there was a tumbler full of liquid in front of him—he drank it.

I once saw him suck the nine lives out of a sleeping cat.

No life challenge was out of his league.

George and Peggy were their adoptive parents.

George was a hard-working man, a handyman, with mad skills reminiscent of MacGyver.

Peggy was a big-hearted crafty homemaker.

They both chain-smoked.

Corrie was academically gifted. Wes needed to be kept alive. Peggy and George often favoured Wes—just a little.

I loved their family. They provided an escape from my father's illness—and comedic release.

I noticed George had stopped smoking. I asked him if he'd smoked for over thirty years.

He said, *forty.*

He told me he caught a cold—and decided smoking was stupid. He never smoked again.

Enter Corrie's best friends: Kleo (Kleo) – Barb (Bub) – Michelle (Flouff), three lovely young ladies.

I accepted their insertion into my support network with enthusiasm.

They're great people!

They comforted me during difficult times.

All we did was love—

Toss in my best friend Darryl Wacker (Whitey); Barb's squeeze at the time—I was going to be okay. Life away from home was sweet.

We became our own "IN" crowd.

We were living.

My father was dying.

One night at Slider's Nightclub I was dancing with my arms firmly at my side. Corrie was shaking it with me.

Kleo approached us, the look on her face was vacant, her voice was panicked; Madonna's *Holiday* was blaring from the nightclub's speakers.

Guys—baseball bat, I was hit on the head.

We laughed.

I was dancing. I spun. WHAM. I was on the floor.

Funny Kleo, nobody hit you with a bat. I said.

No, really. It happened. Is it raining in here? I think they are just washing the roof.

I *holidayed* in Jamaica with Bub, twice (in the future).

The Raddysh house was home to a plethora of parties.

Bub lived only two blocks away.

One night after Club Raddysh shut down she stumbled home.

The story goes: She went to her room, stripped down to her underwear—and headed outside. It was minus -32 Celsius. She began climbing over the fence separating her home from the neighbour's. The clamouring startled her mother, waking her.

Bub's mum shouted at Bub, asking what she was doing.

Bub turned. She looked at her mum like a deer facing headlights. She crawled down off the fence and began sauntering back inside.

Her mother stopped her on the steps of the house—asking again what she was doing out there—*You could freeze to death* she said.

Bub muttered: *Code 649*

Her mother asked: *What's Code 649?*

Bub paused, looked up, her eyes glazed over; she then pulled her hands from behind her back and thrust a pair of socks in her mother's face; and said: *This*

Confused her mother asked: *What?*

Bub, in the calmest of tones, replied: *Lindsay knows.*

THE DAY MY DAD DIED

DATELINE: 17 July 1985: Saskatoon, Saskatchewan – Saskatoon City Hospital

Twelve-hundred hospital visits over five years were about to come to the final one.

Mid-afternoon, my father's doctor called instructing me to round up the family. He made it clear time was at a premium. I had the unenviable task of telling my mother her husband of over fifty years was leaving her. My heart was bursting out of my chest. *LUCKY NUMBER SEVEN* wasn't allowed to wallow in self-pity—I feigned strength for the sake of my mother and Brian.

I was breaking inside.

Shamefully, I was also feeling relieved.

I collected my mother and Brian and drove the familiar route to the hospital for the last time to be at my father's deathbed.

I turned 25 the previous day. I celebrated life with my friends. I did this after staring at my dad's incoherent near-lifeless body for several hours earlier that afternoon. He was now putting an indelible mark on my birthday.

Twenty-five years—strange to say, I don't recall a single family celebration of my birth. No cards – no gifts – nothing. My birthday seemed to be a non-event to my entire family.

In my late teens, I took it upon myself to celebrate, with friends, not family.

In grade school, I lied about my birthday—my teacher threw me a celebration during the school year. An im*aginary* friend named Rudy egged me on. I was terrified I would get caught lying, I never did.

GUILT asked me if I thought I was selfish celebrating considering my father was dying.

Today, my father was going to die.

I was fucking angry.

I can't put into words what riding this six-year torturous roller coaster does to a young man's spirit—my frail, father, was succumbing to his illness. Sadly, I couldn't recall him ever being truly alive—his life burdened with struggle: the industrial accident, the collapsed lung, endless financial worries, and now: *THE BIG FUCKING C.*

The breather *GUILT* gave me was short lived. *GUILT* became a harbinger to remind me of my responsibility to be strong for my mother and brother.

I didn't want the task.

Fuck you. I'm too young for this; too young to lose my father.

GUILT gave me a reprehensible glance.

By being born, I robbed my parents of their golden years. *GUILT* reminded me of that daily.

Brian and I were still living at home, burdened with the daily hospital visits.

The rest of the family lived scattered around Western Canada—far removed from the sterile stench of the hospital—far removed from the ups and downs of Dad's daily rollercoaster.

How's Dad today?

He ate. Things are looking up.

THE NEXT DAY

How's he doing?

He didn't remember my name. I want this to—never mind.

Beat down by six years of visits, I wanted it to fucking end. I said goodbye in my heart over six hundred times. I hated the illusion of false hope. Dad had dropped to eighty pounds from two hundred. I wanted him to die. I wanted the fucking pain to be over.

I didn't want to create a family divide; so, I kept my feelings to myself.

My siblings periodically rolled into town during Dad's illness. Their visits raised his spirits. Each time, upon leaving, they'd complain I wasn't doing enough—*you need to go to the hospital more often*, they'd tell me.

If you've ever visited someone in a medical prison, you'd understand the prison extends beyond the hospital walls and engulfs the daily visitor; whereas, monthly visits brought with them the excitement of something new.

But as quickly as they arrived, my siblings would exit the scene.

You need to go more often.

Fuck off, I mumbled.

LAST GASP: 4:45 PM

At roughly 4 PM I veered off Warman Road onto Seventh Avenue. We were seven blocks away from the inevitable ending. I was speeding toward DEATH. I heard sirens. I glanced in the rear view mirror. A police car was chasing after me. I was pulled over.

The Police Officer asked if I knew how fast I was going. He asked for my license and registration.

Mum was sitting beside me, crying, vacant. DEATH was about to drop anguish and relief upon us. We were ridiculously conflicted.

I asked Mum to retrieve the registration from the glove box. She couldn't find the strength.

I informed the Officer of our journey. His voice cracked with emotion as he wished us well and sent us on our way.

I loved my father. It wasn't time. It wasn't fair. I wasn't ready to watch his death.

I parked the car in the hospital's parking lot. Brian and I took our mother by her arms, Brian on the left, me on the right—gingerly guiding her toward finality. My mum was quivering. Every step forward was one step closer to the end. Once inside the hospital, the familiar stench of clean wafted past us. We got on the elevator. The elevator went up. It should've been down. My broken mother, a half-century of struggles were about to flicker to their completion.

I wish I were never born; their lives would've been so much easier, entered my mind.

I'm not sure what Brian was feeling. He always gave our mother tremendous support. Right now, he was at the end of his rope.

I, on the other hand, avoided home; instead, I'd retreat to Corrie's house in an attempt to escape the heartache.

I failed Brian.

The elevator stopped on the fourth floor. We exited left. When we reached the nurse's station, a Doctor and Nurse met us, ushering us into Dad's room.

At 4:43 PM we walked into the room. Brian stood at Mom's left side. I stood to her right. Dad's skin was devoid of colour. He looked frailer than the day before. He opened his eyes and reached for my mother's hand. He tried to mutter something. *He died.* I witnessed the exact moment his life ceased. I saw his spirit leave his body. I wanted to collapse. Tears exploded from my eyes.

For the first time, I realised: my mother and father were in love—he held on to life long enough to say goodbye—and with the touch of her hand—he was freed.

I think the words he was trying to say to her were: *I love you; I'm sorry.*

Out of the corner of my eye, I'm certain I saw THE BIG C leave the room.

The fucker was *smirking.*

AFTERMATH

DATELINE: 17 July 1985 - Sept 1985: Saskatoon, Saskatchewan

That night I went to Corrie's house to grieve. I made calls to friends informing them my dad passed away. With each call, my voice cracked, and I'd break into tears.

Within a few days, relatives rolled into town. Many of them I'd never met before. My siblings asked me to find another place to stay. I thought nothing of it. I welcomed the opportunity to escape.

A friend's family, the Ellis's; offered to let me stay at their home. My best friend Whitey was dating Rhonda Ellis. Being around the Ellis girls parents' was a constant reminder that I was too young to have lost one of mine.

It often occurred to me the gap between first-born, my oldest sister Bernice, and I—23 years—didn't make sense to me. I told friends I was a miracle baby because my mum and dad were 46 and 56 when I was born.

I can't remember my father's funeral.

I know I was a pallbearer.

The day after the funeral the relatives left.

I'm not sure why most of them came?

My dad was gone.

He was a proud, quiet, brooding man, with a fierce temper.

He was leading man handsome.

His life was hard.

←←←He only allowed me to drive in reverse.←←←

Christmas 1979: Brother Don – Yvonne K (Don's GF) – Dad – Bernice (Photo) - Me

Knock—Knock—Is Your Mother Home?

DATELINE: September 1986: Saskatoon, Saskatchewan

Dad's six-year death march took a devastating toll on my mother's health. Shortly after Dad died, she became ill. She was now 71.

Mum began to suffer anxiety attacks paired with crippling stomach pains only a few months after Nicholas's death. Her doctor told her—her imagination was tricking her.

KNOCK - KNOCK – *FUCKING* - KNOCK

The boom of the knocking rang familiar.

THE BIG C was at the door once more.

I screamed at him *to get the fuck out of here*. I screamed so loudly that my voice echoed—in my mind.

Mum's doctor was wrong—stomach cancer isn't imagination.

The revolving door between the hospital and home was oiled once more.

Brian had just turned 30. He needed to be able to visit Mum at the hospital on his own. During Dad's fight with THE BIG C, Brian never took the time to get his driver's license. I took it upon myself to teach him how to drive. We avoided farmers' fields.

DRIVER'S TEST 1: FAILED. He hit a guardrail in a parking lot.

TEST 2: FAILED. He crashed into a Volvo that was being test driven.

TEST 3: FAILED. He ran a red light.

TEST 4: PASSED.

In January 1987, we had a short break from the despair. Donald got married in Vancouver—in the International Suite of the Westin Bayshore Hotel. The legendary Howard Hughes once spent six months in this suite eating pancakes. I may have made up the pancake part.

The breather was short-lived. Mum's life was going to end—soon.

I'M NEVER GOING TO COME HOME AGAIN, AM I?

DATELINE: 5-10 December 1987: Saskatoon, Saskatchewan

It was my mother's turn to die—but not before Brian and me made another three hundred plus trips to the hospital.

UP... DOWN... *FALSE HOPE*... UP... DOWN... DOWN... DOWN... *up*... *DENIAL*—to be repeated over-and-over again—

Her cancer attacked violently. She too required a colostomy bag.

I was now 27 years old.

UP came calling, traipsing in disguised as PROMISE before the holidays. Mum was sent home on December 5—family spirits soared with fresh hope, the doctors had removed a cancerous tumour.

On Sunday, December 7, I returned home early after an evening out. Saskatoon was gripped in a bone-chilling minus 35 Celsius. When I entered our home, UP cancelled—my mother lay on the sofa; she was experiencing debilitating pain. Brian was breaking. We had to return to the hospital.

I spent nearly a decade as *LUCKY NUMBER SEVEN* watching *THE BIG C* annihilate my parents, and yet; I had to fake strength because I desperately wanted my mother to feel comforted.

We left our house by the front door. I walked backwards down the steps, supporting Mum. When I reached the bottom step, with Mum standing one step above me, we stopped in the bitter cold of the night and looked into each other's eyes. My mother's eyes filled with tears. The tears froze before they could fall from her frail cheeks. She looked at me and said meekly: *I'm never going to be home again. Am I?*

I looked at her and calmly said: *Yes.*

That was the biggest lie I have ever told.

As I share this story with you now, I need to pause to regain composure before typing the next sentence—for the second time in my life, I battled knowing death was near—words escape me—I want to burst into tears.

The UP of December 5 was gone. The only direction left was DOWN. We could no longer linger in denial. I asked her doctor if I should call the family and tell them to come home before Christmas.

He avoided answering my question, hesitating before speaking, and then, in a soft, comforting voice, said: *YES.*

DATELINE: 12 December 1987: Saskatoon City Hospital

I sat beside mother for five hours on this day. She was barely holding onto life. The love of her life wasn't going to arrive to free her from her pain. I held her hand. She gripped mine tightly. Suddenly, her grip loosened. Her pulse slowed. I left the room. I knew she was going to be gone soon. I didn't have the strength to watch her take her last breath.

The last words she uttered to me came the previous day. She looked into my eyes. I lowered my head close to her mouth to hear her speak—she whispered into my ear with her voice quivering: *Goodbye.*

I hated that word. Whispering it to me was Mum's way to let me know the end was near.

When I left the hospital, I knew my mother was leaving.

That night I went out with friends to mourn. When I returned to my home in the morning, Bernice was sitting in the corner of the living room consumed with grief. We embraced. For the first time, I think. We cried. We comforted each other.

Bernice calmed down. She broke our embrace. Her tears stopped flowing. She then asked me: *Could you find another place to stay? We need the house for the relatives.*

I was *LUCKY NUMBER SEVEN* in the lineup of siblings—we'd—I would be okay, I said to myself.

AFTERMATH

DATELINE: 12 December 1987 – March 1988 – Saskatoon, Saskatchewan

For a fleeting moment, our family was whole again, joined in the misery of death.

I found another place to stay. Gord Tank had been a fantastic friend during these trying times. He even visited my mother on his own. His family offered me a place to collect my emotions.

I had made my last trip to the hospital. After eight years my daily routine was about to change.

Like my father's funeral, the events of my mother's funeral were a blur.

After the service, most of the family retreated to their lives. Bernice and Sadie lingered behind. I was allowed to return home. Sadly, my home was, in a way: no more.

Their lingering came with large doses of chain-smoking and judgement.

Christmas came, two days after a job offer came to me—Federated Insurance—a large insurance company based in Winnipeg. They wanted me to move within two weeks. I was given two hours to decide.

I asked my sisters for advice.

Bernice coldly told me if the decision were hers she wouldn't hire me. She said she'd hire someone like my brother Brian long before me. She said I have too many friends, and people with too many friends are unreliable.

I wanted her to get the fuck out of my home and go back to hers. It was time for the grieving to end. I retreated to my room and cried.

Bernice and Sadie finally left at the end of January.

LOVING SUPPORT

How I wished I'd had the vision to realise *LUCKY NUMBER 7* was a fallacy and my dreams of love and support from my family would never come.

I needed my family to step up to the plate and support me more than ever before.

I wish my parents had easier paths through their golden years.

Did they love me?

I need to believe the answer would be *YES.*

With most of my family gone, it was time for Brian and me to pick up the pieces and try to move on with life. My parents' home was quickly becoming ours, at least to maintain, until sold.

In the meantime, the vision of a loving family completely vanished. Our family splintered apart. I was left alone once the monthly hospital visits of my siblings came to an end.

I was LUCKY NUMBER 7—and now, I was wondering:

Where in the hell, has everyone gone?

4

GOING THROUGH

A meta-memoir

LOVE & LOSS

DATELINE: Summer 1987 – February 1988 – Saskatoon, Saskatchewan

In the summer of 1987, smack in the midst of Rebekah's fight for life, Corrie dumped me. Our relationship succumbed to going through—my list of challenges became too much for our love to continue to have legs.

TOO MUCH SHIT = DEATH OF LOVE

We fought.

We cried.

We made up.

We fought again.

We fought.

We fought.

I loved her. I loved her feisty attitude. I loved that she was a borderline vegetarian who loved McDonald's cheeseburgers and minute steaks.

We were too young to handle the pressure of being a couple.

We decided to remain friends.

Since men and women after breakups have so much more ahead of them, staying together—APART—is always the best medicine.

A movie date—cancelled—a new suitor was calling.

A dinner date—RING–RING–RING—a second date with the new man erased me from her plans.

Trying to be friends was unravelling brilliantly.

In September my Siamese cat Guy died of kitty cancer.

Corrie and I were on the verge of switching from love to hate.

I poured myself into my bartending job. I was rebounding meaningfully at work attempting to cloud reality.

Mutual friend pressure began to build. *My mum died.*

Come to my party. Was asked of me by Bub?

Will Vern & Corrie be there? I'd ask back.

Vern was my replacement.

I went to the party. Vern and I hit it off.

Three-hundred are you *OKAYS* later, and my relationship with Corrie officially died.

The following morning Corrie's parents phoned. Corrie had suffered a Brain Aneurysm in her sleep.

Over the course of the next few months, Vern and I became great friends as we passed each other at the hospital—Corrie's near death added perspective.

In February 1988, just as life was taking on a semblance of normal, I blew my left knee apart playing basketball.

Pressed for survival, after three months on crutches, I rushed back to work.

After my third shift back, I went out with my friends Bub and Jeffbo to see a movie. Before we could make it to a movie, my appendix exploded requiring emergency surgery or I would die.

The next morning, I woke up in the hospital – the same hospital where my mother had died.

MORE NAPSHKINS

DATELINE: 19 July 1988 – Regina, Saskatchewan

Federated Insurance hired me instead of Brian.

I moved to Regina eight months after my mother died.

Regina was a blur. I remember it was flat. It has no naturally grown trees or a body of water within city limits.

I was competent at my job. But, I hated it.

In search of social life, I took a second job at the Keg Restaurant.

My dance card quickly filled.

We drank heavily at work.

Hello, Ken. Hello, Rick. It's a pleasure to meet you. Oh, you're brothers; the Gillis brothers.

Drunken debauchery with them helped me erase any sustainable memory of Regina.

We ordered more shooters—and more shooters!

Rick (Slick) slurred and then asked for *more napshkins.*

I was not sure what a *napshkin* was.

CORRIE & VERN'S WEDDING DAY

DATELINE: 23 September 1989 – Saskatoon, Saskatchewan

Normalcy had returned to Corrie's mind.

I was asked to be an Usher and the MC at their wedding. A tremendous honour—I wondered if she remembered I was her ex-boyfriend.

Months earlier Whitey honoured me with being his Best Man at his wedding. He was tying the knot with the Ellis girl mentioned before; Rhonda. The wedding was Royal, complete with a horse-drawn carriage to transport the wedding party from church to reception.

MY WEDDING PARTICIPATION RIBBONS TO DATE

RING BEARER: 1 TIME
BEST MAN: 4 TIMES
GROOMSMAN: 2 TIMES
USHER: 1 TIME
MC: 1 TIME

Never the Groom—I hope I don't die alone.

CORRIE & VERN'S WEDDING EVE: Patrick, a Groomsman; a brash member of law enforcement, Dick the Best Man, and I, bonded.

Dick developed a painful rash. Pat and I rushed Dick to the U of S Hospital's Emergency Room for treatment.

Pat's Irish. He'd chugged a few pops on this night. While awaiting Dick to be given cream to rub on his—

Anyway, in front of the water fountain in the waiting room sat a man in a wheelchair, in agony—his jaw a jumbled mess.

Pat wanted water. He asked the guy to move out of the way.

The injured man's eyes filled with tears. His pain intensified. He moved his chair a few feet.

I changed my mind. I'm not thirsty anymore. Pat casually stated, looking into the man's tear-filled eyes.

I can't adequately describe the peculiarity of watching someone you spent three years with getting hitched; so, I won't try.

Stranger yet: Being the MC.

Vern's relatives were comedy suppressed Mennonites. Corries were fun-loving, hard-living Ukrainians   a tough room.

I killed.

Well, at least half of the room.

We like Vern. But, we'd prefer it to have been you. One of Corrie's uncles said to me in passing.

That was certainly awkward.

Corrie verbally presented me with a NO SLEEP WITH LIST or our friendship will end talk.

By the end of the night: Check one.

Now, where did I put the damn towels..?

SIMPLY IRRESISTIBLE

DATELINE: 31 October 1989 – Regina, Saskatchewan

In the spirit of Halloween: Vern, Corrie, Bub and I, paraded around Regina in slinky tight black dresses. Bub, wore a suit. We were re-enacting Robert Palmer's music video *Simply Irresistible*.

At the night's second stop Vern kept tapping me on the shoulder. He desperately asked for directions to the washroom.

I told him to focus—we were going on stage soon.

His desperation calmed.

Never mind. I don't need the washroom. I puked. I caught it in my mouth.

You're simply irresistible, simply irresistible—

5

THE WORLD OF V*I*CE

V*I*CE is calling with ingredients quivering precariously between experience and broken.
Are you ready for some fun?

A meta-memoir

THINKING INSIDE THIS BOX: WAXING POETIC IN A CONFUSING WORLD

There is a world of difference between truth and facts. Facts can obscure truth. - Maya Angelou

We have a responsibility to one another regardless of whether the world is going to implode today or in a thousand years. I believe part of that responsibility is for each of us to scrape as much of the negative crap as we can off of life's daily plate. Because, if in fact, it's all going BOOM anyway, wouldn't it better to be thinking of something else?

I want to think of sugar plums dancing in the air. A world of never-ending happiness where you can always see the sun, night or day, and when you call up your shrink—

Prince – Let's go Crazy

Technology, the media and fear mongers have despair, heartache and destruction piped into our homes twenty-four hours a day, seven days per week.

It's no wonder we need to escape!

WELCOME TO VICE WORLD
VICE MENU

Ala' carte and combinations are available – ask your provider for details!

MINOR AFFLICTIONS
COOKIES – MARSHMALLOWS – TRAVEL - INNOCENCE - PASSION – LOVE

- COOKIES AND MARSHMALLOWS: The sugar highs will speed you to happiness.
- TRAVEL: Exploration is intoxicatingly freeing. There is always someplace better. *What happens on the road—stays on the road!*
- INNOCENCE: Strip it away and you will eventually bask in the delights of *BITTER & JADED.*
- PASSION: Share threads with Happy. Uncheck it to enter the blissful state where *GREED* and *NEGLECT* comfort you. Try it with a slathering of *SOLITUDE* to enhance the need for additional *VICES.*
- LOVE: The spice of life. What wasn't taught in school or expressed at home, we bring to you here—let it consume you. Add a dash of neediness to make it better. Stir in sex to thicken the—hopefully coming to co-dependent and settling. Once marginal is achieved—we can entice you with elixirs to transport you places where others are *highly* searching for what you crave.

STARTERS
CAFFEINE – FITNESS – SMOKING – VIDEO GAMES
SPEED – ROCK & ROLL – MASTURBATION

- CAFFEINE: Pep up your day with a jolt. Add a dose of sugar for a tremendous one-two punch! Walk a block, have another blast of *JOE.*
- FITNESS: Obsession with body image is healthy. For that matter, obsession is extremely beneficial in every way. We're here to help you obsess!
- .SMOKING: We've added 4000+ mood-lifting chemicals to draw in with each enjoyable puff. Let the warmth of nicotine soothe your lungs. *(Enhance with Booze)*
- VIDEO GAMES: NEW!!! We will help you escape to your DREAMLAND. Add headphones to switch off the realities around you.
- SPEED: Express your masculinity by hitting the open road. The faster you go, the more intense the rush.
- ROCK & ROLL: Allow music to bring you to a vast MARKETPLACE. Once there, you will find everything you want!
- MASTURBATION: Studies have shown it helps prostate health. Obsession and porn are committed companions. *Add a banana for flavour.*

LET *US* TAKE YOU HIGHER!

Remember to Mix & Match. More is Always Better!

The pace quickens
Sex – Greed – Work – Serial Monogamy

- SEX: FUN – DIRTY – HOT – TABOO! Dive in and express love to the fullest. Needy makes it sweeter. Masturbation and porn are perfect playmates. Add several partners to make emotions uncomplicated. Getting off never felt so good!
- GREED: More of everything is always better. Can you ever have enough?
- WORK: Immerse yourself in it to make home life complete. More work means more stuff—more stuff paired with GREED will gleefully bring you to more…
- SERIAL MONOGAMY: Being in constantly questing validation is healthy—choose this option, and we'll provide several outlets to keep you numbed in denial.

The Big Hitters: Big Risks – Big Illusions – Big Fun – Booze – Drugs

----

Remember all options are interchangeable.
To experience the most intense exhilaration: Mix & Match.
Ask us about our Referral Program and Frequent Flyer Points.

Booze is the Crème de la Crème of our Market Place

- It will be around forever. Try one of our infinite varieties until you find your perfect liquid for your flavour palate.
- Prohibition failed to stop the flow.
- It brings sex, love, opportunity and friendship. Allow it to erase inhibition, lower standards, and to enhance personality.
- If lucky you will enter its World on a full-time basis; hopefully becoming a bartender, so the wonderfulness of tipsy can always be on your tongue!
- Put life on hold for another drink. You'll own the stage. Need cash—work a shift. Eliminate solitude—you have a finger on the pulse of desire.
- With proficiency, the day will be for sleep; the night will be for PLAY. Become a Vampire amongst your friends! Vampires are damn hot!
- Don't be shy, latch onto one of the stronger concoctions floating around as the GATEWAY opens the door to new experiences.
- Stay on the Booze Train and become a PATRON until the end. Subtract SOCIAL from the glass. Your new friend will keep you feeling right; SICKNESS will make it a daily requirement of WELL-BEING!
- We dare you to challenge yourself and others. Don't be a quitter. Drink more. Develop a fierce resolve. Drink enough, and we will put a plaque with your name on it where you regularly sit at the bar—who doesn't want a plaque?

VISIT ON SUNDAY FOR ALL YOU CAN INGEST SUNDAY

AND HIGHER!

PURCHASE ONE VICE ON TUESDAY – GET A SECOND VICE FREE

Drugs

- Second only to BOOZE in variety. Take a hit and escape to enlightenment.
- Enjoy the SOCIAL elements with friends as you want more and more and—
- Become part of the Culture—and escape to the AFTER HOUR WORLD where you will find oneness, friendship; and sex.
- Travel to these CLUBS around the GLOBE. With the right mixture; you may do so without leaving where you are.
- Sex will find you, enjoy without release.
- Meth is our most popular—but we encourage you to sample Ecstasy – Speed – GHB – Heroin - Lick-able Toads (only in season) + many more.
- Put them in a bowl and try one of our Hallucinatory VICE BOWLS—and watch your Mother and Father reunite in the new realm you discover.
- Here at VICE WORLD we provide the safest experience. Our trained Staff encourages the right to alter.
- We have experienced VICERS standing by to promote the latest high techniques to new users.
- TRY ANY VICE PANFRIED!
- The DRUG SECTION of VICE LAND is without the aggressiveness of Booze!

SCREWED

You are now entering the Vice Big Leagues. VICE CAREFULLY!

CRIME

Join our CRIME BRIGADE to be able to participate in every VICE on the MENU.
PROMOTE + PROVIDE + CREATE + DEAL + COLLECT + CONSUME + MORE
ASK YOUR SERVER FORE DETAILS.

FEAR MONGERING

- Only for the courageous; are you one of them?
- Strip away hope – Keep the Masses Down – Help them *ESCAPE!*

WORLD DOMINATION

- Be the first to achieve it.
- Delusion is not an ingredient. Sanity is overrated. Ego-driven sociopathic behaviour will look good on you.
- Be the GREATER GOOD – THE GOD OF VICE!

Want a CUSTOM VICE – LET OUR VICE DESIGNERS DESIGN A PERSONAL ONE-OF-A-KIND FORMULA SOLEY FOR YOUR PLEASURE!

COME BACK OFTEN – VICE HEAVEN AWAITS!

*E*veryting on the menu looks so tempting; I need a minute to decide my selection, is that okay?

No problem. Life has a habit of eventually bringing everyone to our door.

Will they harm me?

How many VICES; and how much consumption, is too much?

Nothings risk-free, Lindsay—a taste won't harm you. It may even take you to a better place.

One last question: Once I VICE—how long will I stay on the program?

Lindsay, it all depends on how much you want to experience, and how far you want to get away from reality?

May I suggest: Start with a taste and take it from there!

Intriguing, I think I will start with—

→*SPEED*→

WAYBACK: 1976 – 1978 – Saskatoon, Saskatchewan

After the success of my third driver's test, I was free to launch the 1963 Epic Envoy into high gear.

I hit the highway grinding my way through the gearbox. My locks were flowing. The speedometer after a few miles of floored read an invigorating FREEDOM 65; then snapped. My thirst for speed was not to be satiated by the Epic.

The Epic did, however; provide many moments of joy.

My friend Tony Gagnon wanted to drive. He was 15. I let him.

SMASH

He t-boned another car in an intersection smashing out the Epic's right headlight.

When Dad discovered the damage the next morning, he hooked up a one hundred watt trouble light from the light's housing to the battery.

A few weeks later while cornering hard—

BLIND SEED may have been right. You do have a sardonic laconic wit.

—I went to downshift into second gear; when I reached for the steering wheel, the gearshift was still in my hand. I could see the road passing by under the car.

When Dad discovered the damage he replaced the gearshift with a silver clamp; that just so fittingly happens to have another name: VISE-GRIP.

The girls at school began taking numbers!

Unfortunately, the number machine was stuck on zero.

To stop my *VICE* selection from being an unmitigated failure, I bought a car I couldn't afford, a 1978 Mercury Capri.

Number 17—Please—

I began collecting speeding tickets when I nearly turned the Capri into an incendiary rocket because of my overzealousness—six in one year—two within twenty blocks—on the same night.

The DMV put my speed on hold for one month.

I like this speed thing. A little expensive, but anyway, what goes well with it?

BOOZE

Two is always better than one!

VICE NUMBER 2: was to be liquid refreshments.

I completed my first season of football with Saskatoon Hilltops. We won the National Championships.

My ID stamped: LEGAL—four months before this day, on my nineteenth birthday.

Being a keen observer, I noticed at team parties popularity grew with consumption.

It was time to consume.

I sauntered up to the counter at the tavern in the Sutherland Hotel. My hands were shaking. Sweat was beading on my forehead. My voice was quivering.

Sweat was beading on the Bartender's forehead as well—this struck me as odd.

I asked what kinds brew they had?

He laughed, paused, and then rambled off a list, starting with Black Label.

I never heard anything after Black.

I asked for Black.

I wasn't asked to prove my age.

When I returned home, I turned the lights off in my bedroom, grabbed a flashlight—retreated under the covers pouring two beers at a time into a large mug; then guzzled. In nineteen minutes the last drop passed my lips, slid down my gullet, and began working its amber liquid magic on me.

The next day Mum woke me from my underwear clad, bathtub slumber, at 5 PM, when she returned from work. She escorted me back to bed.

VICE 2 found a willing new host.

Hey Mr VICE-tender, may I please have another?

SEX

DATELINE: 19(??) - ? – Everywhere

UPBRINGING + FOOTBALL = INDIVIDUALITY + NEED FOR VALIDATION + POPULARITY = OPPORTUNITY = SEX

Wrap *it* up—and go!

The above formula offered retreat, along with a full dance card.

Can you mix booze with sex?

Of course, you can. We all have, at least most of us.

To keep following along with this story I need you to assume a few things.

1. I've had several girlfriends; therefore assume—

2. If you're following the flow of the story you'd realise I'm approaching 30; therefore, you can assume: I wasn't still pure.

3. And, as much as I like sex, I like to stay humble, so; I won't share too many yarns about *doing it*. That may suddenly change if we ever get to DRUGS.

While I was partaking, I never missed going to the hospital to be with my father or mother.

The bloom came off my rose late, but once it did, I forgot how to say no. I'm not comfortable sharing my blossoming date.

You may assume whatever you'd like.

Sex is good—sticky at times—*if it ends with a towel*, it's not love.

I have cuddled with sisters in Jamaica.

I was tapped on the shoulder in a movie theatre by a couple and then asked if I'd like to join.

And, In front of an Aldo Shoes Store at 2 AM, I asked two ladies which shoes they preferred in the window. The next thing I knew, I was naked at their place. Wisely, I allowed them to shave off my body hair. If you were thinking booze was in the mix; your assumption would be correct.

Let me rework the equation:

BOOZE + FOOTBALL + BOOZE + POPULARITY = SEX

Booze and sex do mix after all!

BOOZE + SEX

WAYBACK: 22 October 1981 – Saskatoon, Saskatchewan

ACE

Drink and smart are often jiggered together. Booze has one role: to get us drunk.

By this date I managed to get drunk often in the two years I'd been drinking. Booze was working. I liked it!

It became a weekend activity. It never impacted work or school; nor did I turn aggressive. I was a happy drunk; except for one occasion.

After DJ-ING a Huskie football dance—I shone the spotlight of idiotic brightly on myself. I was hanging with three teammates. I shouted "FAGS" at two guys walking down the street.

They weren't happy with my choice of words, they wanted to fight. I tried to calm the situation. Booze encouraged me to call one of the guys *"Ace"*. He didn't like being called *Ace*.

Lost for what to do, I complimented him on his jacket selection. He still wanted to fight. He wanted GO-TIME.

When he began to take off his coat, I decked him—scoring a TKO. I was a buffoon. Coach Schneider cut me from the team over this scuffle.

I made a vow never to behave that way ever again.

CAM: PART 1

WAYBACK: 1982 – Banff – Calgary Alberta – Saskatoon, Saskatchewan

I was on holiday in Banff with my friend Cam and his girlfriend Kathy. We all got sloshed.

Cam and I played football together. His father owned a Greek Restaurant. He offered me a bartending job. I accepted. The position stripped away my bartending virginity.

In Calgary, the night after the sloshed evening, we tried to relive the debauchery of the night before. I suggested I was so drunk I could've had sex and not remembered.

Cam claimed my thoughts were insane.

Kathy piped in: *Lindsay did walk through the hotel lobby naked.*

I blushed.

TWO-MONTHS LATER

I was alone with Kathy when she brought up the night in Banff. She reflected on the debate in Calgary.

She told me when I made it back to the hotel room—Cam was passed out on a bed—they had had a big fight. She said Cam was exasperating. She said I threw all of Cam's toiletries into the bathroom sink in disgust of his behaviour.

She said Cam's stomach was wambling.

Kathy informed me we did have sex. She said we did it while Cam was puking in the next bed.

WATER BALLOON

WAYBACK: 22 May 1989 – Regina, Saskatchewan

Corrie and Vern drove the one hundred fifty miles from Saskatoon to Regina for a weekend visit.

We double-dated with my new girlfriend; her name shall remain removed from this story.

At night's end, upon returning to my home, each one of us tipsy; Corrie and Vern slept on my hide-a-bed in the living room. My name-removed girlfriend and I slithered into my bedroom.

79

In the morning Corrie came into my room to wake us. She entered the room mid-thrust. She hurried away embarrassed.

After a post-sex slumber, I went to the bathroom to relieve myself. The rush of release was pleasurable. I began panicking. No stream was hitting the bowl. The fear intensified.

A few moments later, I realised: I was still sporting a condom.

6

LOVE & A TROPICAL BEACH

A meta-memoir

GOODBYE BERNICE & SADIE?

DATELINE: 15 December 1989 – 12 February 1990

Jamaica – Regina – Saskatoon – Edmonton – Calgary

I travelled to Jamaica for a second time in December 1989; the second time with Bub.

She left her socks at home.

When we returned to Canada on December 15, the thermostat was a bone-freezing, lips-stuck-to-the-light-standard minus 40 degrees Celsius. I landed in Regina. Bub continued on to Saskatoon.

My car had frozen to death. It refused to start for one week. Eventually, I had it towed to a garage to thaw it out.

My disdain for selling insurance brought my career to an end at the sixteen-month mark, just before our trip. I loved my friends in Regina. My liver wasn't so fond of them. Decision time was upon me.

No job – no girlfriend – a dying liver – most of my friends were moving west—it's fucking minus 40.

It was time to move west. The question, how far?

EDMONTON = BROTHER + SISTER IN LAW + NIECES + AUNTS + UNCLES—

— A definite possibility.

CALGARY = 3 SISTERS + 1 BROTHER + 1 BROTHER IN LAW + BANFF—

—I decided to let the thermostat decide.

Before I departed westward, I moved back to Saskatoon to organise my life. In February 1990, I loaded my Acura Integra with all of my worldly possessions including my white cat named: White Cat—and launched my odyssey.

Corrie & Vern, Darryl & Rhonda, and Barb escorted me as far as Edmonton.

Minus 36 Celsius erased OPTION 1.

Tearfully, I said farewell to my friends and moved on.

In Calgary, I visited Bev & Garth, Shannon and Aimee.

Of course, I stayed with my sisters, Bernice and Sadie.

They were now in their early 50s. They were still living together.

The rest of the family regularly tried to judge them by asking what's up with the girls, why haven't they married; are they—?

I had made several trips with friends to Calgary and Banff over the years. I avoided contacting them each time.

Could you find another place to stay? We need the house for the relatives.

Calgary's decision wasn't weather related.

FLASH TO THE FUTURE: Turn on the tube. The Simpson's are on. It's an episode featuring Patty and Selma.

FLASH BACKWARD: Middle-aged + live together + single + both worked for AGT + chain-smokers—

—what are my other options?

VANCOUVER = WES

VALENTINE'S DAY 1990

DATELINE: 14 February 1990 – Calgary to Vancouver

I was trying to sleep on my sisters' sofa bed. It was 5:30 AM. Bernice and Sadie were sitting on opposite sides of the bed. They were both taking long hard pulls on their fags. I cracked my eye(s) open ever so slightly. I pretended to sleep. A haze of smoke rivalling a blues bar was smothering me. They bantered back and forth over top me. Their words hung in the smoke.

MacGyver is one hot tomato.

I couldn't agree more. Richard Dean makes me—

I don't think Lindsay will ever amount to much.

I couldn't agree more—he will never be as good as his older brothers.

He should give up and live with us.

Everything but MacGyver is true.

The door closed behind them on their way to work. That was our farewell. I haven't seen them since.

I'm going to do my best to amount to something.

WELCOME TO VANCOUVER

I love Vancouver.

It is one of the most beautiful cities on the planet!

The pristine mountains melt into the sparkling sea and seduce the soul.

Why don't you come for a visit some time?

By the time I reached Kamloops, it was +5 Celsius.

With less than two hours to go to Vancouver, it started snowing, hard. I thought the snow would turn to rain once I began my descent to the ocean.

It didn't.

I started counting cars in the ditch. I stopped at two hundred.

Two weeks after landing in Vancouver on Valentine's Day, I found a job bartending at Carlos & Bud's, a funky Tex-Mex joint.

Wes and I found a killer pad.

My new life began.

Wes, I'm not certain how happy I am. Life has taken me on a rocky ride. I feel lost.

He tried to encourage me. He asked when I felt the most content.

In Jamaica, I said.

ROAD RASH

DATELINE: 11 July 1990 – Negril, Jamaica

Five months later Wes and I, along with Greg (four-foot-eleven), landed in Jamaica. We were going to rub our nickel collections together and buy a hotel.

Our negotiation began on the patio of one of the suites of the White Sands Resort. Greg's feet dangled. Wes wasn't intimidated by the league we were about to enter.

Steve (named changed) the son-in-law of the owner Henry had been directed to seek potential buyers. Steve was a Caucasian from Virginia. He came across as a good guy.

He told us they'd entertain a $4-million offer, US.

The property was beautiful. It was situated smack dab in the middle of a seven-mile long white sand beach. It consisted of twenty-nine units, a bar, and a Private Villa.

Steve indicated Henry was motivated to find buyers who would keep the place intact.

We sipped Red Stripes together. Steve informed us of the challenges of owning a business in Jamaica. We shared life stories with him. He was interested in our potential.

Wes jumped in saying we were prepared to offer $2.5-million.

I stared blankly at Wes.

A $2.9-million offer was accepted.

We didn't have a clue what we were doing.

We were given six months to secure funding.

Time to celebrate was upon us.

The next day we rented motorcycles. I'd never ridden one before.

Shorty was a wee bit stoked about our looming little adventure.

Wes assured me short shorts and flip flops were proper attire for motorcycling.

Riding was invigorating. The wind rushed through my flowing locks. Heat and humidity were making my body glisten with anticipation.

We rode over hills, past breathtaking seascapes, dodging carnivorous potholes along the way.

PIT STOP: TASTY JERK CHICKEN + TINGS = DELICIOUS

Satisfied it was time to return to Negril

Wes opened the throttle. The *Friendly Giant* trailed close behind. I struggled to keep pace.

Wes had told me we'd go at my pace before we began. Wes lied.

I tried to keep up. I feared spliff wielding Rastafarians devouring me when night fell.

THUD

I hit a pothole at forty miles per hour, dead centre. My body was flying over the handlebars. I figured that was bad—very bad.

I pushed downward, fell sideways, and commenced a fifty-yard slide with the bike between my legs. *It hurt.* My riding gear didn't protect me.

I sprung to my feet. I threw my hands in the air. I screamed: *I'm OKAY.*

Wes and Kareem were long gone.

I turned, looked at the asphalt of the road and began taking inventory:

BIKE: CHECK – SANDAL: CHECK – SANDAL: CHECK – HAT: CHECK – SKIN: CHECK – RASTAFARIANS—

That's odd, the white tape I was wearing on my hand seemed to have peeled off. Oh fuck, I wasn't wearing tape.

My toe was dangling. *That can't be good.*

The shock was setting in when Wes and *Willis* returned.

I told them the sandals didn't protect me.

Shortly after that, I sat in the waiting room of a small village clinic. Wes placed my flip flops on my toe-dangled feet. A fan blew at my face. Every two minutes a nurse would come by to empty the blood from my sandals.

Hello, I'm Dr Babs.

His degree was from the University of Nigeria. He said he'd fix me up good for $100 US. The price would include Demerol + cleaning + stitches.

I had $60 Canadian on me.

He said he'd do the best he could. He then instructed the nurse to grab a batch of purple stuff along with the vials next to the Demerol.

He fixed me up real—

The vials made me hallucinate.

CORRECTION: it was what was in the vials that made me hallucinate.

It was time to return to Vancouver to pull a rabbit out of a hat.

Rocky do want to see me pull a rabbit out of a hat?—Nothing up my sleeve.

During the flight home, my right calve muscle turned into solid oak and my right foot tripled in size—*troubling me.*

In the Emergency Room of a Seattle Hospital, a Doctor scraped beach remnants out of my dangling toe. He then went looking for a Doctor old enough to figure out what the purple stuff was—and he suggested I stay a couple of days to save my foot.

I agreed it was a good idea.

He hooked me up to powerful antibiotics. He saved me from being left with a stump.

When I sent Greg to pick up the tickets, the DAY of the flight, I specifically instructed him to purchase: MEDICAL INSURANCE.

Several months later the hospital bills began rolling in. OUCH. Private hospital rooms in the States are SELL-YOUR-FIRST-BORN expensive.

Not to worry, I'd get Greg to bring over the MEDICAL INSURANCE I'd instructed him to buy on the DAY of the flight and everything would be okay.

Greg came over. He looked distraught. I asked him to hand me the insurance papers.

By mistake, you bought FLIGHT CANCELLATION INSURANCE?

Being patted on the back by Jamaican pavement isn't fun, a painful lesson. What's more painful—I'd better go have a first born.

Wes and I began rolling coins.

→ → →

LET'S MEET GAIL

DATELINE: 28 July 1990 – Vancouver, British Columbia

Love has a way of rearing its beautiful head at the strangest of times.

Back in Vancouver Wes was now my manager at Carlos & Bud's. He insisted every staff member, and every customer, was sufficiently inebriated on a nightly basis.

Wes would fill a cleaning bottle with Tequila and then go table-to-table adamantly delivering quick bursts of tequila.

TEQUILA + TEN CENT CHICKEN WINGS EQUALS:

Lindsay, after eating, I don't know, one gazillion wings, including: 'so hot that they'll slaughter your intestines placing them in a fiery grave only to force hair to grow on your eyeballs,' and umpteen blasts of Jose Cleaning Fluid Flavoured Tequila. I woke in the middle of the night sweating profusely. You'd never guess what I saw. I opened my drapes—thousands of wingless birds were pecking at my windows. How do they know where I live? What was in the spray bottle? Save me!"

I suggest you take a moment to grab a bucket.

I fell in love with Gail at first sight.

She was a delightful mix of exotic ethnicity. She was enticingly gorgeous, ridiculously gorgeous; gorgeously gorgeous.

She dropped into C & B's with friends on this late July night.

Wes made me shotgun a beer. After I attempted explaining the beauty my eye(s) desired. I stuttered and said: *Girl... table... over there, pretty, likes, hair—*

Wes set up our first date.

Why would anyone care about my eye(s) content?

Well, I'm not entirely sure. Maybe simply because we've all been there before—if you haven't: What's going on?

FLASHING BACK ONE WEEK: I blew my knee apart during the inaugural Carlos & Bud's Flaming Hoops TWO-ON-TWO BASKETBALL TOURNAMENT. It was the third time I blew my left knee apart—and the fourth significant trauma to my knees.

My first injury occurred while playing hockey with the football team back in University. I can't skate. I scored a goal. I administered a solid body check by fluke. I was feeling cocky. A two hundred fifty pound linebacker was skating full speed with his head down. Hot on his tail, a gigantic offensive lineman. I was planning to devastate him at centre ice. I skate ankles turned outward with the skates nearly parallel with the ice. At the last second, I determined what I was attempting to do was a bad idea. It was too late. Both of my knees slammed into the ice with the force of impact causing them to split downward.

The linebacker asked the lineman if he felt anything—*did we just hit something?* was his answer.

For the next three months, crutches were useless except for standing.

Adult Surgery Count: 3 Left Knee + 1 Right Knee + Appendix + Dr Babs = 6 Total

DATELINE: 24 SEPTEMBER 1990 – VANCOUVER, BRITISH COLUMBIA

I managed to discard the crutches just in time for my first date with the enticingly gorgeously gorgeous, Gail.

She was a nationally ranked rhythmic gymnast. She was 23. She was in the last year of psychology at UBC. She was adopted. Her parents were Japanese. She was only part Japanese.

Her parents didn't approve of us.

Her father refused to shake my hand.

Maybe the internment camps of WWII had something to do with his disapproval.

I believed my charm and ambition would eventually win her parents over.

I think I'm turning Japanese. I think I'm turning Japanese—

HOTELIERS + MANUEL NORIEGA

DATELINE: 17 September 1990 – Vancouver, British Columbia

Where does one find $5-million US?

Two million nine hundred thousand US million for purchase—the remainder for operations—

FIRST PLACE: We took the cushions off the couch.

NEXT: An Apple McIntosh computer appeared out of thin air. 1990 value: $10,000.

Wes knew a man named Bob. Bob spent his life savings on the Apple. Bob liked boats. Wes also loved boats. Wes told Bob that if we could have his computer, he could run our Aquatics Division.

Have we an Aquatics Division?

~~We~~ I prepared an extensive business plan without any experience working with computers.

It was time to go fund shopping.

Wes went to the store and bought a newspaper with our couch funds. We flipped straight to the Money to Borrow Section.

Metropolitan's offices were plush. They screamed success. Joan was to be our dream merchant. Joan resembled the Elephant Man meets Eddie Munster. Her lack of beauty gave us confidence.

That was a horrible thing to type.

Two days later our funding was approved. I was to fly to Miami—take a cab to Ft. Lauderdale—check into a Holiday Inn—and wait for a representative of a company from Zurich to call with instructions.

Life was sweet. Eternal sunshine was on the horizon.

Being an international business tycoon was fun.

FLY TO JAMAICA—BUY HOTEL—MAGICALLY, A COMPUTER APPEARS—PASS GAS
—A MONKEY AND IN-DEPTH BUSINESS PLAN FALLS OUT—REMOVE SOFA CUSHIONS
—BUY A NEWSPAPER—FIVE-MILLION US DROPS FROM THE SKY!

That sounds believable.

We believed it.

To this point of my story, I'd like to assure you other than the monkey falling out of my ass, most of my story is on point, including the dialogue. Of course, my recollection allows for leeway.

DATELINE: 13-15 October 1990 – Fort Lauderdale, Florida

Final boarding call for Air Canada Flight 123 to Toronto—
TORONTO—CHICAGO—MIAMI—CAB TO FORT LAUDERDALE—HOLIDAY INN

I eagerly awaited the call from the Swiss connection. I decided to try to unwind. I went for a stroll. I hobbled approximately ten miles north up Fort Lauderdale's expansive beach. Nondescript hotels jutted out of the sand marking the shoreline. Beachside the hotels looked like crap—street side they sported lavish facades.

Back at the lodge the phone never rang. I called home. No news was bad news. It was time to return.

The next morning the Miami Herald's cover greeted me with:

Encephalitis Scare Hits Miami Keep Exposed Skin Covered Avoid Mosquitoes at All Cost

It did strike me as odd I was the only person out walking. No biggie—the mosquitoes loved me—approximately 200 times.

Back at the airport, I made a final call out of desperation.

Cab back to the Holiday Inn—Wait by phone—

A heavily accented female informed me the contract was ready. I was to meet the representative outside of a restaurant down by the docks. I was to bring $10,000 cash. She told me it was a good faith gesture. Once I signed the documents and gave them the money we would meet the following day—at the meeting, they'd confirm the $5-million deposit.

I questioned her.

She assured me this was normal business practice.

I suggested they deposit $10,000 into our account as a good faith gesture and we would return it when the $5-million hits our account.

She hung up.

MANUEL NORIEGA

DATELINE: 27-29 January 1991 – Panama City, Panama

Not to be deterred Joan found OPTION 2.

A Panamanian company, Pan Global was interested. A requirement of the potential deal was it was mandatory for us to hire a consultant.

Wes grabbed the Yellow Pages.

In the offices of William L, I pitched our Business Plan. He loved it. He agreed to work with us on a contingency basis.

Bill and I were instructed to fly to Panama. Our company (Shoreline) was to foot the bill.

Wes, pull the cushions off the couch. Nothing up my sleeve—

Joan came to the rescue securing $10,000 in bridge financing.

JANUARY 27 - 6 AM—VANCOUVER INTERNATIONAL AIRPORT

At the Continental Airlines counter, I asked for two tickets to Panama.

The clerk asked for a payment of $3,000.

I sang. I danced. I said we wouldn't be able to pay until noon. I sang some more. We offered Wes's expired passport as collateral. She handed us the tickets. I danced a little more.

Ten minutes later, Bill arrived.

Seattle—Denver—San Antonio—Miami—Fajitas for Dinner—11 PM - Panama

With our luggage in hand Bill and I stood on the sidewalk outside Panama City's Airport, William asked me if we forgot to do something.

We decided to go back inside the airport; we tapped four times on the Customs Office windows waking the Customs Officers—we let them know we'd arrived.

The humidity was nearing 300%. Our cabbie whisked us to our hotel (Marriot). The roads reminded me of Jamaica with the only exception being there was no reggae music pulsing from roadside bars, each home along the way protected by iron bars.

Tomorrow I was going to own a hotel. I was overwhelmed. I turned on the television in an attempt to relax. A warning message emanated from the screen.

WARNING

Tomorrow's humidity will reach 500%.

If exposed to for more than one minute, you will turn into a puddle only to be lapped up by passing mules.*

Stay indoors at all costs.

THAT WASN'T IT

WARNING - WARNING - WARNING

Due to dangerous conditions stay out of the following sectors—
Failure to do so may result in arrest, injury, loss of limb, or even death.
The fighting is intense—the situation is grave.
The humidity will reach 500%.
We've spotted packs of thirsty mules throughout all sectors—

I was startled out of my sleep by knocking. I cracked the door open a whisper.

A muffled panting voice announced it was *Francis* from room service.

I never ordered room service. I fell back asleep.

I noticed as we rode in the cab to Pan Global every business came with a semi-automatic weapon-toting doorman; strangely, not comforting.

I'm Mr Ortega; this is Mr Hernandez, Mr Ortega and Mr. Martinez. Welcome to Panama!

His voice was low and gravelly. After he had given a brief history on Pan Global, it was time for me to present. Mid presentation I paused. I looked out the window. Military helicopters were hovering in the distance. Plumes of smoke were rising from the conflict below. I sheepishly asked what was going on.

Mr Ortega added more gravel to his voice and explained Panama was in a struggle for liberation and justice. He told me what I was seeing was not of our concern. It is simply a way of life. He said they fight weekdays 9 to 5. On weekends they come together both friends and enemies to celebrate life.

At presentations end the funding was stamped: APPROVED.

I hovered above the cab all the way back to the hotel. William and I drank celebratory beers. Afterwards, I retreated to my room to call home with the good news.

THREE TAPS ON MY DOOR LATER

William cancelled the happy news. He had phoned his company's Panama Office; they said, Pan Global and Noriega in the same sentence. They suggested we get the hell out of the country as quick as possible. *Do not tell anyone what is going on. Do not talk on the phone,* were our orders.

He asked me to bring him the airline tickets so we could cash them in and fly out on the next available flight.

Joan had failed to deposit the bridge funding. The tickets had no value. I had to break this reality to Bill.

Bill handled the news gracefully. He understood Joan fucked us. His office arranged our flights home. Bill paid for the hotel.

That night I cried in my hotel room. I phoned Gail to tell her I loved her. I struggled drifting off to sleep because the rotors of military helicopters buzzed all night long as they continually circled the hotel.

Our dream was dying in the humidity of Panama. Henry and Steve gave us an extension.

We met William at his office two weeks later. Stapled to our file was a picture of a military officer with his foot on the head of an enemy, his rifle pressed against his temple. The picture's headline:

ATTEMPTED OVERTHROW GREETS PANAMA

LOW TIDE

DATELINE: February – May 1991 – Vancouver, British Columbia

MEANWHILE BACK IN VANCOUVER: My relationship with Gail was hanging by a thread.

The Shoreline Investment Group had exhausted all funds, including my credit card.

Barring a miracle our dream was dying.

Instead of a Hotel Owner, I was a gimped bartender unable to work. Our relationship paid the price. I was rehabilitating my knee so that I would be able to pour the next drink. Her father still wouldn't shake my hand. We were growing in different directions.

In May, the Jamaican dream died.

27 JULY 1991

When Gail started with *I love you but,* the end was here. *She called me the sweetest ever. She said sorry.*

I cried for the next seventeen hours. Gail had to decide: *press on* or leave our love on a tropical beach.

She chose the beach.

PATHETIC
AUGUST – NOVEMBER 1991

Screw – twist – screw - twist

A giant hand reached inside of my cracked open cranium and removed 70% of my brain, including: *DIGNITY, PRIDE* and *ESTEEM.* I asked politely for my brain matter to be hidden—maybe in the closet beside the Atari.

Soon, I would learn painful lessons about love.

Before love school was to commence, I decided respecting Gail's wishes was ridiculous.

With my brain-lightened skull, I was able to convince myself, I couldn't live without her. *I was an idiot.*

SURVIVING LOSS: NO LETTING GO: NO HOW TO WIN LOVE BACK: BINGO!

Telling her I love her twenty-eight thousand times didn't work. Buying her a ring I couldn't afford didn't work either. I needed a different *angle.* The book suggested giving her surprise gifts on days with no meaning. Not birthdays or Valentine's Day, but instead; random Tuesdays. Sounds like sage advice; I'll do it, I decided.

The plan was brilliant. Gail didn't dump me because she didn't want to be with me. She dumped me because I wasn't buying her random shit. Random crap screams: LOVE.

The Phil Collins song *Throwing it All Away*—provided escape while I plotted.

Better phone Gail and sing.

NEEDY + CRIPPLED + BLITHERING

I managed to achieve all three in less than nine months. *Time to fill the bathtub.*

I even tried to convince Gail I liked rhythmic gymnastics more than football.

It was time to go for the gusto. I rented a video camera and filmed myself reciting *Off to Sea,* a beautiful childrens' book about losing and finding love, in the background I played Extremes song *More Than Words* on my stereo. I placed the video on Gail's doorstep   idiot didn't do me justice.

BLIND DETERMINATION

Thanks to my brains malfunctions I still believed I could win Gail back. My manipulation plan failed miserably. Anxiety attacks occurred daily. But still, I thought I wouldn't survive without her.

I was a dickhead.

GUILT made it his mission to remind me of that daily.

I continued to be a dickhead.

GUILT called me a fool, laughed at me; and then told me.

GUILT said idiots do not deserve to be loved.

It took me one year to realise I was becoming sad, pathetic and borderline certifiable.

*   There have been no reported cases of mules lapping up the liquid remains of melted humans. Though possible—it is highly unlikely.

7

SUPPORT NETWORK

A meta-memoir

FRIENDS + SURGERY + FRIENDS + MORE SURGERY

DATELINE: 4 August 1991 – Vancouver, British Columbia

PATRICK K M

I was alone in a new city.

Gail was gone.

Wes was a free spirit.

I had one great friend to lean on. Patrick, the Irish groomsman from Corrie & Vern's wedding. He relocated to Vancouver to SERVE & PROTECT. He became a member of the RCMP.

Pat is big and burly. Rumour has it his family is from the *Screw* part of Cork, Ireland.

Pat's assignment was to drag me out of the quicksand swallowing me.

He used alcohol as his tool.

We'd meet, he'd let me wallow for a couple of drinks, he'd then increase the pace, whisking me away to intoxication.

He did a stellar job.

KNEE UPDATE
8 AUGUST 1991

Not only was I without Gail, but my knee still resembled spaghetti from blowing it apart in the FLAMING HOOPS BASKETBALL TOURNAMENT. My good Doctor ordered one hour of rigorous physiotherapy daily. I tripled his recommendation.

I rotated between physiotherapy and *balling* my eyes out, with the occasional visit from a Jocelyn, a co-worker from the *Bombay Bicycle Club*, the pub where I was now working. Jocelyn just so happened to be an ex-stripper.

She'd visit with her daughter. Her daughter was 5. She'd instruct her daughter to watch TV in my living room. She'd then escort me to my bedroom, to begin contorting.

Towel, please.

Fortunately, TV was an excellent babysitter.

By the end of August, my life was beginning to rebound.

I asked the good Doctor if I would ever be able to play sports again.

He said: *YES.*

GAME TWO into the Touch Football Season:

SPRINT HERE + CUT + SPIN + PLANT TO THROW = POP = NOT GOOD PAIN

I called Gail out of desperation attempting to manipulate sympathy from her.

She never returned my calls, until—we got back together.

We now have three beautiful children.

THE END

FAMILY SUPPORT

DATELINE: 9 August 1991 – Vancouver, British Columbia

With the *fantasy* of the last sentence never coming to fruition I realised it might be time to reach out to family

Brother Don had moved up the political ranks in Saskatchewan. He was working directly under the Province's Premier. On one of his rare visits to Vancouver where we got together, he had met Gail.

On this day, I was phoning him to tell him about my knee injury.

With my voice squeaking, I said to him, Gail dumped me.

As for his supportive response: *You're the best looking and smartest Wincherauk. Your problem is you are an underachiever. That is likely why Gail kicked you to the curb.*

When I got off the phone, I cried—and then screamed: *FUCK!*

After I had calmed down, I called Bernice and Sadie. Since they work for the Alberta Government Telephone Company (AGT) they had told me if I ever need to call, I can call collect.

The operator asked if they'd accept the charges from Lindsay.

Bernice replied: *Lindsay who?*

My fucking sister, when I needed her love, dumped: *Lindsay who on me?*

I returned to my Doctor who gave me the go ahead to play sports. He was too busy to see me. I was in excruciating pain; so, I went to another hospital for diagnosis of my new injury.

Dr Regan at the UBC Hospital wiggled my knee. I screamed, fainted, and continued screaming while fainting. He mumbled something under his breath. He asked me to come to his clinic in a few days after the swelling subsides.

Dr Regan told me the previous *Surgeons ke*pt taking things out of my knee—they never fixed it—my knee is now fucked, his words not mine. He informed me I have no cartilage left—causing my bones to grind together.

I tore my ACL ligament, which removed my ability to move laterally. That was the root of the cartilage damage. And, I tore two additional ligaments.

I was itching to tell Gail.

·He then dropped the most troubling news for me. He said he wasn't sure if operating was an option. Learning to walk normally was to be my first goal. He then offered an olive branch: Extensive rehab to rebuild my atrophied leg, once I build up enough strength he'd take a look inside to see what he had to work with and to see if there is any point fixing my knee.

I asked about sports.

He assured me he'd do his best, no guarantees. If he saw hope, I would be ordered to do extensive rehab to rebuild my leg's strength—then he'd operate and repair whatever he could salvage.

After surgery—

SATAN'S PURSUIT

DATELINE: 10 August 1991 – Vancouver, British Columbia

Repeated stints of knee rehabilitation sounded like a cakewalk through Hell.

I'd been to Hell before. Going on crutches was going to present different barriers.

I didn't want to burn. I beat the Satanic Demons off with my crutches. I screamed for them to get out of my way. My crutches caught on fire.

Being kicked in life's junk repeatedly helped me develop resiliency along with a sense of martyrdom. I was broke. I couldn't drive. I crutched home from physiotherapy—seven miles. The temperature was +30 Celsius.

Sweat was dripping down my face when a lovely couple stopped to offer me a ride—I was two miles into my crutching journey home. My crutches were sparking blazes on the side of the road. Beelzebub and Lucifer were on my heels. They were salivating.

I said *NO* to the couple as pain shot under my arms, my face broken with anguish. I sternly told them I wanted to crutch.

They seemed to think I was nuts.

Lucifer was catching up.

Beelzebub stopped at a Starbucks because he saw a Zombie he recognised.

OCTOBER – DECEMBER 1991

EXTENSIVE REHAB + UNBEARABLE ANXIETY + TUESDAY GIFTS FOR GAIL + WES AND PAT GETTING ME DRUNK

Unfortunately, no work—bartenders who can't stand up are strangely not in demand. I hurt myself on Sunday—by Wednesday—my cash reserves had dried up.

An angel must've been watching over me; somehow, I survived.

I was, however, tempted to beat young sitting panhandlers who'd ask for change while I was crutching past them, senseless.

SMACK
Did that hurt? It looked like it hurt.

KNEE SURGERY—

DATELINE: February 1992 – Vancouver, British Columbia

The room was sterile and cold. Masked men and women were hovering above me. My ceremonial gown was open in the back. My ass was freezing. Needles dangled from my arms. I was doped up. Satan finally caught up with me. My underarms were raw due to my stubbornness. My sacrifice was upon me. The Epic Envoy was parked waiting with a full fuel tank.

Doctor Regan asked me to count backwards from one hundred.

One hundred – ninety-nine—

I wasn't about to be sacrifice—instead, this was operation number—

In recovery Dr Regan shared the fantastic news: I qualified for another operation. He then said he'd repeat the story later when I kick my morphine addiction.

And, even later, he said there was hope for a healthy life. The rehab bus was arriving in two minutes. He told me if I hurried I might be able to catch it.

My butt was still freezing.

FAMILY DOCTOR (DOCTOR MUSIAL)

My family Doctor is named Alex Musial. His practice is in the upscale neighbourhood of Kerrisdale. The majority of his patients are aged, precariously close to expiring. Wes introduced me to him. He appeared to love us.

I'm certain he loved us because we had long lives ahead, hopefully. On rare occasions a patient would enter his office upright only to leave vertical; whereas, my visits often brought a smile to his face.

Dr Musial would laugh. I'd ask him what was so funny. I'd tell him my knee has swollen to the point where I can't bend it, and the pain was relentless.

He'd continue to chuckle. He'd then ask if I used to have chest hair.

After I'd answer, he'd laugh some more.

He suggested since I was out of commission anyway, why don't I have surgery to fix my drooping eye.

I thought I was visiting because of my knee. I accepted Dr Musial's suggestion.

BLIND EYE(S)

DATELINE: 11 MARCH 1992 – VANCOUVER, BRITISH COLUMBIA

I was instructed to count backwards from one hundred.

One hundred—

My postoperative nurse's demeanour was crotchety. She had no time for my knee injury.

We won't release you until you can make your way to the washroom by yourself, she said.

I was blind. I couldn't walk. For some reason, my nurse didn't care.

I tripped—collapsing to the floor.

She was forced to pick me up off the floor—and then assist me to the loo. She still didn't care about my knee.

REVISED ADULT SURGERY TOTAL

5 LEFT KNEE + 1 RIGHT KNEE + APPENDIX + EYE + 1.5 AMATEUR LOBOTOMIES + DR. BABS
= 8 SURGERIES ADMINISTERED BY MEDICAL PROFESSIONALS

VEHICULAR SOLIDARITY

My sleek, sexy, hot red ride, a Fiat Convertible; with working headlights, suffered from an aversion to turning left. Straight ahead: no problem, right turns: a breeze, left: never—an unfixable problem. Fiats were fun but notoriously unreliable.

Could it have possibly been showing support for my mangled left knee?

I finally bought a car I could afford, and to show its gratitude: it up and dies on me.

By the end of April, I cast the walking sticks aside. I was able to return to work. Unfortunately, I was facing a small problem: my employer had replaced me. Apparently, a *one hundred fifty day* sabbatical was *one hundred fifty days* too many.

My ferocity landed me two jobs: Earl's Restaurant; and the Hotel Cali. Bartending sucked me back in—I was about to CHECK IN—one day I hoped, I would be able to CHECK OUT.

The Hotel Cali was a five-minus-four-and-a-half-star hotel.

Occasionally, the cleaning staff came to my office to tell me of a guest that wasn't doing well.

Lindsay, the man in Room 450, is sitting upright. He has a needle in his arm. He's dead. Did you want to see?

CAM: PART 2

I hadn't seen Cam in several years.

Cam dropped out to the coast for an impromptu visit just before I started my *Earl's* career.

Cam was rebounding from love (not Kathy). His marriage had failed. Rumours were swirling around him about insider trading—change was in order.

Wes was now managing a funky restaurant named *Cucina Cucina*. It was an Italian joint owned by Asians. The owners loved Wes. He packed the place nightly with diners. The owners loved seeing a full house. They didn't like the fact he did it by using the same techniques he used at *Carlos & Bud's*.

One morning Wes arrived at work to find a ransom note. One of the owners had been kidnapped. Wes found this exciting. Wes's excitement upset the other owner—he fired Wes—a severance package was delivered to him. Cam and I were the recipients of Wes's severance gravy.

PARTY TIME: Taking the fast-ferry from Vancouver to Victoria would help to alleviate my knee pain – Cam's divorce pains – Wes's sobriety pains. We bellied up to the bar onboard.

We arrived in Victoria's beautiful Inner Harbour, fifty minutes after departure.

Carry-on luggage in hand we sauntered into Milestones Restaurant Lounge.

SMALL WORLD: Cam knew the bartender.

After several pops, we asked if we could store our belongings at the restaurant.

WE VISITED: Lounge + lounge + lounge + brewpub – and finally + a popular nightclub. *The name escapes me.* Maybe I lost the name because of 3 lounges + brewpub + nightclub.

We were pickled, feeling no pain, two-sheets-to-the-wind—and somehow: we were still remarkably, charming. Painfully, my knee had turned into spaghetti from shaking it on the dance floor.

We ordered food at an all-night eatery. Three lovely locals joined us. They offered to be our gracious hosts for the evening.

Hey, pasta..! I don't remember ordering pasta?

Wes's chicken burger was raw. I informed the server of this fact. Wes ate it anyway. He said his stomach's resolve was unbreakable.

Sarah found me to be cute; she offered to take me home with her.

Wes and Cam left with the other girls.

Sarah changed her mind about taking me home. Sleeping face down in my pasta probably helped her to make up her mind.

I searched my pockets for loot. I found $5. My knee was revolting. I was in a good spot.

The previous sentence wasn't sauced in sarcasm.

It started raining heavily. I needed to think, quickly – *I'm drunk.* Maybe, I needed to—not think at all. Yes, that would be the ticket—escape your problem—the answer will find you. *Those brick walls over there look like bricks.* Not thinking; wasn't going to work. So, I thought some more. *Those guys in the storefronts seem to know what they're doing. Nah, they don't look like me. Damn it*—I thought—*think Lindsay—think. What would Lindsay do?*

Hey, that's, me, I'll just ask.

I *mocked* myself for the pasta move. I then asked my *booze addled brain:* what's the best hotel in Victoria?

It answered the Empress. *I liked my style.* The Empress it was going to be.

I was two blocks away from The Empress. I began to hobble. I started to jute across the hotel's front lawn. I slipped, falling onto my back. I closed my eyes. The rain pounding into my face forced me to open them. I got up. Sleeping on the lawn wasn't an option. I hobbled the last few yards to the hotel. A bellman opened the door for me.

I was dripping with confidence and drunkenness as I limped past the Front Desk before I reached the elevator; I glanced to my left and with the utmost of calm said: *Good evening. Hold my calls, please.*

The Empress has six floors. When I stepped onto the elevator, I punched six.

While riding upward, I checked my pockets—still only $5.

On the sixth floor, I searched the hallway for a resting place where I would be able to avoid eviction. *My brain spun.* I found a series of vending machines. I purchased a coke and a newspaper. I searched the hallway some more until I found a room with my name on it.

FIRE CLOSET

My room for the night was spacious. Approximately three feet wide by three and a half, maybe four feet, max, long. Since I'm slightly shy of six feet tall, the room was a perfect fit —I settled in for the evening.

I used the Real Estate and Classified Sections of the newspaper as my mattress. The Sports and Entertainment sections as a blanket and my coke can served as a pillow. As a bonus: the room forced me to bend my knees at a *ninety-degree angle*, elevating them, a recommendation of my Doctor.

I slept like a baby.

The rumbling of maids in the morning woke me from my slumber. I was leery of stepping out into the hall. My $3.25 remaining wasn't likely to cover my room's cost. I lay—sat—contorted. Paranoia raced through me. It was time to CHECK OUT.

I propped myself upright, tucked and primped in an attempt to gain decorum —I exited my room.

Good morning. How are you? You may do my room next. Have a beautiful day.

I shuffled around the corner to freedom!

I ate at *McDonald's*. Afterwards, I began roaming the streets looking for Wes and Cam. Hours later we crossed paths. They stayed the night at a beautiful acreage. They were served breakfast in bed. They fed apples to horses in a meadow. *They had sex.* Their accommodating hosts drove them back to the city.

You guys will never guess where I slept last night?

Follow me—follow me—a wee bit further—six please—here!

Are you done with the newspaper? Cam asked.

We returned to *Milestones* to retrieve our gear. We shared our stories with Cam's friend. He listened intently.

When I reached the point of where I slept; he looked confused, and asked: *Was it the only room they had left?*

THIEVING SPIKE

DATELINE: 14 April 1992 – Vancouver, British Columbia

NEW FRIEND INSERTION NUMBER 1: Thieving Spike, his nickname will make sense soon.

We worked at *Earl's* together.

Earl's removed the security of the bar by turning me into a server. Carrying hot plates wasn't my forte. Neither was carrying trays of water. I dropped ten glasses of water on a guest at the first table I served.

Sorry, sir. Could I offer you a shampoo packet with your meal?

FLASH FORWARD: 2006

Life was testing me daily. My options were to either hide or grab it by the junk and fight through my challenges, or withering. I'm not immune to fucking up—which brought me to either sink or swim. I knew I was talented with something to say. I needed to find a way to say it.

102

Why this insertion?

Because, I was reeling in drunk; I returned home to my cat's smelly litter box—and a solo dinner. I didn't like the box. I loved my cat. I wanted someone to love me. I'm a big talker. I'm personable. I sound like success. My actions sometimes deal a different hand.

What holds me back?

I'm not sure.

What I am certain of, I need to rise or risk having my story end sadly.

RIVALRY

Thieving Spike and I shared many things in common. We both loved the Montreal Canadiens Hockey Team. We were both avid tennis players and golfers.

'In common' helped our bond form quickly

In May, Dr Regan gave me the GREEN LIGHT to play tennis.

My next operation was two months away.

The GREEN LIGHT came with a few conditions:

1. I must wear my knee brace.
2. If I experience the slightest twinge of pain, stop playing.

Spike and I became rivals on the tennis courts of Vancouver.

SLICK
16 MAY 1992

Enter Slick.

Slick is Rick Gillis. Slick was a transplant from the flatlands, just like me.

He is exceptionally gregarious and personable. He transferred from a *Keg Restaurant* in Regina to manage a *Keg Restaurant* in Vancouver.

He became my flatmate right around the time I added the *Hotel Cali* to my work roster.

With the insertion of old, and a sprinkling of new, life was swinging upward.

I offer nothing but praise for Slick, a great guy with a big heart.

Back in Regina he teetered between one of the best-dressed men in the city and spilling into a *Caddyshack* persona, ala Bill Murray.

Slick was big city suave with a hint of small town sensibility.

He loved the purple cloak of Crown Royal.

More napshkins, please—

Slick was gifted with an infectious laugh, best described as a Hyena squeezing the life out of a Gremlin. With each pinch, the infectious squeals would increase in pitch. Disturbingly, it appeared as if the Gremlins were enjoying their demise.

BIG RED
16 MAY 1992

Fear and disgust were strewn across Carol's face the moment she walked into the *Hotel Cali.* If it weren't for my presence, she would have quickly turned and sprinted away, never working her first shift. During the shift, my running commentary on our customers started our friendship.

DIVE BAR = OLD + MISUNDERSTOOD + DRUNK + CROTCHETY + WANING HEALTH = OCCASIONALLY POOPING...

—is what I told her.

We acted as the customer's guardians. We'd reset their alarm clocks with each beer served for an additional fifteen minutes—waking them up to order again.

Carol (BIG RED) is adroit. She is slim, beautiful, and funny, with a lust for life. BR was equally at ease with climbing a mountain or lying poolside with a margarita. And, she's a gifted writer and polished businesswoman.

Big Red has crawled through caves, repelled down buildings, swam with crocodiles, and has overcome a fear of sharks. She basically—lights up life, taking on all challengers, taking no prisoners, unless they volunteer. Most important: she became a good friend.

Big Red also contained in her menu of characteristics a love of the Agave's nectar. She could handle it. Under the table, we'd often find her friends who tried to keep up with her drinking pace.

Carol loved and learned from the sharks she once feared.

That fucking hurts! Stop—I'd scream.

I'd shake my ass from side-to-side. The clamp was on tight. I'd run frantically.

Big Red locked onto my ass, sinking her teeth in firmly—so strongly denture moulds were being created.

When I tried to break free by running, Big Red would fly, horizontally, behind me.

No Blood – No Foul

DATELINE: 30 June 1992 – Seattle, Washington

It's time to speed down the I5 to Seattle.

Corrie & Vern were visiting from Calgary. Corrie wanted to go to a Seattle Supersonics basketball game. Wes, Pat, Dave and I, more on everyone except Dave, later, joined us.

Our night's lodging was on Mercer Island; home to Bill Gates.

Drinking was a constant. This time it broke our posse into two groups. Wes and I were on our own.

The separation occurred in Seattle's entertainment zone, Pike Place.

Wes and I were swimming in inebriation, only a tad. My clothing selection placed *me at* an 8.5. I was recovering from my most recent knee surgery.

We developed an alcohol encouraged hunger. Tacos from a street vendor fit the bill nicely.

Wes shot his wrappers in a high arc toward a trash can, thirty feet away. I followed suit.

Both of us: Nothing but net!

We were called *candy-assed* white boys by two guys leaning against the wall behind us.

Blindly, I rebutted righteously, we'd kick whoever was chirpings sorry *black-asses* any day.

Their names were Terry and Ryan. They happened to be black. They asked us to get in Terry's car.

We hopped into Terry's Datsun B210.

Terry's place was in a questionable neighbourhood. Terry served us gin & juice. They flipped on the TV selecting PORN for our viewing pleasure. I was certain this night was going to be my last.

Wes and I hinted we needed to get back to our friends on Mercer Island. They reminded us of *sorry—black—and asses.*

Forty minutes later, after offering to wake their next-door neighbour so we could pursue flesh, we were fully geared up: Shorts – shirts – shoes – a knee brace for me (gear pulled out of a closet rivalling a Foot Locker Store—all new)—and we were on a schoolyard basketball court. Terry parked the B210 facing the court using the headlights to light the court—and with rap music blaring—starting at 4 AM—we engaged in a spirited battle of TWO-ON-TWO hoops.

No blood – no foul rules.

GAME 5

Terry knocked me to the asphalt, hard. I cried for a foul. I shrieked: *Rodney King didn't have it that bad.*
We were going to die.
A bad joke huh? I whispered meekly.

After our victory, they drove us back to Mercer Island so we could reunite with our friends. Along the way we made a couple of pit-stops:

1.   A neighbourhood convenience store so they could steal the newspaper drop (Seattle Times). They said they were going to sell the papers down in Pioneer Square.

2.   A gas station's convenience store where they suggested: the best way for us to mend International Relations was for us to pick them up a six-pack of Lucky Beer.

MORE SURGERY + HELLO KITTY

DATELINE: 31 July 1992 – Vancouver, British Columbia

It was time for another surgery!

On this day, Doctor Regan cracked open my leg and rebuilt my left knee. He inserted scopes—borrowed parts from other regions of my body—slapped them together—and then—sewed his creation back together tightly.

Once again, no walking translated into no working.

Thankfully, I had refilled my friends prescription left empty by Gail:

Pat & Wes supplied inebriation, Rick constant companionship, Big Red the soft touch of a woman, and Thieving, free meals at *Earl's*.

When October rolled around, I cast my crutches to the side, three months ahead of schedule.

I also convinced Dade I'd make an excellent manager for the Hotel Cali.

5 SEPTEMBER 1992

HOTEL CALI EVICTION POLICY

Drugs – Hookers – Pets = **EVICTED**

Dead with a needle dangling from your arm = Please Follow the Flashing Lights

Dade would still cash the deceased's next two scammed welfare cheques. I wondered if the ambulances ever came.

Ah, why is there a kitten in my office?

The maintenance man, Walter, found her roaming on the lower roof of the hotel.

Maybe she was dealing drugs.

She was about two weeks old.

I named her Fuzzy Nose & Toes.

I took her home and promptly attached her to the arms of *Slick's* couch.

CHASING NEON

DATELINE: 24 October 1992 – Vancouver, British Columbia

With my work passport affably stamped: **MANAGEMENT**, it was time to celebrate. Spike and I borrowed the Sport Family Truckster from Slick and blasted down to Seattle to *CHASE NEON!*

The Truckster's gravitational pull vehemently sucked us toward Wal-Marts.

MEETING GREG FOR THE FIRST TIME—

To succeed at *CHASING NEON* all one requires is desire and a pair of soft-soled shoes. Then they must follow these steps:

1. Identify target.
2. Check window advertisements.
3. Walk in—order drink—relax.
4. Repeat often.

Thieving and I, had hit twenty-three NEON establishments.

En route to twenty-four, Spike told me he was dying of cancer.

That was fucking odd.

Upon returning to Vancouver, I rushed to *Earl's* to regroup. Greg greeted me at the door. Greg was from Nanaimo on Vancouver Island. He's part Slavic, Hungarian, German, Croatian, educated, and slightly nuts. I found this to be an intriguing mixture.

He also loved scotch, beer, wine, gin, helium—

I dumped the news about Spike having *THE BIG C* —on him. We've been great friends since.

He even bathed me once after Big Red plied me with a horde of tequila, causing me to go off like *Old Faithful* all over myself during one of my birthday celebrations, a proud moment.

I think he may have even given me a tongue bath!

KNEE UPDATE

DATELINE: January 1993 – Vancouver, British Columbia

Young man, I'm impressed. Professional athletes would have trouble getting back in shape this fast.
Doctor Regan said: *YOUNG MAN*—sweet!

WALLY & DANIELLE

DATELINE: March 1993 – Vancouver, British Columbia

Kevin & Danielle were walking at a rapid pace, arms firmly at their sides, steps elongated, focused—in the same cadence. I mentioned this to Danielle. She added an arm sway afterwards.

Kevin (Wally) was my new best friend. I met him at *Earl's*. With my knee rehabbed I started a touch football team. Wally was on the team.

The three of us hit it off. I became Kevin & Danielle's third wheel. I played third fiddle for seven years.

Danielle became my stand-in-date at work functions. And, I would often fill in for Wally because he lived by the credo: Can't make plans; a better offer might come along.

Wally was a comedy gold mine firing several gems our way.

When Greg came to him in need of emotional support because his girlfriend dumped him suggesting he may end his life, TONIGHT. Wally casually said *what—look—soccer*…and then stared lovingly at the game on the tube.

In Seattle, he screamed at the top of his lungs: *Fuck—shit—crap—bullshit—fuck—fuck*!

When asked if he was okay, he sheepishly said: *Damn Irish flag, never mind.*

And, my personal favourite: Wally was driving my car as a designated driver. Greg and I were beating each other senseless in the backseat like a couple of brothers fighting just because we were like, brothers. Wally would hit a bump. The road became green. Tree branches began to caress the windshield. Slick sat speechless in the front seat.

Greg and I screamed: *Wally!*

He hit another bump. The road returned to asphalt. Wally then said: *Didn't there used to be two lanes here?*

Wally eventually became an engineer.

FORESHADOWING: January 2000 – Vancouver, British Columbia

Wally & Danielle's relationship lost its lustre as 23 years of age turned into 30.

When it ends, Wally may end up on my doorstep?

COCAINE OFF A HOOKER'S TITS

DATELINE: November 1993 – January 1994 – Vancouver, British Columbia

I was hired to bartend. After my second surgery, I used my charm to help me land a position in management. I had no choice. I needed money. And, I was sure bartenders who could only sit, well, they weren't of much use.

My style was nepotistic. My style worked. I managed to turn a *dive bar* into a great success.

Dade, the owner, piled responsibility upon me. Everything from accounting to inventory control to personnel decisions. When I became overwhelmed, he would dish out more responsibilities.

I'd discover the cash to be $1,000 over one day. The next day, $2,000, short. I'd inform Dade.

He told me not to worry about it.

After a little more than one year in the role—I was fired.

Why? I asked.

He said he wasn't sure why. I seem to do a lot he said.

He said a reason would eventually come to him.

Three days later he accused me of stealing the hotel's nightly deposits. He said he was going to launch an investigation.

Later, I found out; I was stealing somewhere between $1,000 and $30,000 per month. The story varied depending on the audience.

I pulled the cushions off my couch. I found a Cheezie.

Law enforcement came calling. Often at 6 AM. A detective knocked relentlessly on my door for hours on end. I avoided him.

Slick, my roommate and our neighbours were becoming restless of the early morning wake up calls.

I decided to find the real killers myself.

One Thursday morning, I let Detective Gadget in.

Nice place—beautiful couch—very expensive! Detective Gadget said.

I pointed to the phone books for legs, and my cat was hanging off one of the arms.

Those stereo speakers look high-end.

I ranted:

They're five years old and belong to my roommate. To spare your precious time, I ate Macaroni & Cheese last night without milk or butter—my bank account reads negative—barring magic I'm going to lose my place. My only indulgence is I like snorting cocaine of hooker's tits using $100 bills for the straw. And, oh yeah, I don't snort cocaine.

He asked me to take a lie detector test.

I don't know what Dade's deal is? Perhaps cashing two or three welfare cheques from the same tenants monthly, is clouding his reality. I said.

I agreed to take the test.

You're not lying.

Prefuckingcisely!

Sorry about this. You're free to go.

Dade hired three people to replace me. He made me jump through hoops to obtain my last pay cheque.

Eventually, I called him explaining what I was going to do.

I asked for only what I was owed, by the following day. If he refused to comply—I was going to enlighten his business partner on hotel practices. I calmly said I would phone the Labour Board. I finished making it clear I only wanted what I was owed.

He screamed words I've never heard before into the phone. He called me a lying thieving blackmailer. He said he would take me down. He said he would never give me a cent.

I let Slick listen. He said Dade didn't seem very friendly.

I serenely suggested Dade reign in his excitement. I rhetorically stated: *you know I never stole from you, don't you?*

Fucking, asshole, bastard—

Ten minutes later he called to tell me the cheque would be ready the next morning.

I picked up my last paycheque at his business partner's office the next day. He made me sign a non-disclosure document regarding their business practices.

Therefore, please disregard the last few pages.

If I implied Dade to be a drug user, I don't know for sure. I do know, I'm not: *A fucking asshole bastard—*

My former staff would invite me to the bar on occasion after my firing, in Dade's absence. They'd never allow me to pay for a beverage. I drank to the tune of $30,000 per month.

FOR HONESTY'S SAKE: Dade is not his real name. But it does rhyme with—

WAYNE

DATELINE: February 1994 – Vancouver, British Columbia

There is a good chance he's the best man I've ever met.

After the struggles with the *Hotel Cali* complete with the *CSI Investigation*, I landed a career with *Mutual Exchange Canada* (MEC) as a consultant.

MEC brokered deals between companies dealing in a virtual currency called Trade Dollars. My job was to bring companies together to trade, *Trade Dollars*. MEC is where I met Wayne.

Part of our remuneration was in *Trade Dollars*, Wayne and I became drinking buddies at any *NEON Establishment* that accepted *Trade Dollars*. Fortunately, there were many.

Lindsay, you're blowing this for us—go, talk to them now.

Wayne issued the order for me to talk to women; so, off I'd go. I'd use my gift of gab, every night. If I became bored—Wayne would slither in.

He'd ask women if they liked travelling and expensive things.

The answers were always affirmative.

Wayne in an unassuming fashion hung in the shadows on most nights.

He mixed effortlessly with the other members of my support network.

He was simply a drinking buddy—that seemed to be enough—for the time being.

RASTAMAN VIBRATIONS WITH WAYNE & GREG - MAY 1996

Greg and I scored flights to Jamaica for $290 Canadian. I told Wayne about the deal. The next day he informed us he was coming with us to Jamaica 'mon'.

DRIVE TO SEATTLE—MEET OLYMPIC FIGURE SKATERS AND SWEDISH GIRLS AT THE AIRPORT—RED EYE TO MINNEAPOLIS—PLAY *XARCON* (VIDEO GAME) @ AIRPORT—GREG'S LIGHT BEACH READING: *THE GENTRIFICATION OF NAZI GERMANY*—MONTEGO BAY—TAXI TO NEGRIL—COUNTLESS RED STRIPES—BARB B' BARN HOTEL

We were flying by the seat-of-our-pants, drunk, by my doing. Without a reservation in tow, I negotiated for the room. The Barb B' Barn front desk clerk started at $1500 each for fifteen nights?

By the end of my haggling, we landed us a home for $600 total, for the three of us.

Sleep-deprived, it was time to talk to girls.

My friends were ornery—they dumped excessive amounts of pressure on me to talk. To appease their needs, I spoke to—everyone.

PUBLIC SERVICE ANNOUNCEMENT ON WHAT NOT TO DO IN FOREIGN COUNTRIES

1. Don't start out blithering drunk.
2. Don't leave friends alone when they are not familiar with the customs of the country.
3. Do not invite strangers into your hotel room, while blithering drunk.
4. Do not fall asleep (pass-out) on the beach with all of your money and identification on you (Greg), or in the chair outside your hotel room's door (?)

Luckily, we escaped, unscathed.

VACATION ~~HIGH~~ LOW POINTS

Greg and I packed *three hundred pounds* of luggage, each. Wayne brought *one blue shirt*.

On the second day, we met a hot girl from Ontario. She was hanging with three large, gruff, girlfriends.

I was interested in Ontario.

I went to the washroom. Upon my return, Greg was dating her.

Wayne drank and laughed.

Something stung me causing my temperature to escalate. The gruff girls disappeared into the jungle with Rastafarians. Greg's gal moved in with us.

Wayne drank and laughed.

With my fever hitting critical, Greg and *Ontario,* checked in on me every twenty minutes—waking me each time.

Wayne drank and laughed.

His shirt began to change colours.

THE NEXT SCENE HAD BEEN DELETED—IN THE SPIRIT OF FRIENDSHIP

Take this time to grab yourself a snack.

I'm back.

Wayne drank and laughed.

My health returned. I determined *Ontario* was off. Greg disputed my arguments.

FAST FORWARD TO THE FUTURE: One year later: Greg was studying at McGill University in Montreal. *Ontario* contacted him. She said she was dying of cancer. She asked him to return to Jamaica to marry her.

Wayne drank and laughed.

Then, in an instant of male bonding, the three of us became more than acquaintances. At the Negril Country Club, Wayne was about to golf for the first time.

He rented clubs. After twenty minutes on the driving range, a course worker approached to call us to the first tee.

Wayne casually stated to the worker: *I think I might be left-handed.*

Greg and I competed intensely.

Wayne not so much, he asked his caddie if using a tee on every shot was okay.

Yeah, mon. Irie. No Problem was the answer.

The scent of Ganja wafted through the air.

Wayne asked his caddie where he should aim.

His caddie layered more '*mons*' and '*Iries*' on him. He then said to Wayne: *For the blue patch in the sky right, right about—now, mon!*

From that day forward we became family, sharing life, death, marriage, and birth.

We discovered the secret to friendship longevity:

THINKING INSIDE THIS BOX: THE SECRETS TO A LASTING FRIENDSHIP

All that matters is to be there for the events from two sentences ago. The rest is nothing more than noise.

ONE LOVE

Mancy was the Rasta version of Keith Richards, born with a spliff in hand, not a day under 200. We were off-the-beaten-path in a jungle cottage. Mancy and four of his Rasta buddies were packing gigantic *spliffs*. With each toke the air *filled* with the fragrance of *high.*

BOW, was shouted by one of the Rasta's as he slammed a domino onto a table; breaking it in two.

Wayne suggested: I had ties to Satan. Wayne would then point at me →

Bumba clot, ras clot, we believe in da power of Rastafari, Hailie Sallase. G'wan boi. The devil has no place here. We will git—a Rastafarian chanted.

Rasta's happen to be religious. I didn't think this was funny.

BOW, another domino shattered. Smoke filled the room, much like a thick, dense fog caressing a coastline. We were experiencing contact *highs*.

Mancy was babbling in his *patois* to Greg. A beautiful young Jamaican woman sauntered out of a back room. Reggae music pulsed.

You, not de Devil 'mon, ' that's good.

Wayne smirked, coyly.

One of the Rastas offered his sister to Greg.

G'wan 'mon. You like? She's sweet like candy. Me sista. G'wan boi. Don't be shy. You may have her for 200 J. She be yours. Sweet like candy. G'wan boi. Touch her.

A blip passed. Greg refused the generous offer. Instead, he walked into the woods. Mancy was close behind, wielding a machete.

BOW, Devil, Rastafari!

Another domino shattered. Then another *BOW*, the shattering pieces flew though the room.

Greg and Mancy returned. Mancy had been teaching Greg how to cut hashish.

My hand began to *morph* into different shapes.

One love, one heart, let's get together and feel alright—

The room filled with music—volume increasing with each beat.

We danced, one hand raised in the air reaching for the sky. The three of us + four Rastafarians + Mancy + the Sista, all marching to the sound of a Jamaican God, *one-two-steps-forward—one-step-two-steps-back*—hands reaching toward the sky. At that moment we all became one. Culture married culture.

One love, one heart—

TRIPS END—RETURNING HOME—

For the remainder of the trip Greg and I decided it was best to join Wayne drinking and laughing.

Wayne ate all three of our breakfasts, every day. He drank copious amounts of alcohol. Wayne only weighs *one hundred forty pounds*; he consumed so much booze deceased alcoholics started to become squeamish in their graves.

We met sisters from Chicago, an ageing Super Model from Spain, and; of course, Jamaican beauties.

With the combination of new friends and old, my friend network was complete. Life was *GRAND*. The *pieces* were interchangeable except for the one piece that held it all together:

ME.

UNRAVEL

DATELINE: May 1994 – Vancouver, British Columbia

As quickly as my friend roster became GRAND—it began to fall apart.

Thieving's moniker was given to him officially. During his battle with *THE BIG C*, he managed to scoop one of my Bank Cards and began helping himself to cash from one of my Bank Accounts. Our Friendship: **CANCELLED**.

Who'd lie about having THE BIG C?

I haven't spoken to him since finding out. However, my friends have.

Spike sauntered into the *Planet Restaurant* on a night when Wes was the managing. Wes slammed Spike's head into the windows at the front of the restaurant and then threw him out.

And, Greg kissed him on the forehead in a nightclub one night. He then informed Spike he couldn't be sure the precise moment it was coming, but when it came, it was going to involve unbearable pain.

RESTING ON MY SHOULDERS

Two years passed since Dr Regan reconstructed my knee. There was nary a problem, until:

CLICK – CLICK - CLICK

I asked the Doc if the strange sounds emanating from my shoulder were normal.

Three weeks later: he reconstructed my right shoulder.

SOUTH PACIFIC

A few weeks after my shoulder surgery Wes fluttered away, Vanuatu in the South Pacific, was calling his name.

Vanuatu was—

~2-YEARS OF RELATIVE CALM~

Hey, Where Is Everybody Going?

DATELINE: February 1997 – Vancouver, British Columbia

Work Related Uncomfortable Unravelling Moment

I was entering my third year with MEC. I had managed to secure a prominent list of clients. The success carrot was *dangling* within my reach. I was a top performer.

Norm Friend, our Sales Manager, called me into his office. He swivelled his chair. Norm glared out the window. He then told me about how his wife (T) was out having fun. She was racing Dragon Boats he said.

He went on to tell me about how his recent foot surgery had left him hobbled.

He said his heart was breaking. He then repeated: *T is out having fun.*

A week later he called me into his office again and fired me.

Wayne quit MEC that day in a show of support.

Days later, one of the principals of the company offered me a position running a district.

I DECLINED.

Phoenix Rising

Like Wes, Slick's tribal roots were also in Saskatchewan.

Slick has told me he has a long line of crazy uncles. The first one I met was Leo. Leo was a salvage baron and a hoarder. On one occasion, Leo suggested: we should hook up for beers. When Slick and I were about to depart his company, he handed me his business card. On the card there was only a single word, nothing more.

LEO

Slick was now leaving Vancouver because a second crazy uncle wanted Slick to bring his restaurant expertise with him to help him open a restaurant in Phoenix Arizona.

Slick left our flat and headed to the land of the rising sun.

La Belle Province

What's going on? Am I swimming in cold water? Why is everything shrivelling up?

One month after Slick, in September 1997, Greg left Vancouver to finish his Master's Degree at McGill University in Montreal.

ANUS

DATELINE: October 1997 – Vancouver General Hospital

It's probably nothing to worry about; I must remove these growths to assure they're not cancerous, Dr Aldice said calmly.

Dr Aldice mentioned *THE BIG C,* and *nothing to worry about*; in the same breath.

The waiting time for surgery was six months—two days later—welcome to VGH—not comforting.

During pre-op, I discovered my resting heart rate was *forty-one beats per minute*. I thought that was cool—I found out, it may not be.

The night before the surgery *THE BIG C* was peeking through the window, smirking.

Cold-assed and on a gurney once more, my nurse rounded the last corner before the operating room. Just where the corner broke toward the operating rooms a second nurse was playing a piano—*seriously*. We made eye contact.

She smiled at me and then said: *Do you have any last requests?*

Moments later: *One hundred—*

DEEP COVER

The splintering continued.

Pat took an undercover *post* fighting the war on drugs in January 1998. He was forced to distance himself from his civilian friends.

POOF—everyone important to me was KEYSER SÖZE'D as quickly as they arrived.

I began to flounder.

GUILT chimed in telling me to quit feeling sorry for myself. *GUILT* said people are simply living their lives. People come and go all the time he said.

I told *GUILT* to fuck off.

My friendship network took four years to construct, in reality, eight years since I arrived in Vancouver in 1990—had been almost entirely dismantled in less than four. Except for Wayne, and Kevin & Danielle, everyone else seemed to have vanished in what appeared to be the blink of my one functioning eye.

I was once again struggling. Work was woeful. I was taking menial jobs to survive. Love was absent except for the occasional—

In March 1998, I landed a job with a software company named *Timeac*. I sold POS (Point of Sale Systems) to bars and Restaurants. I sold a system to Judy and Dale the owners of the *Sandpiper Pub* in White Rock. In June they offered me a bartending job. I quickly turned bartending into management.

Life was trending upward once more.

Russians Clowns & Drag Queens

DATELINE: 20 July 1998 – Vancouver, British Columbia

Monday night in Vancouver is usually sleepy.

On this Monday, the summer heat turned the night into sweltering.

With my living room approaching the temperature of the sun's surface I decided to hazard a night on the town alone with my shadow was in order instead of melting into my sofa sweating profusely.

One... two... three bars into my night, I entered the *Odyssey Nightclub*. The Odyssey caters to GAY.

I focused my GAYDAR toward the dance floor—I'm not sure I have GAYDAR?

Anyway, I drew undisputable conclusions from my focus.

THINKING INSIDE THIS BOX: GAY—STRAIGHT—IN BETWEEN—WHO CARES?

STRAIGHT: Stiff in movement, shoulders shrugging, hands planted firmly on the hips.

AT EASE SEXUALLY: The groove flows loosely with every step.

FLAMBOYANTLY GAY: Hands gleefully raised above the head, at all times?

Just as I finished my thesis, a handsomely attractive, deliciously slim, girl—approached me. She took a shine to me. She plied me with drinks. She invited me to accompany her to a raging party. Her name was Carla.

I accepted her invitation.

We flagged a cab. Carla and I exchanged cute smiles. Upon closer inspection I noticed Carla had an Adam's Apple. I chuckled sheepishly, she asked why I was laughing.

I told her about her Adam's—

She said she was in Drag.

We crisscrossed streets and alleyways as the cab driver followed the instructions Carla gave him. After about thirty-five minutes we arrived at our destination, which happened to be about a five-minute walk across the Granville Street Bridge from the *Odyssey*.

Carla paid our driver. We hopped out of the cab at the back of a nondescript white warehouse. Carla tapped an elaborate code on the back door—after three minutes passed the door finally cracked open—a bearded man sporting white overalls emerged from the darkness. He spoke with a strong *accent'* – which later, I was informed—was Russian.

While I waited patiently for Carla to negotiate our admittance, a cab rolled up to us in the laneway. Three men in clown suits jumped out.

Pounding music filled the warehouse. Attractive, scantily clad people danced.

Carla excused herself to retreat to the washroom. She asked me to guard her bag. In her absence a continuous line of individuals glided up to me, asking me when Carla was going to be returning.

One hour passed. I put my thesis cap back on—could Carla be selling, drugs?

Carla returned.

With my senses overloaded, I decided: it was time to go home.

On my way home I wondered if the heat of the night, mixed with the drink from the bars, had led me to an excellent title for a book or a movie.

Concussion Protocol + New Flatmate

DATELINE: 21 -24 January 1999 – Phoenix, Arizona

Wayne, Kevin and I, flew the friendly skies to Phoenix to visit Slick. The flight was three hours, just enough time for us to get sufficiently pickled.

Slick retrieved us from the airport. He took us to his restaurant, the *Armadillo Grill*. We drank more.

He then took us to a *Strip-Joint.* He bought me a lap dance. I wasn't sure where I was supposed to look during the performance, so, I looked into my lap dancer's eyes. After the dance, he took us to watch him play in a beer league hockey game. We drank more.

After the game, we finally made it back to his place—where we were going to, drink more.

Before our next beverage, I'd like to back up a few moments. Slick pulled his Jeep into his carport. His carport, like most carports in Phoenix, consists of steel girders holding up the roof to protect the—in Slick's case: Jeep, from Phoenix's unrelenting sun.

That brings us to another—

SEED PUBLIC SERVICE ANNOUNCEMENT (PSA)

Jeep Doors swing wide open.

Be careful when exiting Jeeps.

Hammering your head into a steel girder while exiting said Jeep is very painful.

Don't bang head into steel beams.

When I exited Slick's Jeep, my head slammed into the beam creating a loud thud that echoed throughout the neighbourhood.

Was that the Jeep's door? Slick askèd.

Concussion protocol states:

DO NOT LET THE CONCUSSED PERSON SLEEP

They let me sleep.

I spent the next three days travelling around in a fog. I was also sporting a goitre on my forehead. And, even though the temperature was in the high 80s Fahrenheit, I couldn't stop shivering. And, oh yeah, I don't think I wore shoes for the duration of the trip.

On our last morning shortly before flying away from the land of the rising sun, Slick said to us: *Hey guys, I'm not going to shower today. Want to grab a hot tub?*

I chose to shower.

ROOMIE

I'm breaking up with Danielle. Can I stay at your place for a month? Kevin asked me on the phone in December 1999.

I said he was welcome to stay as long as he needed to.

He replied: *I wouldn't be able to stand living with you for more than a month.*

Our friendship began to evolve difficultly, living with a good friend can likely only lead to one outcome—ex.

118

Anyway, Danielle and Kevin's breakup—~~their~~ our breakup was going to impact me significantly.

8

↑DRUGS↑

A meta-memoir

↑Can I Take You Higher↑

DATELINE: 10 February 2001 – Vancouver, British Columbia

I was 40. I thought intelligent. I didn't start conversation announcing what I'm not.

I'm not a doctor—I'm not a scientist but here is my opinion on global warming—

I decided I wanted to try ecstasy. My IQ remained silent.

TIME OUT

Was I facing a life crisis... perhaps?

Did I just want to get high?

I don't know—I guess I was just attempting to evolve by letting experimentation eliminate judgement from my ethos. Tripping into my dark side was to enlighten the path leading me to what was missing from life.

QUEST FOR ECSTASY: AFTER HOURS

It was time to begin my hunt for experimentation.

Now, where do I begin?

I headed to a questionable part of Vancouver—logic told me the establishments located in this area would be excellent starting points. How could they not be with names such as *Blunt Brothers* or *New Amsterdam*?

Just imagine: I'm 40, clean looking, fashionable, shaved head, and I'm often mistaken for the law. What could go wrong?

My first stop was *Blunt Brothers*. I nervously sauntered up to the counter. I whispered to the tattooed, purple haired, pierced girl, behind the counter—stuttering more with each word.

Excuse me; I'm looking to try new thing—

I then cupped my hands over my lips and emphatically mouthed *ECSTASY*.

I sauntered out of the store, empty-handed.

ALTERATIONS

On this chilly Saturday night, I was about to enter a *WORLD* where naivety goes to face its demise, a place where reality and fantasy live in reckless abandon. I abnegated my beliefs about drugs.

I must have walked past the door thirty times before finding the courage to enter. What if someone saw me?

How could I explain my presence?

If seen, how would I mask my embarrassment?

I wasn't buying a dirty magazine where I could sneak it in with other items.

Oblivious to what was in store for me I took the trip down the stairs.

Bass music pumped. Glow sticks swayed rapidly. The room was pulsing with energy. Stylish people at different points of inebriation and dress, danced. I had entered a den of indulgence.

Had I known the presage of liberation ahead, I may have turned around and walked the other way.

Inside, I felt safe.

The interior consisted of an open area filled with couches covered in throw pillows. A heart occupied by gyrating bodies. And, a back room for chilling and processing *one's* selection of alteration.

I knew no one. I didn't belong. I stood out.

I sat on a couch in the front area. Conversations floated freely all around me. People flashed in and then quickly flashed out.

A girl to my right complimented my selection of footware. Her voice was relaxing. We hit it off. She asked me what I was on.

I said alcohol. I asked the girl the same question.

She recited the alphabet starting at e. Her name was Samantha. She asked mine.

I started saying my name—*broke it off*—and introduced myself as Mark.

I then cringed and murmured: *Do you know where I could get e?*

My lips barely stopped before Sam was back with an offering. She told me to buy water.

Water in hand, I asked what I need to do.

In the chill-out room, known as the *Red Room*, she instructed me to pop—wash it down with a swig, and soon I would be travelling to a new reality.

I popped and waited. Sam remained with me, sharing stories of where the chemicals had taken her before.

Sam was half my age. In the club, age evaporates with paid admission.

The tiling on the ceiling wavered—morphing into different shapes. Countless worms wiggled in perfect synchronisation with the charging music—wheels in a rainbow of colours started revolving.

My heart began spiking. My body became lovingly warm. I belonged here, I thought. I felt complete. Illusion and fantasy shared oxygen with reality. The urge to dance came over me.

Sam left my side when she felt me rise.

I was *dazzlingly* fucking *high*. *Drugs are great!* I thought.

People slid next to me. People slid out. People slid in.

What are you on —was the common question.

Thoughts swirled into a deep crevice in my brain. Kissing strangers seemed reasonable. Friends came and went in a POOF!

I found this to be infinitely better than under the covers with a flashlight.

My need for sex(uality) oozed.

In the heart of the club, I found a rhythm. The chemicals transformed me into a great dancer. I'd step three times—shake my ass—step three more—shake again. Occasionally, I would flip my water bottle in the air.

I ripped my shirt off. I permitted myself to be groped and kissed. Lips felt like heaven. I found Samantha dancing next to me. I began licking her arm.

She covered her arms.

At mornings end (7:30) the club closed. I was unfathomably horny. Going home was going to bring with it pain.

SPECTRAL SOCIETIES

I thought I had fulfilled my desire to experiment. *One trip* would surely suffice.

The night was a veritable menagerie of the bizarre. My mind opened to new realms.

The deviant behaviour disturbed me.

What I once condemned became acceptable. My essence was ripe for cultivation.

I vomited in my mouth a little bit when I typed the last line.

I vowed never to return.

The phone rang. On the other end of the line was *HIGH.*

I researched the evils of drugs. For each article I found denouncing usage, I found one saying *NO-BIG-DEAL.*

My mind was easily swayed.

On Thursday, I thought: maybe—

Come Saturday, I'd go out with friends. When the opening of the *AFTER HOURS* approached—POOF—I'd vanish, tripping down the stairs once more.

Pop—swig—wait—hallucinate.

Why is everyone wearing opera glasses and draped in bubble wrapping?

What was in my head to have the club filled with people donning goalie masks while wearing sumo suits?

I glanced to my right.

Hello, Scottish Andy. You don't say. One minute you were on the dance floor—the next on the flight deck of the Starship Enterprise with Captain Kirk and Homer Simpson. I hope you had fun. Welcome back!

While you're here, beautiful opera glasses by the way, can you help me get off the dance floor? Every time I make it to the edge, a wall magically appears.

One—two—three shake my ass—

Hallucinating was fun. *LOGIC* suggests it might be harmful, fuck *LOGIC*.

What's that *high guy, drugs aren't bad for you. The couple openly fucking in the corner is sharing a beautiful expression of love, sounds reasonable.*

The physical violence associated with alcohol rarely reared its ugly head here; however, I have a hunch this *World* may be far more aggressive. Maybe my server isn't being completely honest.

That's nonsense. How could drugs possibly rewire a brain—they'll never destroy who I am, will they?

This social experiment plays out weekly. Participants would sing the praises of chemicals. One-by-one they seemed to crash—burn-out—some becoming addicted to harsher choices on the menu, until they fizzled out, incapable of returning to norm again.

High started becoming cut with judgment.

I kept returning.

I ignored the evil side.

People desperately tried to find a place of belonging, *high* brought with it the desperation. *Club goers* were desperate for acceptance. The most beautiful rarely granted it. As quickly as drugs opened options—they slammed them shut at a fiercer pace.

Paranoia shared fabric with usage. Paranoia's interpretation sends many over the edge. Lips moved—the conversation was about you. Goblins and ghosts crawled out of the walls or from beneath the floor.

A SHORT TRIP INTO THE FUTURE: Andy and Mike experienced life-altering visions. They collapsed on Trish's bathroom floor. Trish hovered above them. Dr Ken flew alongside. Mike and Andy heard voices. Trish was close to collapse. She asked everyone to leave so the voices could dissipate.

The DOCTOR asked if we were doing the right thing.

Leaving three incredibly fucked-up people who are hearing the devil talk to them to fend for themselves, how could that possibly be wrong?

I returned to the club the following Saturday night.

9

~~Trash~~ Trish

A meta-memoir

~~T̶R̶I̶S̶H̶~~ TRASH

DATELINE: 10 November 2001 – Vancouver, British Columbia – The World After Hours

It only took me ten years to find new love after Gail. You will be meeting her soon!
Round and round we spun. Much like dancers in an awful music video, we continued the circular motion to the rhythm of the pulsing music. We were locked in a passionate kiss. Fireworks exploded. Chills shot down my spine. Electricity fired through my veins. The lips of this smashing young vixen were full and supple. Her kisses melted me.

With the chemicals rushing through me, past loves were being washed away by the beauty of *high*.

Life was about to change.

High = Change

Some say change is good.

A MOMENT OF REFLECTION

All of my past loves seemed to fit a similar profile.

CORRIE: adopted.

GAIL: adopted.

WHEN I WAS WITH CORRIE: My parents were dying—school was a struggle—because my parents were dying. I was bartending. I had suffered numerous athletic injuries that required surgery.

WHEN I WAS WITH GAIL: I was trying to buy a hotel in Jamaica—direction was a struggle—because—I'm not entirely sure—I guess I was just directionless. I was bartending. I suffered numerous athletic and life injuries that required surgery.

Likely just a coincidence, wouldn't one think?

ENDLESS KISS

The club was closing. Our spinning stopped. We unlocked lips. Our amatory dance was ending. We needed to find elsewhere.

This Saturday was no different than any other, sweaty, drug-fuelled, scantily clad people, were about to disperse into the morning light.

I wanted to *fuck* Trish.

It became my routine to escape to the club after a night out with friends. Every week at 2 AM—I'd vanish.

On this night I sat in the *Red Room* waiting for the alcohol to wane and pharmaceuticals to kick in. A sexy young girl sashayed into the room.

The person sitting next to me asked me if I wanted to meet her. *I did.* He arranged the meeting.

Victoria was her name. She was attached. It was time to press on.

A friend of Victoria glided into the room. Victoria encouraged me to kiss her. It's her birthday she said.

The chemicals took hold. We lost track of time. Seven hours passed.

I was befuddled. I struggled with comprehension. I wasn't looking for a relationship.

Fuck, I thought, my head was spinning—fireworks were exploding inside of me.

I hoped Trish was experiencing the same sensations.

GUILT'S friend *LOGIC* dropped in for a visit. He said: *She kissed you for 7-friggen-hours.*

He made a good point.

I felt something more substantive than chemicals were at play.

My first attempt at cranking out this history on Trish, well, let's say an epically long kiss was the root of my written drivel.

It was decision time. Call it a night or find a way to continue.

FUCKED-UP directed us to continue. Trish's place was off limits. She was hosting a visitor from Edmonton, spineless Dr Kenny.

And, my flatmate, Wally, was inclination free of my soirees into darkness.

I didn't want to blow this case of *something more*. Of course, touchy—feely—horny—and my desire to press flesh, with her, wasn't hurting.

That's right, press flesh.

It's time to break away from my Grade B porn description—shifting us through more naked pursuits—taking you only a few steps down the road toward pleasure.

LOGIC told me I was nothing more than *high*.

I told *LOGIC* to ingest something magical.

I didn't want to blow my discovery.

A hotel screams romance, I thought. Hornily, Trish agreed. We were going to *explore* the possibilities.

Mr Desk Clerk, we need a room, I said.

I then shook my brain in search of the magic words to kick the morning into gear. Three shakes later, and the best my altered brain came up with was: *I'd like to get to know more about you, your family, your dreams—*

Too corny, I decided.

I shook my head three more times.

Tell me about your views on the future; career, love and life?

Nah

I have an *erection*—thrust into my mind. I found the magic words. I took Trish's hand placing it gently on my excited nether region. My thoughts were gold, I thought. I thanked my brain decipher. I looked into her eyes—this was going to be good, brilliant. I encouraged the *mint-magical* words to flow. I knew my mind wouldn't lead me astray. It instructed me to lower my voice. Make it sultry, saucy, and hot.

Feel this. It is going to be your toy for the next several hours.

She didn't run.

I think my friend *LOGIC* met her friend *LOGIC* and they were getting busy in the next room.

We clicked. Trish's supple lips were sweet. My pulse raced. I slowly undressed her—one button at a time. I kissed and licked along every inch of her neck. I nibbled her earlobes. I licked down her spine. The heat intensified. I slowed my caresses as her clothes fell slowly to the ground like a dancing feather fluttering in the wind.

We continued. I wanted to devour Trish, to taste her. I felt my heart was going to quiver and stop. Her kisses sparked it back to life. I longed for every inch of her. We were stripping away boundaries. We were going places I've never been. I licked my way over her clavicle. Her nipples hardened. Her breasts heaved. She moaned as our chemistry whisked us away.

I could barely contain myself. I kissed and licked every inch of Trish's gorgeous body. Beads of sweat formed on her chest. I felt as if I was about to explode only to drown in her arms. The intensity increased. I derived pleasure each time she squirmed. I licked the inside of her legs, slowly at first. My strokes lengthened. I increased the pressure.

Trish was sent into orbit, consumed by ecstasy. She begged for more. Eventually, I licked and caressed until I reached—

Anyway, we clicked. I have a video to prove it.

Feel fortunate, my first attempt at describing the night ended with: Gentle waves of the ocean lapping up against the beach.

Aren't heaving breasts better?

Pursuits completed, we headed back to her place.

I told her my name wasn't Mark as we climbed the stairs to her front door.

She was okay with my revelation.

And besides, she seemed to have taken a shine to her new toy!

THE SANDPIPER PUB

DATELINE: 16 November 2001 – White Rock. British Columbia

Cowardice entered my psyche. It took until the following Friday to call Trish.

I was managing a seaside bar in White Rock, a beautiful resort setting minutes from the Washington border. The owners were divorced. Judy was an ex-Olympic swimmer, Dale an ex-professional football player. *Owning a bar while divorced—*

Dale liked (....ing) a blonde waitress who had a bit of a booty.

Judy searched for ways to make Dale jealous. Her first effort was breast enhancement. Next, she married an (...sive) dentist.

The first two attempts didn't work; so, she had a child with the (...sive) dentist.

Dale kept (....ing) the blonde waitress. *Server,* if you'd like my story to be politically correct.

She tried playing the staff against each other.

Dale didn't care.

She dumped her son's primary care on Nester. Nester is a cross between *Mr Rogers* meets a *Priest* meets *Jack Nicholson* from *The Shining.*

His body odour was far past rancid.

He'd rub his index finger in a circular motion on the inside of his knee and then express Judy's undying love for Dale. His voice scratched piercingly. Somehow, it was still meek.

She won't let him go. Nester said his index finger circling.

Judy asked me to transport him the fifty kilometres from Vancouver to White Rock. Oh yeah, Nester lived only a few blocks from me.

He'd look over to me while I was driving, finger circling rapidly and with his voice cracking: *I used to watch her swim every day. We used to go out, platonically—only if Dale was gone—They've been (...king) the books. One day, Dale will be gone.*

I mentioned his stench to Judy. She informed me he doesn't like to bathe. She said he uses his bathtub for storage.

The news about *(...king)* the books was far from a secret. For the past eight months, my management mandate was: DON'T RING IN A SINGLE SALE.

Judy asked me to drive Nestor again. I said, NO.

BACKUP 2 DAYS: 14 November 2001 – White Rock, British Columbia

Judy fired me.

FLASHBACK: 31 May 2001 – Vancouver, British Columbia

Lindsay, you're *fired—*

The POS company I mentioned in a previous part of this book. While plying their wares, I was the top salesperson. Anyway, they hired a sales manager named Ryan. He was an ass. Salaried employees were ordered to come in at 6 AM, three hours before their regular start times for meetings.

It's 8:30. We don't have time for questions. I know you are all eager to get to work. Ryan would say.

I'd grab Ryan's attention, gingerly suggesting they've been at work since 6 AM.

One week later, Ryan presented me with a letter instructing me to keep my mouth shut.

Two weeks later he fired me.

One year later, I ran into the owner of the company at the airport. He told me he lost everything: his wife, business, health; everything. He then said he's bouncing back—working for a company out of Dallas. He thought I'd be a perfect fit. He said if interested, he would highly recommend me.

I reminded him of the day he and Ryan fired me.

I made a mistake he said timidly.

Dale gave me a glowing reference letter after my dismissal from the Sandpiper.

Maybe I need to open my own business so I can figure out why I will eventually have to let myself go.

FIRST DATE

The World After Hours – Vancouver British Columbia

Thanks to my firing, I was free on Friday night to phone Trish. We planned to meet at the club on Saturday evening.

I was about to strap myself—I'll stop there.

Trish is Chinese; yet, somehow, not Asian.

She earned a psychology degree from the U of A.

She was an FA (Flight Attendant) with Air Canada.

She also worked with autistic children.

Her family disowned her, but for some reason, they still paid all of her bills.

She made a killer first impression, perhaps, because she made it while everyone was *high*.

She was a seven-year veteran of the party culture.

She was only 25.

I wasn't 25.

She played hard.

I think I was falling—I'll stop there.

MARY

This First Date Ditty is For Adult Entertainment Only

I was entering virginal territories.

The more trips I made down the stairs into the club, the more skewed my morals and values became. Everyone who partakes in recreational—tries to erase human from living.

Everything was okay if it happened at the club. Nothing was meant to follow you home.

It was a bad place for anyone trying to hold onto who they truly are—an emotionally violent place. The reasons for escape may seem to be different on the surface. In reality, they all blend together.

ESCAPE = PAIN

Escape is a sign you no longer belong. The more you go, the more you sacrifice your soul. It's all bullshit. The only thing relevant is getting *high*.

I was about to embark on a relationship that's existence depended upon the substances readily available inside the confines of the club. I believed we'd be the exceptions. We could partake without becoming hypocritical. Because of the justification—you don't accept how ridiculous the proposition is.

Son, if I catch you smoking, I'll kick your ass. Here's a note. Now, go pick me up smokes.

Trish was a seasoned veteran of alteration. I was a rookie, still wrapped in protective latex.

Our relationship was about to kick into full gear. I was going to have to allow Trish to make mistakes knowing full well, one day, she'd eventually: settle into my arms.

Yes, I said settle into my arms.

My previous relationship taught me entering into a relationship jobless was incredibly smart. I entered.

Our second-first-date unfolded smoothly. *Up* we went, it was time to sabotage. I met Mary in the *Red Room*. She is a hot Croatian. We kissed, intensely. Round and round—

GUILT called me a *high*, idiot.

Mary invited me home. I declined. I took her back to Trish's instead.

Sam joined us. *She put on a long sleeve shirt.*

We were lying on Trish's bed. My mind was racing in an attempt to find *LOGIC*. I undressed. I started to—

Mary snapped some Polaroids. She left with an uncomfortable feeling in her gut.

Build

Trish and Mary guessed my age that night at the club.

They guessed 29 and 30 respectively. My guess was slightly *higher*.

Once Mary and Sam vamoosed and Trish and I were alone, we did it—all weekend long.

On Monday morning Trish gave me a key to her place. I began living out of a suitcase, only going home to feed Fuzzy, sporadically.

Fuzzy, I found a girl to replace you. Like you, she has a touch of the Far East in her bloodlines. If it's okay, I'll leave you in the capable hands of Wally. I'll visit often.

BACK TO MY SUITCASE: I loved Trish. I believed she was the one. *I was ripe for—*

I never felt this way about a relationship before. Different was good.

During the week, we did couple things. I spent my time with Trish and her friends. *I kept her from mine.* I wasn't going to allow my friends to judge my relationship with a 25-year-old Asian that started while *high*.

DATELINE: 1 December 2001 – The World – Vancouver, British Columbia

Another Saturday at the club, I wanted it to end. I wanted our weekends to mirror our weekdays. Unfortunately, the lifestyle is hard to break.

I'm not going, usually turns into: *Hello, I'm glad to see you out.*

It was easy to find (insert name), as if (insert name) can't possibly pop a pill without you, as an excuse for going.

Sacrificing Saturday's for drugs wasn't delusional.

On this Saturday Trish sat in a chair near the front of the club, eyes transfixed on a neon sign reading H_2O.

I looked into her eyes and said: *I love you.*

She gazed into mine.

We went home, *high*.

THINKING INSIDE THE BOX: SEX-FILLED MEANINGLESS ROMP—OR SOMETHING MORE?

Every love quest has ups & downs.

Where do you want to eat? What do you want to do?

In our case, our ups & downs were rooted together, the club. Drugs were the foundation of our relationship. I had to accept that. If I didn't, we'd have a passionate sex-filled romp, ending prematurely. For the relationship to have legs, I was going to have to change.

Fuck off LOGIC. I don't want to hear another peep.

The club is a toxic wasteland. Friends are spectral in nature. People go to escape only to come out more scarred. Saturday morphs into Sunday Sketch Parties. Sunday Sketch Parties were a time for "pretend" friends to talk in unison while they unearthed the secrets of the universe, all too busy with what they were saying to listen to anyone else.

Monday/Tuesday is time for the brain to try to restore itself to happy.

Trish always hosted the after parties. The parties grew old, fast. Guests would flash in.

Michael – Jeremy – Toni – Andrew – Kim – Kim – Jeremy – Patrick – Stephen + + +

Each transposable, most short-lived, some; would burn out needing to find reality again.

Trish was the one constant. I hated that. If I wouldn't go—she'd go without me, so, I went.

She assured me the party meant nothing. She told me one day it would end. She told me—

Sweetie, the only way I'd ever break up with you is if you cheated on me.

ENTER PATRICK

Why is there a Patrick phoning you from San Francisco? You met him for two minutes while high. I asked Trish in a visibly upset manner.

Trish met Patrick at the *World*, the Saturday be*fore*.

BLIND ~~EYE~~

I'm not sure why she needs a new guy-friend in San Francisco. She told me cheating is not an option.

After *LOGIC* had piped in with his two cents, saying, *let her be*, I decided to let it slide.

Even though, I wasn't sure if *LOGIC* was making *logical* sense?

Trish was a contrast between artificial and natural, illusion and truth.

By the time March 2002 rolled around, we had made it six months. Our relationship found balance. Trish appeared extroverted. In reality, she's a shy introvert. Whereas, I'm an extrovert who chose to be introverted, if that makes an ounce of sense?

Trish makes a killer first impression. She craves to be the centre of attention. But once she is, she retreats into the mist of *high*, rarely contributing anything of substance.

Whereas I like the individual, not the pack, I find the pack to be emotionally vapid. Life's gems when it comes to club-related are derived from letting *high*—take you places with other likeminded lost souls you've never been before and will likely never find again. In reality, it's all BULLSHIT. Typing this paragraph highlights that point

Friendship for Trish relied on the next pill.

During the week her friends would come and go—most times, without the pace of the medicine she'd retreat to the computer while I entertained.

In March, I became sick. I kept the severity of my illness to myself. A *Specialist* was afraid my situation might become grave. There was a chance my liver might fail. He believed I might have developed a rare liver ailment that is prevalent in individuals of Asian descent.

Trish continued going to the club.

Magically, I woke one day, my illness was gone—no explanation found.

HOW'S IT GOING, TONIGHT, FAG?

DATELINE: 8 April 2002 – New Westminster, British Columbia

I started a new job as a bartender at the *Fireside Pub* in the backwards community of New Westminster—at least the *Pub* was backwards, the *Fireside* belongs in the seventies.

The walls were velour. Patrons wore shirts emblazoned with beer logos. Solo musicians playing *Van Morrison* were part of the nightly entertainment. The clientele consisted of heavy-set blue-collar men sitting at the bar reliving past glory, avoiding home.

The nightly activities included: talking about the big game, reciting sport jersey numbers—and intimidating newcomers.

Many regulars snorted cocaine with the bitchy unionised female servers who were out of their league: as if cocaine snorting negligent single mothers play in an elite league?

I wore shirts with collars, an invitation to be taunted.

How's it going, tonight, fag—what's it like being a fag—fag—

After seven days and fifteen thousand variations, it grew tiresome.

My work schedule was Thursday through Sunday nights. A challenging task when one considers:

SATURDAY NIGHT (WEEKLY) EQUATION

FINISH WORK AT MIDNIGHT—> THE WORLD + POP A PILL + POP ANOTHER PILL—>
SKETCH PARTY 7 AM UNTIL—> LEAVE SKETCH PARTY 4 PM —>ARRIVE AT WORK 5 PM (SLEEP DEPRIVED)
LEGEND: —> = RUSH TO

This particular weekend followed the same formula. Trish hosted the party. On Sunday afternoon I'd hit the road to work at precisely 4 PM sans sleep. A sketched out fifteen-minute drive later I'd arrive back in the seventies.

Luckily, for my regular customers—change that—fortunately, for me—sleep deprivation and the continual processing of chemicals provided me with a bitchy edge.

Jamie, a bus driver, tipped the scales in the neighbourhood of two hundred sixty pounds. Facial fat produced a youthful artery clogging sheen.

Without question, he hadn't seen his feet for more than a decade or his penis for that matter, without the help of a mirror.

I hope one day the *Fireside* crew read this. I hated everything about the place.

On this night, Jamie, in a smooth-crackling almost pubescent tone, asked me where I lived.

I responded: *Vancouver.*

In Gayville, he chirped back.

I called him a dipshit. Next, I sarcastically confirmed all one million residents of Vancouver are fags. I asked to see his Mensa Card.

I said I live in Yaletown, and that *Gayville* would be the West End.

There are too many faggot weirdoes in the West End. He stays away from them, he said

Thanks to the processing, I ranted: *Well, unlike this area, which is rampant with panhandlers and heroin addicts, the West End is clean and liveable. One of the big differences is the people dress better. And, oh yeah, I have never seen gay sex acts breaking out there. Another thing Jamie, when the 'gays' come up to you and ask to have sex because the 'gays' are attracted to obese middle-aged men who are about to drop dead from a coronary, you can always say, NO.*

In a Mensa moment, he fired back: *You must be one of them because you're defending them.*

Another regular Ryan *tinkled* in saying he spoke with a Lesbian couple once. He asked them if they knew an unborn child was going to be retarded, would they abort the birth. Ryan said they replied *yes*. He then said he asked them the same question substituting *gay* for *retard*. He claimed their response was the same.

He then shouted*: See, gays* and *retards, the same thing!*

I recoiled and fired; edge intensified: *Look around fags. There are ten of you and one toothless woman in here. Collectively, you're pushing the scales at ambulance crashing massive coronary levels. There are stained beer posters on the walls. You've likely not had sex with a sober woman in years.*

I began laughing.

There's velour on the walls. Are we in a Holiday Inn Lounge in the 70s? Let's not forget the musician is playing "Brown Eyed Girl" for the zillionth time. Oh my, look, the toothless lady is leaving just as two fat guys enter upping the count to twelve. Do you guys get where I'm going? I didn't think so. Anyway, you guys are in a 'GAY' bar right now, just not a good one.

They never called me *fag* again.

14 JUNE 2002 – NEW WESTMINSTER BRITISH COLUMBIA

I transferred pubs in New West. The treatment remained the same, shoddy. The poor treatment ended when I forcefully removed a humongous ironworker who was about to bend a mouthy regular into twisted rebar.

A regular in an angry tone told me to cut off the Ironworkers, calling me *Fag* in the process.

I have things under control. I said.

I was the lone worker. I needed to handle things delicately.

The ironworkers agreed to leave, quietly—if I bought them a shooter.

The regular noticed the shooters, barking at me to kick the clowns out, now.

The ironworkers didn't like being called clowns.

Who are you calling a clown—wasn't that your whore wife I saw down on the corner on twelfth?

The regular, the ironworker's ire was directed at, flashed a single digit. The ironworker was about to twist.

I intervened; addressing the whole bar: *Shut the fuck up*!

I explained what was going to transpire as I spoke loudly in my octave-lowered voice.

I explained the shooters would be drunk in silence. The ironworkers would then leave—and, if anything escalates, there will be losers. I just won't be one of them.

The ironworkers were at the exit when the loud mouth regular flashed the digit again. I was in the middle. I blocked a man twice my size. He spun, placing his arm on the edge of the pool table. I pushed my right hand down on his arm. His arm snapped.

From that day on, *the reg*ulars stopped calling me Fag.

I couldn't wait to get home to Trish.

BOMBSHELL: NUMBER 1

24 APRIL 2002

FROM: LINDSAY
To: Trish (Sweetie Pie)
Message: Greeting Card

Sweetie, tonight when I get home I want to undress you and throw you onto the bed slowly. I want to caress and lick—

Love

Lindsay

FROM: E-GREETINGS.

To: Lindsay

Message: Your card has been received by the following recipients.

Trish

Patrick

To view, the greetings click on the link below.

(link)

Regards

E-GREETINGS

FROM: TRISH

To: Patrick

Message: Greeting Card

Next time I see you I want to undress you and throw you onto the bed slowly. I want to caress and lick—

Too hot to handle

Trish

When Trish came home from work, I told her I was going to hate the conversation we were about to engage in; I asked her: *What the hell is this? You sent the fucking card to Patrick; why?*

She lied. She told me it was merely a joke. She said she sent it to all of her friends.

I let it slide.

LOGIC jumped into the mix. *LOGIC* told me I couldn't ignore reality.

I chose to ignore fucking *LOGIC*.

FORK IN THE ROAD

I love you. I love you. I don't want to be with anyone else.

Those words flowed from her mouth as we were in the throes of—

Take that *LOGIC*.

BOMBSHELL: NUMBER 2

19 MAY 2002

Another Sunday = Another Sketch Party at Trish's

I retreated to the computer.

Trish's email was open on her computer screen—we shared her computer. She'd been exchanging emails with some guy named Rod.

FROM TRISH TO ROD:

It will be hot when we get together. You won't be able to handle the intensity.

We could've this morning, but your girlfriend and my boyfriend were watching like hawks.

She said I love you? LOGIC sarcastically piped in. He called me an idiot.

137

Tell me your boyfriend's schedule, and I'll come over when he's not there, climb under the covers and send you places you've never been before.

That fucking sucked—crossed my mind.

LOGIC told me to walk away.

Maybe she can explain? I argued.

LOVE joined in, calling her: *A manipulative attention whore...*

I was flying *high*. I didn't enjoy *LOGIC* and *LOVE* ganging up on me. In my deluded state I believed they were jealous of what I had. They didn't like my defensive ways.

SCREW – TWIST – SCREW - TWIST

Let me scoop out a little more brain, don't worry—we'll keep it in a safe place.

Effortlessly, Trish denied the emails. She claimed somebody was trying to screw us up. Trish believed her performance. She was—

I didn't have the credentials to diagnose.

Her friends bought her performance as well; they too went searching for the real—

She cheated. She hurt me. I let it go. I'm just as bad as her. Please don't try to convince me—

I met Rod at the club one week later; I asked him if it was true?

He ran.

Paranoia entered the fray.

Pop a pill for a blast of elation; just teasing. I'll rip the moment from your mind. Everyone in the club will be after Trish. Feeling crazy, yet? You'll have visual and auditory hallucinations. Elaborate hand signals will be exchanged between everyone and Trish, all night long. The beauty: you'll think what's happening is real. You won't be able to escape. She cheated, but you'll become the villain quickly, fun, hey? She cheats. You pay and pay and pay. Keep thinking she loves you, sucker.

I never embraced *PARANOIA*. He swallowed me.

A handsome guy across the room touched his cap—patted his chest twice—winked—looked upward—touched his inner thigh—winked again—and double clapped.

I stole home.

I think he was telling Trish his work schedule.

Another pill would surely fix things.

PICNIC IN THE PARK

DATELINE: 13 July 2002 – Vancouver, British Columbia

Saturday thru Tuesday sucked.

Trish was young, beautiful, and evil, with a tremendous upside.

Have I gone mad?

Bedlam was about to ensue.

I'll eagerly await your diagnosis. Keep turning the pages

My birthday was in three days. Trish planned a picnic in the park with friends, mostly hers.

She gave me a card filled with love and affection. When I read it, I became weak. I believed every word.

Hello again, do you mind if I take another scoop?

SKETCH PARTY

Two taps on the front door.

Trish answered, her Grandpa was on the other side. *Oh fuck.*

Not good, out of seven people present—nobody, not even me, was capable of speaking an understandable dialect or sentences consisting of words.

I was sitting at the computer.

Grandpa asked Trish if she was okay.

Galywilbeens. Trish said.

Michael (more on him later), *high* on a combination of drugs, solidified with pot, couldn't stop laughing, hysterically. He'd been laughing uncontrollably for five hours.

Spineless Kenny attempted to help by saying: *Parandg thig eryed si ko l'il teg Tris ot.*

I was still sitting silently at the computer. I was positive *Parandg thig eryed si ko l'il teg Tris ot* was meaningless. I also thought: maybe Grandpa would like to pop a pill.

Grandpa shook his head and then said in broken English: *Stay in school. Make sure you rotate your tires,* then left.

INTERVENTION

Four days later

Jeremy, a regular party acquaintance, called. He asked me to give him a ride to pick up some furniture. I reluctantly agreed, leaving Trish behind. When I returned home to Trish's, I found a note on the door:

I'm with Grandpa—I will be back shortly.

Love Trish

I had left my key behind at Trish's. I couldn't let myself in. So, I waited nervously. Ten turned into 11 PM. One eventually arrived at 4 AM. Trish returned home shortly after 4. She told me they figured things out. She said they were doing an intervention.

I hugged her. I drifted off to sleep thinking: *The club days were finally coming to an end.*

Trish would never fall board-like face-first toward the floor in the *Red Room*—only to be saved at the last moment by me jumping forth to break her fall, an occurrence that happened on several occasions while Trish was tweaking in the midst of *high*; again.

Two days later

When Trish and I were out having dinner, Trish's cousin phoned. Her cousin happened to live with Grandpa. Trish chuckled and then said: *Yeah, bad timing; Grandpa must think—No, no, I haven't spoken to him since Sunday.*

NOVEMBER 2002

It was time to insert new sketched-out antagonists into our lives to replace the ones that had crashed.

It was an easy proposition because FRIENDSHIP = whoever is sitting next to you when the chemicals rev up your circuitry.

Harish became Trish's sixth new best friend of the year. Harish enjoyed being single. Harish loved prowling for sex.

Their friendship would certainly bode well for our calmed love. *Fucking Harish—*

Late in the month, Trish flew to Miami for work. The flight is approximately nine hours. I dropped by her place at 9 AM.

She was already home—this struck me as odd.

BOMBSHELL: NUMBER 3

I made a pit-stop at Trish's between bar gigs. Trish was out with Harish.

I went to open my email. The computer screen was resting on Trish's inbox. I opened it.

There was an email from Patrick. I opened it.

I discovered her trip, wasn't to Miami. When she returned with Harish, tears were pouring down my face.

Somebody is trying to fuck us up! She barked.

I questioned my sanity. *May I take another scoop? Thank you.*

GUILT, LOGIC and SELF LOVE told me to take care of myself. I left for work. I was still crying.

This revelation made it paramount I leave her. We had no relationship. Instead of running, I hung on.

I sent an email to Patrick, asking him WTF?

He pleaded innocence.

I told him to fuck off.

He said he'd step away. He said he wanted us to work things out.

I bought his bullshit.

I was becoming borderline certifiable. I wanted to work things out. Trish did as well. For her it was easy, just lie.

COHABITATE

If you happen to be wondering what's wrong with me? – THE ANSWER: a lot.

If you're wondering what's wrong with Trish, thank you.

Penning this part of my life was an intimidating, emotionally excruciating task. It's obvious our love was flawed. She was spoilt, selfish, manipulative, with zero regard for anyone but herself, and even that's, questionable?

What I've shared has damaged me. Trish became my drug.

I needed to let her go—to crash. I didn't. Instead, I convinced myself if I don't love her now all she'll ever be is a liar and a cheat.

So, to keep the ride moving, we moved in together on December 1.

DATELINE: 15 February 2003

Against all the odds, we made it. The drama subsided. Trish was off to Montreal for work.

She phoned me on this chilly Saturday night to say *I love you. Thank you for not leaving. I can't wait to get home.*

Twelve days after Trish and I beat all odds, life was spiralling upward. I was out with my good friend David. David was privy to some of Trish and my relationship histrionics. Despite our flaws, he was cheering for us.

At nights end, I felt an urge to share my feelings. I looked over at David and casually stated: *David, life is great. We made it past our problems. I forgave her. I'm the happiest I've ever been—*

10

FREE FALL

A meta-memoir

PEOPLE MATTER

DATELINE: 28 FEBRUARY 2003 – VANCOUVER, BRITISH COLUMBIA

A s day turned to night; it was time to go home. After my last pint at my favourite local watering hole, I began stumbling home. I took a breather on a bus bench at the halfway mark. A 75-year-old man sat beside me. Together we watched people pass by while we discussed the world around us. He was pleasant, bearded, wearing a winter jacket; sort of Santa meets the streets. To my surprise, he was homed—not homeless. His pension left him scrambling for survival.

Can you buy me a coffee, he asked.

I offered $2, only if he promised not to spend it on drugs.

He laughed and said: *Drugs don't allow you to play to my age.*

I asked him: *What do you think matters most in life?*

Stoically, he said, while pointing to the passers-by: *That's simple. People matter. Sadly, I believe that we've lost sight of that.*

He firmly grasped my hand, smiled, and then, thanked me.

Trauma is hovering on the story horizon. Change is about to alter life's course once more.

Buckle yourself in, the amperage of life is about to be cranked to eleven.

Thank you for joining me.

I may need a hug at the end.

DUMPED

DATELINE: 3 March 2003 – Vancouver, British Columbia

8:30 AM the alarm rang.

My eyes peeped open; I rolled over and said: *Good morning, sweetie.*

Good morning, was Trish's reply.

She then dished out: *I'm dumping you.*

I pried her for clarification.

She clarified she was breaking up with me. She walked out the door on her way to work. She came back four hours later and confirmed her earlier sentiment; claiming she wasn't as happy as she could be.

My voice cracked. Trish had just moved in. She loved me yesterday.

*Fucking drugs—destroye*d us, I thought.

She was committed to "us" being over.

You just moved in. What about our living arrangement? I asked.

You're an amazing man. I want to keep living with you.

LOGIC pressed me to throw her out; you must end this bullshit, *LOGIC* emphatically stated.

I decided this will pass.

Harish asked—you are not 30. I deserve more. You're not as successful as you should be by now.

Somehow, my age trumped her lies.

I was stuck on *this will pass.*

More of my brain was scooped out, leaving barely enough for me to make it through a day.

I pulled from my memory banks on what to do when dumped. I came up with serenading *I love you* from every possible angle.

LOGIC sternly offered: *Shut the fuck up.*

Distraught didn't do my emotional state justice. Being hit by a bus might have been a blessing.

At work that night, the bar was robbed.

A past-shady character walked in and calmly announced he was a robber.

In a deadpan fashion, I replied: *You're a robber? What is it you want? Is it the cash drawer? I have an idea: how about you sit back and relax while I make you a drink. Of course, since you are robbing the joint, you will not have to pay, nor will I phone the police. When you finish your drink, I'll hand over the cash—sending you on your merry way. How does that sound?*

He looked at me in baffled manner and said: *My name is Robert. There is a meal set aside for me.*

BRANDON

DATELINE: 7 March 2003 – Vancouver, British Columbia

It was a postcard perfect Vancouver spring day. It was time to break free from the angular *I love you* serenade.

Brandon was 18. A block from home I ran into him at *Choices Market*. I met him two years prior at the club. He was artistically gifted. Two years prior = 16.

The Club doesn't serve alcohol, and since drugs don't require ID, age becomes shamefully; irrelevant.

Brandon was a good *kid*. We, *responsible* adults, had no fucking business hanging out with him.

Outside of *Choices*, I asked him how he was doing.

Not so good, you? He replied.

I told him likewise. I said to him Trish and I broke up. He adored Trish.

He trembled as I hugged him adding: *I've got to go. Life sucks.*

I cry as I write this.

We broke our embrace. And then, Brandon back stepped two times, looked directly into my eyes, and repeated: *My life sucks.*

He turned and walked away.

Brandon went home that postcard perfect beautiful Vancouver spring day—and hung himself.

Brandon was a good kid.

We, society; failed him.

Every time I walked into *Choices* for months after, our conversations in *THE CLUB* played in perfect clarity in my mind. Brandon was gay. He was trying to fit in while at the same time being isolated from his family. Everything was urgent to him.

Brandon, you don't need to be in a serious relationship, you have your whole life ahead of you.

Brandon, stay young as long as you can.

Brandon, I'll call you to make sure you got home okay.

I told Trish the news. She was unfazed.

I hated that week.

LOGIC and *LOVE* chimed in telling me to stop the self-torment and throw her out?

Who's, Matthew?

Trish met Matthew on her last night in Montreal; moments after she called to say *I love you so much.*

She was attempting a long distance relationship with him. He's a lawyer. I'm not. Trish pointed that fact out to me.

Hey, this time, do you mind if we remove your spine, of course, you don't. I added stupid to my list of accomplishments. I called Matthew and introduced myself as Trish's boyfriend. He said he'd cut off all contact with her.

He lied.

Living together was going to be heavenly.

SKETCH PARTY MICHAEL

DATELINE: 15 March 2003 – Vancouver, British Columbia

His quest was to get into Trish's pants. I hated him. We tolerated each other. I gave him credit for honesty. Trish discounted my interpretation of his intentions.

Until, until they went for coffee together and he painted the picture, she declined his advances.

Michael and I became friends, defying all odds.

My home life sucked. Home felt more like a prison than a home. I avoided it. I went for drinks after work every night after finishing my bartending gig to prolong my inevitable need to go home.

On this night, I ran into Michael at the *Odyssey Bar*. He ushered me to a quiet spot. He told me Trish doesn't deserve me. He told me I am a good man. He said he considers me a good friend.

He then dropped a bomb on me.

Remember, at the club, I always said I would never make it to 30. Well—I have cancer—I'm—

AUNT PRISCILLA

DATELINE: 29 March 2003 – Vancouver, British Columbia

Aunt Priscilla was my favourite relative. She lived in Edmonton. She occasionally called to say *I love you*, nothing more.

On this day her call was different. She told me she was cutting my *evil sisters* out of her *Will*. She said they disrespected her, showed zero gratitude for all the things she'd done for them.

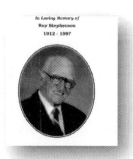

I didn't like hearing this. I asked Priscilla why she was telling me.

Because I love you, you've always been my favourite. Ever since your mother and father died, you've been on your own. We all need a family. I'm yours.

She went on to tell me she was going to find out today she was dying. She said she was going to be reunited with my Uncle Roy: her true love.

I cried uncontrollably. I told Priscilla *I loved her*. I let her in on the events transpiring around me. I collapsed to the floor sobbing. Priscilla and I only spoke two more times.

THE BIG C took her away just over one month later.

THE BIG C ragged me, saying *IT* had become a permanent fixture, a close friend, *IT* jabbed me reminding me of the roster of pain: Father—mother—friend—aunt—and, even yanking my chain with a close call. *IT* guaranteed *IT* would be back again, soon.

Two weeks before Pricilla's death, my brother Jim called. The family wanted me to drop everything and travel to Edmonton to watch Priscilla die.

I expressed my life was in shambles. I told him I cry every day. I said I didn't have the strength; I said we said our goodbyes. I reminded him I watched our parents die. I told him I didn't need another reason to cry on queue.

Having to defend my emotions was fucking sucking.

PRINCE

DATELINE: 7 April 2003 – Vancouver, British Columbia

When you've been dumped but still live with your ex—allowing her to get a dog—is **SMART**.

Really: **SMART**; with no reeking of manipulation written all over the gesture, seriously, how could there be?

Trish selected a Border-Collie from an animal rescue. We don't have sheep or cattle roaming through our downtown apartment; therefore, a Border-Collie made sense. Trish pleaded. I gave in.

When we brought the eight-month-old Border-Collie home, Fuzzy gave up one of her nine lives when her kitty heart stopped on sight.

Trish left for work. The dog began to bark uncontrollably while repeatedly throwing itself against the sliding glass door of the sunroom.

The dog had to go.

I was instantly labelled: BAD GUY.

The party was over, and I refused to accept that fact. Self-destruction was part of the pain.

Somehow during my downward slide, I never missed a shift at *Pat's Pub* (NEW JOB) and the *Old Terminal Pub*; an unhealthy accomplishment. I also never missed a shift at the club.

Michael's chemotherapy was kicking into full gear when he told me of his illness. After he had confided in me, I made a point of contacting him on a weekly basis to offer support.

I ran into him in the *Odyssey* again. He said he valued my friendship. He said he had something important to tell me. He also strongly encouraged me to kick Trish out.

I hate telling you this—we fucked, Michael said.

Instantly, I became consumed with misguided hatred. It's hard to remain compassionate to a dying man when he's just told you he's *fucked* your girlfriend.

He apologised, suggesting he should have remained silent.

He's fucking right. Relinquishing his guilt was selfish. I hated him for that.

When I arrived home, I confronted Trish. *Trish, Michael told me. You fucking cheated on me. Did you ever love me?*

She barely looked up from the computer when she said: *I was trying to get you a job. I did it for you. I thought Michael would hire you.*

I grabbed her by the back of the neck, threw her into the hallway, slamming the door in her face, never allowing her back into my life ever again, a momentary, *unfulfilled fantasy.*

Unfortunately, I was spineless.

LOGIC & LOVE gave up on me. They were tired of looking at the train wreck of my life.

It was time to manipulate with kindness. A lady at the *Terminal Pub* was being forced to give her dog away. I phoned Trish with the news.

Sweetie, would you still like a dog?

She declined my offer.

When I arrived home from work, I went to use the bathroom; I opened the door—a baby Jack Russell Terrier greeted me.

Prince stopped at my feet, looked up, and went, ~~meow~~, *ruff.*

The dog experiment continued—

TOUCHED BY AN ANGEL

DATELINE: 27 April 2003 – New Westminster, British Columbia

The *Old Terminal Pub* sits in a remote parking lot in a bad part of New Westminster. Sharing the parking lot is an adult video store. One week before this night, thugs beat a store clerk to within an inch of his life. It was a random act.

The patrons of the pub consist of longshoremen and construction workers, most lacking refinement. As mentioned before, since I was the lone male employee—until the arm snap—*FAG*, was my pet name.

Most nights the regulars would be liquored by 7, and then on their way home to their wives and kids.

Marginal sprung to mind.

Most nights, when the last Neanderthal slithered out—I'd be left alone.

The Terminal is located in the middle of a large empty parking lot, far from civilisation, with two entrances—and just me in inside.

I'd often lock the doors, allowing only the odd late comer in, only if I knew them.

The fog was dense on this night. Fifteen minutes shy of closing I heard a knock at the door.

The knocking began cascading like the rain beating down outside.

Standing at the door was a large man, well over six feet tall, many pounds over two hundred. He was dishevelled, rougher than the regulars; I had never seen him before.

I let him in.

He told me he'd never been here before; he'd driven past the pub on several occasions, he said. He wanted to case out the inside.

He asked me to shoot stick.

We ambled toward the pool table, stopping to grab cues, our arms brushed, *I shuddered*—he looked skyward, paused, and began a sermon.

His voice was deliberate. His life was tough, fuelled by alcohol, tobacco, and drugs.

His words resonated with me.

I rarely drink now. What time do you close? Are you often left alone? That's scary. There are evil people out there. I've spent time in prison. I developed a significant taste for heroin and crack. I've done terrible things. I've hurt people.

I remained silent. Strangely, the words were comforting.

My wife is gone—she's too far gone—demons have taken her away. My wife and I royally fucked up—we lost our children to dope. My wife lost her mind. She crashed. She burned.

My kids have become my life. My wife is too far into the world of 'hype' that normalcy is not an option anymore.

His voice cracked.

She's the love of my life. I introduced her to the destruction—I'm paying a self-inflicted high price. She can't come back. I'm responsible for her flaws. That's my ticket to misery.

I racked the balls.

He asked me to break.

I slowly pulled back the cue, thrusting it into the cue ball, sending it fiercely into the tightly racked balls. The balls scattered—the *eight ball* shot into the corner pocket—instant victory—a rarity.

Regardless of my new friend's outward appearance—he had a quality of understanding about him. He'd fallen far, but his resolve was still present; still strong.

147

I've come to an understanding—I've had to let my love go. She can't come back. My children—their future— that's all that matters now—my life is belongs to them.

He asked me if he could make an observation. I nodded, looking directly into his bloodshot eyes.

You're broken and confused. You're struggling to find meaning. People are dying. People are leaving you. You want to hold on. You've lost love. I see the pain in your eyes. My friend, all I can offer—it's not your fault. You must believe that. People lie. They sabotage the good in life. That's just the way it is. You're part of what's right in this world. It's going to get worse for you—for a while at least.

I listened, speechless.

Your lover made a mistake—she's not coming back. Sorry. You'll survive. You're a great man. I can see that in your eyes. Cry. Cry every day. One day the crying will end and you'll wake up a better person. Don't let life destroy you. You won't. I've come here tonight to tell you this. That is my mission.

He walked to the door. He asked if I'd ever seen him before. I shook my head.

My friend, you will survive and come back stronger. That is your mission. Believe it.

I gazed out the window cut in the middle of the pub's entrance as this man I'd never seen before walked into a dense fog—vanishing into the unknown.

That night when I drove home the fog intensified. My heart was pounding. My chest felt like it was about to burst. My legs were shaking so violently it was hard to control the gas pedal and brakes on my drive home. My mind fixated on his words. *My mission* kept coming to the forefront.

I skipped going to the *Odyssey* that night, choosing to go directly home instead. When I arrived, I went straight to my bed, undressed, crawled under the covers, and continued to tremble. *I gasped for air as I drifted off to sleep.*

Farewell + Evil + Crack Whore

Goodbye Priscilla

DATELINE: 24 May 2003 – Edmonton, Alberta

Evil Sisters

DATELINE: 4 June 2003 – Calgary, Alberta

Uncle James was my last living uncle.

Merely three days passed after Priscilla's funeral when my sister Bernice phoned. It was our first conversation in years. I thought she found out about the *Will* and was about to layer guilt on me.

Uncle James died last night. I thought you should know.

My pig-headedness to continue my trips to the club were counterproductive to my recovery. Both Trish and *high* needed to be expelled. Too many traumas were zapping my strength. Living in delusion was providing false hope.

I'd see Trish hanging out at the club with *The Big C*, laughing. I was certain of it.

I needed a hug. Instead, Trish paraded potential replacements in front of me. *Paranoia* paid me regular visits. I was tripping in a vicious weekly cycle.

Trauma—Followed by Pain—Chased with Drugs—Enhanced with *Paranoia* and Isolation

Man's Best Friend

Every day I took Prince on long walks. He became a great friend.

Usually, after about two blocks, he'd sit down, refusing to move. Thus, in reality, I took Prince for long carries, often six plus miles.

We'd stop for lunch. I'd ask him for answers.

He'd tilt his head to the right. Ears flopped inside out. Then he'd look up at me and say: *Ruff!*

After a substantial carry, I lay down. I drifted off to sleep with Prince by my side on the lawn at *English Bay* with my knees bent at a *sixty-degree angle*. When I woke, I found that Prince had crawled onto my stomach and fallen asleep. A stranger took pictures. He offered to email them to me.

An RCMP Officer who happened to be a friend of mine approached. His name was Duane. He asked how I was doing.

I explained I was in the midst of a difficult time.

He told me my boss from the *Sandpiper Pub*, his sister, Andrea—was found dead in her apartment the previous night.

Mommy and Daddy love you. One day things will return to normal, I promise.

He'd tilt his head to the right and—

Crack Whore Jessica

DATELINE: 23 June 2003 – Vancouver, British Columbia

Gifted artist—lousy human being, *Crack Whore* was my pet name for her.

I don't apologise for giving her the moniker; she's, mean, aggressive, and a bitch, at least to me.

She appeared out of *high,* immediately sweeping Trish and a mutual friend, Noel, off their feet by promising to use them as models. *Vanity* led her to favourite.

Noel was a rare mutual friend from the club. Our bond appeared stable.

As my life was withering, we drifted apart because I was drowning in emotional quicksand.

The party continued around me. The party doesn't mix well with despair. Jessica's insertion turned the three of them into *MEAN GIRLS.* Jessica was a gin-loving party girl who dabbled in more illicit substances.

My party was crashing.

They didn't care.

They knew what was unfolding in my life.

It didn't matter to them.

Crack Whore knew we lived together. She bombarded potential replacements in front of me by blasting email-after-email of new candidates for Trish to replace me with.

Throw her out; we give up; you're on your own.

LOVE and *LOGIC* sauntered away.

Jessica's *mark* was derived, because she has two children, her ex has custody; periodically, they stay with her. Occasionally, Jessica, I mean *Crack Whore,* would break out lines of Crystal Meth on my *fucking* kitchen counter—that's why I gave her the name.

What the fuck are you guys doing? Trish, you told me you'd never do this shit. You said you have limits. Why are you bringing this garbage into our home? Jessica, what if your kids need you? I wailed!

Don't judge me. You don't know what's best for my children.

I reasoned it wasn't a cracked-out mother. I offered to give them a ride to wherever they were going.

They declined.

Jessica almost died from an overdose several months later.

I continued to make monumental mistakes. I continued to cry every day. I punished myself by going to the club. Afterwards, I'd end up in precarious—soul-sapping encounters.

I disgusted myself.

Often we'd go the club as a group of "pretend" friends—once inside I'd be cast aside, ostracised for the night. At closing time, Trish would host *Sketch Parties* at our place.

DESPAIR shuffled *GUILT* aside.

He said he'd take care of me for a while.

I'd sit—lost—alone—longing to hear Priscilla's *I love you.*

11

COLLAPSE

A meta-memoir

PASSPORT

TIME OUT

On March 3, 2003, it started with Trish dumping me—it was now two weeks into July.

Four fucking months—only *four months* had passed. BREAKUP—SUICIDE—CANCER—ALIENATION—INFIDELITY—DEATH—CANCER—DEATH—DEATH—AND—*FUCKING* DEATH; had entered my life.

I wanted to die. The medicine was to provide the solution. The prescriptions were never potent enough.

I continued the destructive cycle.

The demons kept picking at my being; they were now nearing my core.

I was continuing to fall down this dark, lonely tunnel. The tunnel was narrow, but strangely, had no sides. The pace quickened. I passed *level after level* reaching out frantically grabbing for relief, something to hold onto—I only grasped air. I passed *GUILT, LOGIC,* and *LOVE.* They were reaching for me—an invisible force was holding them at bay. The velocity reached a lightning pace. I wanted this to end. I imagined my body slamming into the ground with such force that it would explode leaving nothing more than an unidentifiable stain on the cold asphalt, only to be washed away by the next rain. Everything changed overnight. I was positive I had reached the precipice and falling down the tunnel and dying, was next.

DATELINE: 19 JULY 2003

It was time to fight for survival.

I decided to implement a **2 STEP PLAN.**

STEP 1: Leave my environment.

Europe popped into my mind.

STEP 2: Escape the Club.

I failed miserably—with STEP 2.

SHOWER—RINSE—REPEAT

I kept imbibing in illicit.

My friend Dave had worked with me at the *Sandpiper*. He decided to come with me on my adventure to Europe. I was not sure what his motivation was.

He quit the pub, eagerly anticipating our journey. The only thing slowing our departure was renewing my passport.

Sir, we can't issue you a new passport. Oh my, you have a tear in your birth certificate. You'll need to get a new one. A civil servant at the passport office said to me.

You can expedite the process the staff member said. It takes two days. All I needed to do was contact *Vital Statistics* in Edmonton, the city where I was born, and provide them with both of my parents' names. I phoned.

Two weeks passed. Dave was getting antsy. I phoned again to inquire about the delay.

A female civil servant answered, and drably stated: they couldn't issue me a new birth certificate. She said the information I provided doesn't match my birth records.

I began to cry. I asked what was needed. *I pinched myself.*

She then asked me a question in the same drab emotionless timber as before,

Could you phone your parents and ask them who your real parents are?

I stepped off the edge of the cliff. My fall continued.

INTENSITY + CONFUSION + FRUSTRATION + DESPAIR + HOPLESSNESS came forth in unison.

Could you phone your parents and ask them? I asked the civil servant.

I gasped.

What do you mean? What does this mean? I asked.

An eternity passed. In real time, two seconds.

I watched them both die; take their last breaths. Up until seconds ago, they were my real parents.

The civil servant lacked empathy. She asked me if I could ask one of my older brothers or sisters.

I told her since I didn't know who I was anymore, I guess, they wouldn't be brothers and sisters, would they?

I asked if she could make that call.

She replied, *no*, and then transferred me to a supervisor.

Before she transferred me, she informed me unless I could prove who I was—they wouldn't be able to issue me a birth certificate.

When the supervisor came on, I was still crying. She seemed to care. She asked me a plethora of questions.

What are the names of your siblings? What schools have you attended? What sports have you played? When did you masturbate for the first time? How many times have you masturbated? When did you get your driver's license? Who's Mark? How many rolls of toilet paper have you used?

At least she seemed to understand how difficult it would be to call my older brothers and sisters to ask them, who am I?

Hey Jim, while I was renewing my passport I found out—anyway, who's my fucking father; and, who the hell are you?

The supervisor told me, once she confirmed my identity there were a series of steps I would need to follow: 1) Once I received my birth certificate, I was to send her a copy; 2) She would then send me my official birth records listing my real parents.

Less than one hour earlier, I had spent over 43 years as the son of Nicholas and Rebekah, brother of Bernice, Sadie, Beverly, James, Donald, and Brian. Now—now, I didn't have a clue what this meant or who I was, I felt betrayed, lied to, and cheated.

When I informed Wayne, he was shocked, for the second time in the last couple of weeks.

Next up on the newswire, Dave—I updated him on the delay.

Dave took the news in stride:

I love you man; your life is so not boring!

I speculated on the potential identity of my father: perhaps a mass murder, maybe Mick Jagger; please don't let it be an uncle, I thought.

Hello, Lindsay, I see your support network has vacated. You seem to be in some disrepair; so, my friend, I'm going to do the driving for a while, if that's okay, with you?

I'm not going to give you a choice. It's going to get messy. I'm going to fuck things up. There's going to be a significant amount of damage. You will become lonely. When I'm all done you'll have only one way to go. Without most of your brain; and your other allies not present, you're going to have to trust me.

Hey, if you're here to help, why did you hit the down button?

And besides, *who the hell are you?*

NEXT STOPS

DESPAIR – ISOLATION – INNER TURMOIL – DEATH – ALL ABOARD
THE CONDUCTOR BARKED!

Unlike the young girl behind the hoarding of the construction site (coming later), I wasn't banging needles into my arm; I boarded the train anyway.

DESPAIR

Each new day in Vancouver's summer was a high-resolution copy of the last, perfect.

Every day brought fresh opportunity. I needed to hold on to something. My life was out of control.

My vital organs, my heart, my soul, along with LOGIC and LOVE were ripped from my body and placed on the asphalt. The summer sun scorched the pavement. The heat was wavering intensely in the air, clouding the future. Its hue was opaque with a reddish tinge as blood escaped from my heart. My essence left my soul. I began to sense the end was near. Escape was finally on the platform. A magnifying glass stood between the asphalt and the sun. The heat intensified. The pain increased as the pavement began to bubble, soften, and burn.

I could feel the sun's rays sear then pierce. Living became unbearable. Agony confirmed: I was alive.

PAIN = LIFE

Suddenly, as the searing turned to charring and the burn became blackened and hard, friends or complete strangers would reach out and pull the magnifying glass away. The heat cooled, my expiration was cancelled, leaving behind scars as a constant reminder of life.

Delusion was kicking into full gear. I ignored the positives; instead, I focused on the traumas. My dear friends Wayne and Fiona never wavered, even with me keeping them in the dark. I refused to reach out.

I wanted to crutch...

Fiona hated Trish because she caused me pain. She relieved me of the responsibility.

Fiona is stunningly beautiful with sparkling eyes and long flowing strawberry blonde hair.

She is feisty. She's Irish. She's a great friend. She's an amazing wife and mother. Wayne and Fiona have always had my back through good and bad.

FLASHBACK: 27 May 2001 – Vancouver, British Columbia

Wayne prodded me to talk—*talk I did.*

They've been together ever since.

She likes travelling and expensive things.

The two of them bestowed life honours upon me: Pallbearer at Wayne's father's funeral, Best Man, *tipsy* in their living room, and Godfather of their son Aidan. I love them dearly.

INHERITANCE

DATELINE: 27 June 2003 – Vancouver, British Columbia

Aunt Priscilla bequeathed me what I believed to be an never-ending sum of money—$63,000. Her generosity sent my emotions into a spin. Her generosity was a blessing. It allowed me to flee my circumstances. It allowed me to escape myself to find myself. As much as money is often ephemeral, Priscilla's inheritance—was her final— *"I love you."*

Upon depositing the money, a twinge of *guilt* came over me—I wasn't there for her at the end.

TO SEEK OUT THE HELP OF FRIENDS OR: I WANT TO CRUTCH

DATELINE: 19 - 23 July 2003 – Vancouver, British Columbia

I needed help, desperately.

I was drowning in my despair.

I needed to reach out to friends.

A close friend Greg was in Germany—too far for us to have face-to-face talks.

I still kept Wayne & Fiona in the dark.

Danielle, Dave, and Carol, were only a phone call away.

I lost sight of the way out of the tunnel. *LOGIC* was painful and correct.

Even with an incredible bounty of friends, complete strangers played a huge role in saving me from total collapse.

Gio—Dale—Scott—Michael (a new one)—and many more—I was too stubborn to realise there were people all around who'd come to my rescue.

Gio worked in a clothing store.

Dale, a stranger I met on the street (remember the hospital visit).

Scott was a bartender.

Michael, a stranger I met in a park.

Each one of them saw the pain on my face and asked if I was okay?

In turn, I'd hang my traumas on them like clothes on a clothesline.

How did they save me?

By not running when they saw me coming.

Sadly, I continued to crutch—

ISOLATION

DATELINE: 24 July 2003 – Vancouver, British Columbia

The moment Trish dumped me was the moment she stopped cheating. After that, my only responsibility: was to take care of myself.

The first part of the healing process was to listen to *LOGIC* and kick Trish out. There was no point of us continuing the charade of roommates.

As summer's thermostat cranked up so did the party season. I regularly subjected myself to every aspect of the party, including the crash.

Prince offered escape: one walk per day turned into four.

When Jessica broke out the *Crystal Meth*, it wasn't Trish's first foray into *Meth*. I denied reality for a long time. She boasted once about using during a University exam, as well as doing lines with a passenger on a flight she was working on, back from LA.

WORK – AVOID HOME – PUB STOP TO VISIT SCOTTY—became my daily routine.

When I'd return home, I'd bring *PATHETIC* along with me.

Honey, let me sit on the edge of the bed for a bit. We don't need to talk. I just need to relax. I don't want to be alone.

No, get out now, Trish would y*ell.*

Please. I don't want to be alone. I'll leave when you fall asleep.

No, get out now.

Calm down.

Trish would shove me out the door. I'd push back. Her eyes changed. They became filled with rage.

She'd repeatedly scream *Get out now!*

Our interaction became a war of five words.

Get out now and *calm down.*

A series of photos hung on the bedroom wall above the bed.

Trish ripped the pictures off the wall and threw them at me, smashing them into the wall behind me. I'd push on the door. She'd push back. *PATHETIC* would tire, not without desperate pleas before I'd retreat to my room.

The end is nearing—we couldn't pretend anymore.

As the tragic escalator kept moving downward with its teeth violently chomping at my soul, Trish began to have guests sleep over.

I'd be asked to walk Prince—Trish was called into work.

One hour later, I'd return home. Trish was already back. I grabbed a shirt out of the closet in the bedroom. Barely tucked under her pillow, lay a condom.

I couldn't help but think: she'd put it there for me to discover.

I'd ask her why she was punishing me.

You've got to accept it. I'm going to see other people. She said.

I asked her to have the decency to keep it out of my *fucking* home. I then called her, *a sick bitch.*

The end is near—

INNER TURMOIL

DATELINE: 26 July 2013 – Vancouver, British Columbia

I lent Trish my car for a trip to Seattle.

Don't say a word.

She left on Friday.

I phoned Sunday to ask when she'd be coming home.

She told me Tuesday. She was extending her trip to go to Victoria.

She told me she was visiting Patrick.

You know, from San Francisco. She said.

I called her a liar and demanded my car back.

I threatened to phone the police to report my car stolen.

She hung up.

I phoned back. Patrick answered.

Calm down. We're just friends. Don't worry; it's not going to be a fuck-fest here tonight. He said.

The end draws nearer. I spiral downward more—

Jessica, Noel, and Spineless Kelly became fixtures in my home, without civility toward me. I'd say hello. They'd ignore me.

Jessica or Noel was present at all times. Noel doted, and Jessica—

How about this guy?

I'd go to work—come home, Noel. Go for a walk, Jessica. Noel, Jessica, Noel, Jessica—

I returned from work one night, Noel.

Do you always have to be here, stop reminding me of how I no longer fit in—Trish invited me, Noel barked at me.

I clasped his neck.

Does it have to be every fucking night?

Downward I go, soon—

Out of a dense fog, the Conductor appeared again:

FINAL STOP—

$\rightarrow\!\longrightarrow\!\rightarrow$

DEATH OF ROMANCE

DATELINE: 14 August 2003 – Vancouver, British Columbia

T rish volunteered for a summer festival, so did I; the same festival

I did it out of spite, admittedly, with motive. Being *fucked up*—punishing myself by trying to be everywhere Trish was—became second nature—watching her move on right before my eyes—stupid. It wasn't enough I was subjected to it at home, like a tragic addict, I needed more.

Volunteering framed my isolation for the world to see. Avoiding life issues became paramount to me—for my survival.

I was focusing on the destruction of love that ran its tumultuous course instead of finding a way to cope with tragedies life was delivering—screaming at me to pay attention to them.

Trish was the object of my focus. Like said, I was *fucked up*.

The festival was a huge success. This night was an appreciation night for our efforts. I went solo, isolated once more. The *MEAN GIRLS, Crack Whore* Jessica and Noel walked in, they walked within a few feet of me, I didn't exist to them.

I chatted with strangers off in the distance. They laughed as a group. Hours passed. Beers were drunk. I returned home.

Fuck, she's here again.

They were sitting on Trish's bed.

I went to escape to my room. I couldn't.

I sat face-to-face with Jessica.

Go home. Why do you always have to be here? Don't your kids need you? I screeched in a confrontational manner.

I pressed my finger against my nose and sorted, mocking her drug proclivities.

It's Trish's—

I interrupted: *It's my fucking place, too. You treat me like shit. My life's been hell. You don't fucking care. All you care about is getting high.*

I pressed my nose to hers. *Get out. I'm fucking sick of you.*

I escorted her to the elevator.

Trish screamed at me when I entered the apartment again: *Look what you've done?*

Done what—I don't care. I'm sick of this. Trish, sweetie, my life is falling apart, and all you care about is the party. She's a fucking bitch. You fucking said you loved me. I can't let you hurt me anymore. I can't punish myself anymore. I need to be good enough.

I spiral down further—

She claimed I crossed an invisible line—I've changed she said. My behaviour was impacting her friends.

These friends are fucking drugged-out-losers. They're users. You're better than them. I hate seeing these fucking lowlifes. And fuck, yes, I've changed. Are you daft?

She said this was the last straw.

Trish receded to her room. I followed. Above the bed was a shrine of her past loves: including Matthew, and, *it's not going to be a fuck-fest,* Patrick.

My picture was glaringly absent.

I asked her if she understood how much fucking pain the shrine inflicts. I told her again that I loved her. I reminded her people were dying in my life. I suggested I needed compassion.

She called me unbearable.

Fucking people right in front of me is the punishment I deserve? Then you rub my face in it.

She bellowed: *Get out. I'm moving on!*

I pivoted to my left—grabbed a picture of Patrick, and tore it apart.

Trish was leaning against a dresser. Her photo albums were on top of it. She pulled out *picture-after-picture* of the two of us and proceeded to shred them *one-by-one*.

My heart shattered. I leapt at Trish throwing my arms around her. I lifted her. I placed her on her bed. She screamed. I gathered her albums. I ran to my room. I began throwing them out the window. They smashed on the courtyard below.

She came rushing in.

Stop it. Stop it.

She began flailing frantically, repeatedly hitting me. A punch connected. She was wearing a ring. My lip sliced. Blood started flowing. Pain rushed into the cut. My mouth began to pulse. It swelled. She continued pounding, screaming. Another punch landed tearing into the skin above my left eye. My blood spurted covering my face. My blood splashed onto her shirt.

I dropped to my bed covering my head. I never once raised my hands. She continued kicking me alternating between stomach and head.

Eventually, she tired. The insanity of the situation subsided. She raced to her room, slamming the door.

I lay still in the darkness. Silence resonated. A pin drop or a feather's flutter would've been audible for miles. Emptiness flowed into the apartment. It no longer belonged to anyone. It became an emotional graveyard.

I picked myself up—blood was flowing steadily from the cuts on my face—painting my face. I went to the bathroom to inspect my wounds. As I passed Trish's room, our room, I softly uttered—my voice was tear-stained:

SWEETIE, WE CAN FIX THIS—

→ → →

BOTTOM

DATELINE: 14 August 2003 – Vancouver, British Columbia

*T*ap – *Tap* - *Tap*

The night was fucked up. It escalated rapidly. Trish and I had reached a boiling point. We were perilously close to passing no return.

The knocking at the door confused me. I spun toward the door. I calmly opened it. Two police officers were waiting on the other side.

It was time.

The uniformed officers awaited the invite to enter. A gigantic **PERIOD** was about to be slammed into our relationship. The pain was about to ease.

I asked them who called.

They said my neighbours. I knew they were lying. I invited them inside.

Emotionless, I backed up to let them enter and then slumped onto a chair a few feet away from the door. I focused my eyes on the floor.

Things got out of hand. Fast. Five people died. My family lied to me. Trish lied to me. She said she loved me; she cheated, put up a shrine of all of her lovers, excluding me—above our bed—I saw it every day. I want to hold onto something. There's nothing to hold onto—I love her. I'd never hurt her—this is so fucked up—it isn't me.

One of the Police Officer's disappeared into Trish's room.

This has to end—it must end. I understand. I'm smarter than this—this was my first—I'm hurting badly. She has to leave—I don't want her to, but—I do love her. I need to take care of myself. Take care of her. I'm sorry.

The officer offered an olive branch. He asked me to go easy on myself. He understood my life was changing from what I said. He understood this was the combination of everything. He told me they would take Trish away. She could pick up her things another day. He finished by encouraging me to take care of myself.

With the closing of the door, the page was turning. This chapter was drawing to finality. It had to. Trish was a flawed lover. I stooped to her level. I hated myself for doing so.

Alone, calmness washed over me.

Blood tears dripped from my cuts.

Drip – Drip – Drip—

Puddles formed on my leg, only to flow, then drop to the floor below. I didn't stop the flow. I sat, stared blankly ahead, my slate wiped clean. It was time to come to terms with what transpired. I loved her. I lost that love. I needed to accept that it wasn't my fault.

Drip – Drip – Drip—

It wasn't all bad. *I loved her. I loved her. I loved her.* I allowed myself to experience the vulnerability associated with love. I'd been through a ringer filled with debilitating pain. The pain was invigorating; freeing.

I crossed grounds disrespecting my morals and values. I realised I must accept responsibility for my disgraceful behaviour.

Trish was responsible for hers.

Drip – Drip—

I smiled, meekly.

I wouldn't have hurt her.

I acted out of character.

I was bleeding.

She was in character.

I put blinders on. *I loved her.*

I replayed the good times in my mind for hours as I sat in the chair, motionless. The memories were wonderful. I'll miss them. They're mine to keep.

Drip

I apologised to myself. I vowed to be kinder to me. I'll miss her. I truly will. We're not supposed to treat each other this way. This wasn't supposed to be part of the script.

I reached up, caressed my eye, then my lips, the blood-tears clotted—the flow ceased—four hours passed. I picked myself up—tomorrow—depended on it. I retreated to what was once our bedroom. *I undressed.* The blood hardened on my skin. I lay down, naked.

For the first night in more than five months, I drifted off to sleep, instantly, without tears.

TOMORROW THE SUN WAS GOING TO RISE AGAIN—THE CONSISTENCY—CHANGED

12

TRANSITION

A meta-memoir

↑Up↑

DATELINE: 24 August 2003 – Vancouver, British Columbia

I lost my happy.

My biggest fear: I'd never find it again.

Life is a continuous struggle. During youth happiness is easy: it's out of our hands. Mum and Dad are in charge if life hasn't already broken them.

Enter school. *Easy* changes: school brings with it a pecking order—where you fall impacts your development. Barriers appear from nowhere. Rich hangs with rich, poor with poor, beauty with beauty—changing status, daunting at best.

At home, you witness struggle and competition. Struggle to provide for your family. Competition to keep up with the neighbours, Dad works *twelve hour days* to put food on the table, or to buy a boat, or car—to give an illusion of status, lost in the shuffle, you.

You begin to want what other kids have, the rich kids. Unfortunately, it's not an option. They've become products of advertising. They've bought into consumption. It defines them. You crave the same definition. Your parents can't afford the dictionary.

Enter death, first the grandparents. Your parents shield you from the sorrow. You see the pain in your mother's eyes. The protection is faulty.

If you're unfortunate, death comes again while you're too young to process it. In the meantime: you're struggling to find your place in the pecking order. Technology advances rapidly—images of products promising bliss become part of the daily noise—we're manipulated to buy. We're becoming *Stupid Girls* and *Stupid Boys*. Marketing and rampant consumerism are massive parts of this transition. You don't have to play along—as you do, dealing with death leads to depression.

What do most people do when they're depressed?

They consume more. The marketing works.

The problem is consumption doesn't eliminate the pain of death. You must grieve. But you're too young to grieve, let alone comprehend the significance of the changes transpiring in your world around you.

You have no choice, so, you pick yourself up, buy more stuff, and vow to persevere, doubting if it is possible.

While you grasp desperately for meaning, you decide to consume more, and for brief moments the consumption provides elation—the moments pass. You realise: NEW eventually needs replacing, and you couldn't afford your purchases to begin with—you long for old.

Love seizes the stage. It confuses. Your upbringing saw to that. Instead of providing comfort it becomes part of the struggle. You project your will—rarely accepting who your loved ones are—you only see who they may become. Your upbringing defined the parameters. You move on casting many aside. You think you deserve more. You rarely look inward.

Our parents taught us this lesson. The more we follow it the more likely *needy* will become a fixture. Eventually, love loses meaning. Its essence is a casualty of consumption.

We become greedy. Like sheep, we're herded—cloned in a sense. We continue to be desensitised consumers. Love takes a beating in the quest for more—

People matter. I think we've lost sight of that.

With age, the hurdles grow. The euphoric hits of consumption addict us. Corporate giants move us around like pawns.

We become exactly like our parents: *twelve hours daily* to both survive and maintain an image. Lost in the shuffle: your children—also lost in the shuffle: you, and sadly: happiness.

There are *one hundred sixty-eight hours* in a week. Working *eighty* is common—leaving *eighty-eight* for life. You spend *fourteen hours* commuting. You're supposed to allow *fifty-six* for sleep—my God, you're only left with *eighteen* for your wife/husband, the kids, health, fitness, and relaxation.

We broke the fucking formula. We sold our souls to pursue STUFF. The pursuit of NEW STUFF leaves everything that matters, including people, fragile—and at risk of suddenly vanishing—in a heartbeat, those who matter most disappear through death or of their own accord because they've believed that they're entitled to more.

The Human Race continues. What the hell are we racing to? I'm not sure if making, seeing for that matter; the finish line, is an accomplishment. Every creature on this planet uses up their resources until extinction, or until humans speed up the process by invading their environs. Urban sprawl bursts to mind. The big difference between us and all other creatures: we can see the damage we're inflicting; yet, we choose to live in denial.

The next generation can fix it, we think.

Unfortunately, each generation is a product of the *last*—and the *last* liked to consume. The *last* still needs children to buy in so they can continue stuffing their own pockets.

THINKING INSIDE THIS BOX: STUFF IS NOTHING MORE THAN WINDOW DRESSING

Our challenge is to put down our wallets, stop buying the propaganda and remember what's truly important. It doesn't matter what you have; it is what's in your heart that counts. We need to slow down, say *I love you,* and mean it. Continued happiness depends upon it.

Life is a tremendous struggle. Death, sickness, lost love, financial crisis, infidelity, entitlement, just to name a few, will rear their ugly heads, testing who you are going to become. They'll visit early or come along later. We can't prepare for them. They don't follow a schedule. They'll eat away at you. They'll influence your future. Your happiness will be a wounded soldier sent to triage during life's journey. For happiness to have a chance, it can't be a product of buying stuff.

If you're fortunate enough to have taken a beating, gotten up, and realised; nice *STUFF* is nothing more than window dressing, consider yourself lucky. 'Cause, one day, like love, when you least expect it—you'll breathe a sigh of relief, crack a smile, and understand: *happiness* comes from within, it is a derivative of how you treat the people in your life who matter most. Then and only then, you will have stepped off the consumption bandwagon, you'll say, *I love you*, and, you'll mean it.

Does happiness exist?

I know it does. I experienced it firsthand. It may have been fleeting, but it was real.

I hope one day to find it again if I let my guard down. Next time I do, I think I will sprain my ankle on my way home.

BOTTOM OF THE TUNNEL

When I slammed into the tunnels bottom, I'd been crying for *one hundred sixty-four* consecutive days.

My existence shattered into pieces, just shy of *one million.* I needed to retrace my steps to collect the pieces. I needed to start rebuilding me.

It took slightly over *six months* to annihilate the first *five hundred eleven* months of living—and then, my life came crumbling down—

When the walls—Come tumblin' down—When the walls—Come crumbling' crumbling

—leaving me back at SQUARE 1, this time without the support of family

GUILT and *LOGIC* came scurrying back.

They snapped a portion of my brain back into place.

15 AUGUST 2003

When I woke the blood tears of the horrific night before were hardened on my body. I saw a faint flickering light. Up was going to be taxing. The only way for my story to become relevant was if I began the climb to sweep the unimaginable assault of trauma to the side.

What's that *Drama Police*: you think I'm exceptionally melodramatic?

Life is dramatic, how else would I tell my story, well, how?

Life beat me down. Most things were not in my control. Fortunately, my core remained untouched, if it had been—*I don't want to go there.*

With each passing day, the light out of the tunnel shone brighter. The exciting part: I was starting anew, the luxury of setting the parameters, belonged to only me.

Sometimes it takes extreme events to emblazon their characteristics into your broken spirit—allowing you to see you need outside help.

I was fucking lost. Two events brought me to conclude *HELP* was necessary.

Wayne informed me he was going to be a father. I faked happiness.

The second event: *Sweetie, we can fix this—*

It was time to reach for a crutch. It was time to stop sinking into myself. It was time to open the door to those whom truly love me.

IT'S ABOUT TRISH

19 August 2003 – Vancouver, British Columbia

My life was conflicted. Love was gone. I was alone again.

My support network was vanishing. Trouble was lingering around every corner. Problems came with every phone call. I was trying to hold onto a love that was no more. I desperately wanted to stop crying.

My few amazing friends did the best they could to help me through the turmoil. I instinctively knew if I didn't understand what was happening all around me, how could anyone else.

Wayne and Fiona are two of my dearest friends, my rocks. They took care of me when no one else was listening. They did so, judgement free. They never abandoned me.

Wayne is a brilliant friend. Our friendship is effortless. No conversation is ever too important that it can't end when it became stale. We avoid pressuring one another. We know we'll be there for each other when life matters.

Wayne became a combination of FRIEND + BROTHER + CONFIDENT + PARENTAL INFLUENCE – without motive.

I never allowed Wayne and Fiona to meet Trish. At first, it was a bit of a joke. Trish's absence became more thrilling as a fantasy instead of real.

There was always the tease of a potential meeting, to be cast aside by an elaborate story.

Wayne never pressed. He looked forward to the day they'd eventually meet.

Fiona on the other hand pressed.

In the wake of my *COLLAPSE*, I realised it must be incredibly difficult for them to show sympathy when I kept them at a distance. I finally broke down. I summoned Wayne to meet me for drinks. I needed him to understand how Trish was intensifying my pains.

We drank a few drinks, ate wings, and drank some more.

With a revelation on the tip of my tongue, Wayne sensed my trepidation and told me I didn't have to tell him. He said he was going on holidays and I could tell him when he returned.

I stressed I needed to tell him. I've been trying to deal with everything alone, alone wasn't working.

We switched bars.

I crawled inside myself digging, trying to find the words. I dug deeper. I knew Wayne would understand. Of course, he would. They love me, I thought.

I finally found the courage. I was shaking. I was scared. I looked Wayne in the eyes and calmly said: *Wayne, it's about Trish—*

A VISIT WITH DR MUSIAL

What can I help you with? The good doctor asked.

Well, my life. It's spinning out of control. I don't know how to slow the revolutions. Can I tell you about the last six months? It all started March 3—that is what brings me here today.

Dr Musial was amazed. He said it was a testament to my resolve. Dr Musial asked if I was okay. He told me he was proud of me.

I *fretted,* I break down often.

Go easy on yourself; honestly, I've never heard anything so extreme—be strong, and be kind, to you.

I told him I hate my family. I said I'm not sure they can be—

He asked me to breathe deeply. People screw up. Try to take a step back. Don't judge too hastily. He said I might be right in attempting to eliminate them from my life.

I told him I was going to a counsellor.

He was impressed with my sanity. He was also impressed with the fact I wasn't willing to dump everything on friends.

You'll be okay. You just can't see it now. I'm not even going to ask you about your chest hair.

A smile broke on his face.

MY VISIT WITH DR SAULNIER

Well, my life. It's spinning out of control. I don't know how to slow the revolutions. Can I tell you about the last six months? It all started March 3—that is what brings me here today.

Where does one find a counsellor?

The newspaper seemed reasonable. I contacted Dr Saulnier on August 15. His office was one block from my home. He assured me he understood relationships similar to mine.

The good Doctor said everything is confidential unless a crime is involved.

At the end of my tale, he asked how I have survived this far?

I assured him I felt out of control.

He stressed I was doing well. Both my relationship with Trish and my new family realities were extreme, especially since they were new realities for me. He found that in itself, astonishing. He said specifically: Speaking of Trish, it was something most people take a lifetime to come to terms with, *the fact is, your relationship with Trish was abusive. You may not see it. It was harsh.*

His words were comforting. He thought it was unbelievable I hadn't snapped long ago. As for the gory details, he told me he has never heard of a series of events so extreme in such a short period. He then added: *I don't think I've heard of events this extreme, in a lifetime.*

As I was about to leave—he asked me to stop for a moment. He then continued with one last thought in an unassuming manner.

Your ability to assign meaning and to go through the appropriate emotions is amazing. You'll be okay. Let's meet again next month.

30 August 2003

The last night Trish and I would spend together under the same roof.

Trish's posse had the audacity to brand me as a bad guy without a single one of them questioning why I was bruised and battered while Trish was unscathed.

High wore blinders.

After the dust-up, Trish darted to Jessica's. A few days later, she escaped to her parent's home in Lethbridge, Alberta. Before she left, she asked if I could take Prince for two weeks.

Fifteen minutes later she arrived with *Crack Whore Jessica.*

Bad Guy = Care Provider for a beloved pet—somehow, the formula seems: skewed.

I said hello to Jessica. She sneered at me.

I promised *Logic* this would be the last time.

He called me a liar.

Is it not baffling her great friends would allow her to spend this night alone with me?

I cried myself to sleep. Trish slept peacefully in the next room.

Moving Day

The last call arrived. The curtain closed. A rented van was rented. Trish was leaving—she rallied her friends to help her move.

To keep up the bad-boy façade I wasn't allowed to help, or to know: Trish's new address.

I took Prince on four epic walks to spare the punishment of watching her move. Saturday morning was perfect. The light was breaking at the tunnels bottom—walls began to form.

I'd sit on a park bench with Prince at my side. Tears flowed from my eyes. I thanked Prince for taking care of me. I said goodbye. I kissed his head.

I expected to return to emptiness after the fourth walk.

Trish, where are your helpers?

She was angry. Her lovely fucking friends partied the previous night, rendering themselves, useless. She looked at me sadly. She asked me to help.

I blasted out: *If I help I'll know where you live. I thought I was the fucking devil.*

I helped. Each trip cut sharply into my spirit.

I escaped to the club that night. The movers were present. So was Trish. I spent the night unacknowledged, alone. The curtain closed, almost.

One Week Later

I'm going out of town for a week, can you look after Prince?

Dr Saulnier: Part 2

I poured out detail-after-detail of my life, painting my ordeals as the most grievous kind.

He drank them in.

When I completed my tale of despair, Dr Saulnier asked if he could offer his opinion.

I don't know how you've done it, but you seem to be well-adjusted. It's as if an angel has guided you, helping you to develop an astonishing sense of what is right and what is wrong when interacting with others. I can't help but bestow upon you the utmost of praise for coming to a place where you don't blame others for what's transpired around you. You must go to Europe. You must allow yourself to smile. You must lose yourself. I believe that when you do, you will find yourself once more.

I walked to the door of his office; I *raked* the room with my eye(s) stopping at his.

His eyes were soft, calm.

On your journey, if you find out who your parents are, call me, anytime.

A single tear rolled over my right cheek—and then fell to the floor.

25 SEPTEMBER 2003

My new Birth Certificate arrived. Stuffed inside the envelope was a second Birth Certificate. Vital Stats accidentally sent me another man's as well. *Another lost soul had a piece still missing.*

My heart began pounding once more. I EXIST—filled my mind. I became flush. My pulse raced. I clamped onto the wall to maintain my balance. I wanted to cry.

I flashed back to the instructions of the Supervisor.

1.   Renew my passport.

2.   Send it back to Vital Statistics in Edmonton.

3.   When my official Birth Record finally arrives—I will be able to stop asking complete strangers if they are my mommy or daddy.

Pause for breath. How emotionally draining pulling myself up to find out the truth—possibly be?

Please let my father be Mick Jagger?

Dave, good news, my Birth Certificate arrived. We can make travel plans and go. Don't be too mad. I'm emotionally fucked up. I'm stupid. I still think I love Trish. Smack me, please, I don't know if I want to go, but, I will, I'm terrified of going, I'm such a flake, I don't want to ruin the trip for you—I'm so sorry.

Dave said with controlled force over the phone: Listen to me: cut yourself some slack—

He then offered a dose of perspective—

—discovering who you are, witnessing death, and losing love all at the same time, come on, quit trying to be superhuman.

→ → →

13 14 15

ESCAPE

A meta-memoir

HALFWAY HOME

SEED'S IDENTITY TOUR

i·den·ti·ty - noun

▪ What identifies somebody or something: who somebody is or what something is, especially the name somebody or something is known by.

▪ Somebody's essential self: the set of characteristics that somebody recognises as belonging uniquely to himself or herself and constituting his or her individual personality for life.

▪ Sameness: the fact or condition of being the same or exactly alike.

Dr Saulnier told me to go to Europe and lose myself. He asked me to escape my realities.

It was abundantly clear if I was ever to find me:

~I NEEDED TO DISAPPEAR~

MONTREAL

DAY 1: WEDNESDAY - 8 OCTOBER 2003

VANCOUVER - CALGARY – MONTREAL ✂✂✂

The alarm rang at 7:45 AM. Wayne arrived to whisk us to the airport. He was wearing a blue shirt.

Dave and I wisely went out the night before and got sauced. Fortunately, Wayne was acting as our guardians.

While *pickled* the night before, I packed. Eighty pounds of luggage seemed light. Wayne brought me bigger suitcases. I filled them with every garment in my closet.

We arrived at the airport with four minutes to spare. Sleep deprivation was allowing us to ignore the horrors of hung-over.

FIRST STOP: CALGARY.

We met Corrie for lunch during our two-hour layover.

I asked her how her kids Dave and Chucky were doing.

Jordan and Ethan are excellent. Corrie answered.

I introduced her to Dave as my *ex*.

Corrie then said, after fourteen years, we could dump, *ex*.

Back at the airport: West Jet was to fly us to Montreal.

The Flight Attendants loved us. They were curious to know what our trip was about; I made them laugh.

Karenna asked me my age.

Before I could answer, she guessed 31.

She pegged Dave at 28. I'm 19 years older than Dave. I will always be 19 years older as long as we're both alive.

What is the reason for your trip?

She unwittingly became the first victim of the story of my identity.

On March 3—Four days after that—eight days after that—that's why we've embarked on this trip.

She became flush, at a loss for words. She couldn't understand how I could be okay. She exalted Dave for being a wonderful friend.

The other FA loved us as well. They both thought my tale would make a fantastic book.

We arrived in Montreal. The night was balmy; +15 (Celsius).

Having no place to call home for the evening we decided to fly by the seat-of-our-pants. I was about to discover how the ingredients of sleep deprivation, drunk, and hung over, would affect Dave's predilection for winging it.

Dave was cranky and lost. I was hoping to find lost. He took the proverbial bull by the horns. One phone call and a cab ride later, we arrived at the *Hotel de Paris*—the hotel steps were steep—carved at *a ninety-degree* angle. The door of or our room, Room 101, almost touched the front desk.

Dave wanted downtime. I wouldn't allow it.

He suggested he might die.

I didn't care.

We ventured forth to find sustenance. We picked a direction and began walking. In the *Plateau Section* of Montreal, Dave suggested sushi.

I reminded him we flew from Vancouver—the sushi capital of the West Coast.

QUIRKS

Once the laughter brought on by the sushi suggestion subsided, we discovered a recurring trip quirk.

Like married couples, we developed an inability to pick a place to eat. This quirk wasn't quirky—it was painful. We'd walk past place-after-place.

Finally, we stopped at *Three Brassieres*. We chased drink with drink forgetting about food, blaming it on the language barrier.

NEXT STOP: *THE MONKEY BAR*—where drink followed drink.

The drinking program continued when we stumbled into the *St Elizabeth Tavern*. Monique, our server, was a babe. She feigned admiration. She served up an indoctrination of Montreal women's *je ne sais quoi*; show interest, and upon the interest return volley, turn coy.

Dave told me he was *drunky* and must eat now.

I promised the next place we came across.

I'll have a Whopper with cheese combo and poutine.

Gastronomically satiated, we flagged our fourth cab of the day and went to *The Village*. We dropped our asses onto stools in *Le Stud*.

Le Stud was full of leather. It was dark and creepy. We ordered Smirnoff Ices from a shirtless bartender. A few sips in we drew the conclusion: *Le Stud* may be a gay-friendly establishment, that and, we needed downtime.

We flagged a *Sherpa* to help with the climb to our room.

Home by 3:30; off to dreamland by 6 AM.

Before sleep came, I flashed back to the Calgary airport: The security staff asked to check Dave's bag.

Dave, you brought a harmonica and bicycle tire repair kit. Why?

DAY 2: THURSDAY – 9 OCTOBER 2003

Thursday morning drowned us in beautiful sunshine. It was hard to believe we were in Montreal.

For the first time during my litany of tragedies, I was able to escape. My terrors of the past were momentarily set to rest. There would be no bawling my eyes out this day.

Slumber was kicked to the curb at 9:30 AM.

QUIRK 3: *Seed, ME,* laced with infinite wisdom packed far more energy than Dave. I found myself waiting for him to refresh on a regular basis.

Finally, at noon, we were back in *The Village*. The sun warmed us with a toasty +20 (C).

Surprisingly, for what likely was to be the only time, we ate at the first place we found.

We asked customers where we should party that night.

Je m'appelle Lindsay. Il s'appelle David, party..? Where should we party? Bon retour guimauves.

They handed us a stack of Gay Guides.

Our day's itinerary consisted of four goals:

1. Find a TD Bank.
2. Buy a camera.
3. DRINK!!!
4. Secure transportation to New York City for the following day.

Oh yeah, and:

5. Find my lost *happy.*

Trish entered my mind.

I told her to get the fuck out.

She replied she was from Montreal. She decided tormenting me would be fun.

She was a manipulative bitch.

Montreal sparkled in the daylight.

We visited: St Catherine's Street—McGill University—Crescent Street—Stoogies—three-levels, one-toilet.

I glided across the street to a travel agency to finalise our New York plans. The one hour flight was going to cost a nightmarish $1000 for the two of us.

We decided drinking would provide a solution. So, I bought a camera, and we began to drink.

We were flying New York to London return for $300 on American Airlines. They certainly must have a better deal, I thought. I phoned. Fuck. Wrong.

The camera needed a drink. We ordered two at *Parking Pub*.

Slightly revved up we stopped at an internet café. The internet was to be our saviour.

I asked the man sitting next to me how to log on. His name was Larry.

Your voice is exquisite. It turns me on. If you use your voice over the right channels, you will—

I stressed to him I simply needed to log on. I'm not fond of my voice; however, comments like his have surfaced before.

The internet café was a rousing, failure.

On the way home, we grabbed takeout—booze. Once home, we began making calls.

CALL 1: *What are you wearing? Perhaps you'd like to loosen your belt and slowly run your hand—that wasn't it—we need to get to New York tomorrow. How much to rent a car, a limo, a pony? Rent—sip, sip, sip—we don't care how we get there. Do you have a cab, a plane, a train; a helicopter…?*

Dave decided *Dreamland* was in order—just as quickly as he decided—he concluded: it was futile.

TIME TO PARTY: Before we did, after *fifty-phone-calls,* we figured: taking a limo for $500 would elevate us to rock star status. We forgot to book one.

Tomorrow was going to take care of itself, in liquid, magically.

QUIRK 4: While on our mission to the night's partying we stopped at the Bus Depot. We paid $100 each. Our bus would leave at 11 AM. The trip to NYC would be *eight and a half hours*.

We slurped our way from the *St Elizabeth* to the *Parking Club*, filled with a mixed crowd.

We sauntered up to Linda's bar. Linda was jaw-droppingly beautiful.

I offered to rub goo all over—

She asked us the purpose of our journey.

The curtains opened.

It all started March 3—that's why we're here today.

Linda hung on every word. At times she looked confused. At stories end confused turned to despair, she was on the verge of tears.

She suggested we were *shitting* her. The story is too bizarre. She wondered how I could be able to function.

I let her know I shared only the short version. I assured her it was true. I thanked her, another piece was discovered, and strangers were allowing me to find hope: The FA's on the plane and now Linda, condition free, let me grieve. They taught me it was OK to be fucked-up. They also taught me it was OK if it took a long time to process and get over my series of events, if at all, possible.

They restored the faith that my supposed good friends back home stripped me of; by acting as if recovery timeframes exist.

RECOVERY TIMEFRAME (DAYS TO GET OVER)

Infidelity – 2 days to get over; break-up – 2 days; suicide – 1 day (3 days if it's your own) - A young-friends battle with THE BIG C – 1.5 days; death of a close relative – 2 days; death of your last uncle – 1 day. Finding out the parents' you watched die were not your real parents and everything in your life has been a lie – 0 days. Finally, being run over by a train – oops; you're dead.

CORRECTION: 1 day for the life is a lie category; just because it occurred at the end of all of the other traumas, in my friends' estimation: recovery should've taken, roughly - 9.5 days and life would simply return to normal.

In fact, Noel, playing the role of *MEAN GIRL,* while I was in a moment of despair said: *You've seemed to have changed over the last four months. Maybe Trish cheated on you because she wasn't getting enough attention from you.*

I HAVE CHANGED. I'd like to stress firmly to anyone sharing threads with that opinion: **FUCK OFF.**

I want you to take my message personally. Does my scorn seem too harsh?

I could've wished miserable unsatisfying lives to engulf the lot of them. I didn't. Maybe, I should.

Linda informed us highballs were $2. We began a gin & tonic parade.

Two gins in we decided to up the party ante with a voyage to the pharmacy. I started hunting for ecstasy. I asked Linda's brother who happened to be the night's promoter if he knew of a supply chain.

The question bothered him.

I flashed back to *Russians & Clowns* by approaching a *Drag Queen*—wrong again.

I asked five random shady looking guys, once again, to no avail.

A man sashayed up to me. His name was Alex. He was a delightful English fellow. Alex took a shine to me. He thought I was smoking hot.

That was fun to type.

We exchanged banter. Alex found me to be intoxicating.

I assured him it was the gin fumes escaping from my mouth. I did so in a bastardised British accent.

Alex swivelled in a fashion similar to a stir-stick. He was without question, mixed.

Another man, named Y, since I forgot his name, circled our table. Like a vulture, he was waiting for one of us to have a weak moment. Weak moments had become my thing. When he approached he told me he thought I was incredibly hot.

FLASH FORWARD: March – July 2003

TIME OUT

I'd like to make it clear the HOT theme is real. I do not think of myself in that way. In fact: At times, I'm afraid of my reflection.

Being called HOT became a recurring theme over my time of despair—not only HOT—but, I am a man of incredible depth!

To date, my two favourites occurred while out for avoid-home-drinks.

FAVOURITE 1

Brandon ended his pain two days prior. On this evening my eyes were swollen shut by tears. I was tattered. Across the smoked filled patio of a crowded bar, I noticed a lovely young lady scouring my body. She traipsed toward me. She tapped my shoulder. I turned. I wiped tears from my eyes.

You are a good-looking man. There is something in your eyes. Character—I wanted you to know that.

After the final eloquent word escaped her mouth; she simply turned, and walked away.

FAVOURITE 2

I shared my views on love and life while sitting at the end of the bar at the *Granville Room.*

179

I often share my views.

To my left sat a beautiful brunette, she became my eager audience. I excused myself to go to the washroom. I was standing at the urinal when I felt hands on my shoulder. She'd followed me. She sharply twisted my torso. She kissed me full on the lips.

When our lips parted, she brazenly said *you're an amazing man.*

She strolled away.

When I returned to my seat, the girl two seats down from the bar from me handed me a note.

Call me in twenty minutes. I overheard your conversation.
I'd like to see you again.
Call me. xxx.xxx.xxxx

S

I CALLED.

Our visit was relieving.

I walked past *Milestones Restaurant* on my way home. They were receiving a delivery. It was 2 AM. A five-gallon drum rolled down the truck's loading ramp. It came to rest at my feet. I looked around; no one was around. I took the drum home, opened it, *pickled beans.*

I can't recall what I said to the girls at the bar.

GROPE

Now, where was I?

Alex liked stuffing his hands down my pants. I let him, to a point.

Alex was an FA with British Airways. I assumed all FAs knew how to find a chemist. I asked him. He was back before I finished my question with pills to pop.

One hour later the assault from the combination of gin and vitamins began taking hold. The assault was peaceful. Alex began to grope. The pharmaceuticals gave me the go ahead to allow him.

I pointed just below my belt line. I insisted: this was my do not cross point.

He found my honesty to be deliciously HOT.

He gingerly called off his offensive; bought Dave another gin, then offered us a place to stay in London at month's end.

We shared our table with a male/female couple—they made me an offer—asking *me to join naked, elsewhere.*

I declined.

THE PLOT THICKENS

Seed, I'm leaving for the evening. Dave said.

His face was muddled, pixilated, pulsing.

Before I could process his words—he was gone.

I was going to use his absence to get to know myself. A blip passed. Dave reappeared.

I spun the calculations of a blip in my mind—VOID was the outcome.

I might have been *high?*

Dave said something along the lines of *Girl—very hot—washroom—got heavy—take me places—rock my world—kissing—she wanted sex—I couldn't—I want more.*

I was still *high.*

180

I looked at him and said *soccer*

I may or may not have called him: IDIOT.

Parking was closing. We had nowhere to go. A congregation formed outside the pub. I tried to levitate—after I had failed—I tried to read the masses' minds. Someone suggested partying in Laval. We couldn't, could we?—Laval is near Quebec City, I thought (my thinking was incorrect). We're heading to the Big Apple in the morning. Dave and I like apples. Laval would've been a mistake.

We flagged a taxi, jumped-in—a blip later we reached our destination. We travelled half a block. We reversed the jump-in motion.

The bass was thumping in *Stereo*. We stumbled into the opening party for *Black & Blue – The Jock Ball*. The crowd was less than mixed.

GET HIGH - TAKE YOUR SHIRT OFF - GROPE SOMEONE & DANCE TO THE CONTINUOUS THUMP OF HOUSE MUSIC!

Those were the instructions floating through the air.

Our prescriptions began to fade—as if *high* can determine when more *high* is required. I checked the label; it was marked: REFILL.

Gone was *DISCRETION* and *LOGIC*.

Between you and me, I think *LOGIC* may have been a little bit, *high*.

Strangely, with *PARANOIA'S* absence, *LOGIC* was slicing me some party slack.

I asked the first person I saw if they could refill our prescriptions.

The first person was an ex-Vancouverite who was friends with another ex-Vancouverite named, Mike. I knew Mike. He directed me to where I could fulfil my quest.

Dr Creole set a price for two pills, very smooth he said. Sensing we wanted to travel further he suggested a product with more kick. We liked the sound of kick.

SEED PUBLIC SERVICE ANNOUNCEMENT (SPSA)

Drug dealers deal drugs. When high on drugs questioning skills disintegrate—even the right questions regarding the additional drugs you are about to ingest won't matter as you're dealing with drug dealers. So, at the risk of sounding hypocritical: Don't buy drugs from drug dealers.

DAY 2: WRAP UP

I hawked a hot Floridian on the dance floor with a smoking body.

Kicking lead to hitting it off, we danced. Florida invited me to come to Florida. Before tasting the sweet OJ—Florida dissipated into thin air.

The medicine *kicked* more. The dance floor started to dance, morphing between: *packed – empty – round – square – truck stop – and Palatial Palace*.

It became abundantly clear to me: I'm Jesus. Not of the Latin American baseball variety, but instead; the real deal.

OMG, my good friends would be my disciples, I thought.

Jesus sounded like a pressure-filled gig.

I let Dave in on my discovery. He didn't care. He said he was trying to figure out if he was a porcupine. Instantly, I started seeing quills.

To make sure I didn't imagine things I parted the top of his head with my hands and dove inside his brain to listen. He was a porcupine.

He asked me to leave.

Abruptly, the night (morning) ended. It was time to go home. It was 7 AM. Our bus was leaving at 11.

Outside of the club, I developed a bloodcurdling feeling if we stepped out from the awning we'd freeze to death. I believed a force-field was protecting us from becoming ice only to be vaporised if a flash of light was to hit us. I looked up; a tiny blue flicker was trying to peek out from the clouds.

The light scared us back to the hotel. Dave crashed. I ventured forth. Experience taught me the kaleidoscope which would certainly play in my brain while pretending to sleep was going to bring futility.

I came across a panhandler. I stared intently at him trying to read his mind. His eyes were dishevelled. He was downtrodden. My stares turned creepy.

My mind was sounding like a playing card stuck in bicycle spokes.

What happened next is only for adult consumption. FYI: The panhandler wasn't involved.

I've decided this page is not the place or time to reveal. All I will say is it may or may not have included flesh.

Hey Dirt, come over here. Do I have a story for you!

The only things I know for certain: If this were to be the pace of the trip—I wouldn't return home upright.

That and, say no to drugs.

ESCAPE TO NEW YORK

DAY 3: FRIDAY – 10 OCTOBER 2003

MONTREAL – ALBANY – NYC – DEPARTING MONTREAL

Where would you like me to place my towel?

I lay prone, hovering in the air above my hotel bed, beside the check-in desk; spent and sticky from the night before. It was 9:30 AM, which allowed me one-hour of hallucinating before we were to discover teleportation and the bus depot. Five hours of sleep in four days—the bus was going to be a treat.

I was holding my camera. I may have been holding my camera all night long. It was going to be able to prove my hallucinations were real. I turned it on. I accidentally touched: ERASE ALL.

I floated down to the mattress; the coils swallowed me. One nanosecond later I sprung upward.

PREVIOUSLY ALTERED SEED told me not to risk tripping into the unknown.

The sidewalk kept flowing away from us during the three blocks to the bus depot. I hated my fucking luggage. It was sunny and swelteringly hot. The path flowed faster. I began to melt. My luggage's unquenchable appetite rendered it gluttonies.

Dave wanted to cocoon. My inability to remain quiet was on a different frequency. We met a cute girl from Winnipeg—and another cute girl from Syracuse.

One of them asked me why I was sweating profusely. I gave my bags an evil glance.

Megan was from Winnipeg.

The other girl introduced herself to us.

I'm Lindsay.

Cool, my name is also Lindsay. You do know you have a girl's name; don't you?

S SUCK: ACT I

Life was about to enter crummy.

Highly excited and sleepless meant pain was to spin with each rotation of the buses tires on the asphalt.

I suggested to Dave the countryside whisking by reminded me of Bellingham.

Her hair was circa 1956. It looked as if it rarely leaves the salon. An overabundance of spray caused her hair to rival the weight of my luggage. I imagined her doing neck curls. Hazmat teams concluded her hair to be susceptible to open flames.

She sat three rows in front of us, to the right. She commanded the stage. She was primed to entertain the silent bus. She was ready to go for hours on end.

Dave pulled out his harmonica. He introduced her with a little ditty. His musical flair was cut short by a cyclist on the side of the road with a flat tire.

Her voice scratched excruciatingly. It was Jewish Manhattan. It was soul-sapping. She began laying out every detail of her life itinerary for the rest of her life. The passenger beside her started to act out a scene from *Deer Hunter*.

On November 13, I remind you this is October 10; I'm going to have a Diet Sprite at the Diner on Sixty-Third Street. Helga or Mrs Goldstein may be with me. Do you remember Mrs. Goldstein?

Her son Harvey is a lawyer. She has sciatica. Did I mention: I might have basted eggs, only if Rudy cooks them? I've heard he's had problems with his feet. At precisely 2:15, are you listening—Tom will drive me to my hair appointment with Blanche. He'd better not be late. I hate it when—

On November 14—

Stephan Segal sprung to action in a fashion straight out of *Marked for Death*—SNAP, she was gone. He mistook granny for a *Jamaican Drug Lord*. Revenge was a dish served cold, like *Spanish soup*.

We arrived at customs—who says drugs are bad?

CUSTOMS

Customs provided an intermission. Customs while zooming, well—at least I thought we were at customs; suddenly it had vanished—fortunately, when we stepped down off the bus, customs returned.

We couldn't blink. Dave and my jaws were threatening to shatter our skulls because we were clenching them together so tightly. We drifted to the counter at the same time without lifting our feet. Dave and I each had our own Custom's Officer.

The officers in harmony, in droned-out voices, asked if we were aliens.

I *willed* Dave to fire his eye lasers. I crumbled my words together spitting out *I'm Canadian. I'm from Vancouver. I have a furry kitty.*

I tried desperately to blink. I glanced toward Dave. I saw quills sticking out of his jacket.

Chicken for dinner tonight, that's what I'll have.

They set us free—

🚌 s SUCK: ACT II

Stephan failed us; granny was back to inflict more pain.

Three people jumped out of the bus windows. Three more hung themselves in the buses washroom because they couldn't handle the timber of her voice.

The bus stopped in Albany for a short respite.

We reunited with Megan after consuming a rubbery cheese covered *cardboard-like delicacy* in the cafeteria. We held each other, trembling, fearing Act II.

Dan, the driver, hated the continual whine of bus passengers. Dan was a big burly man. I'm confident he shot a man in Reno once just to watch him die. Bussing was his sentence.

Dave asked him to kill her. He told Dan if he did, we'd have his back.

Let's get our stories straight—she tripped right?

Dan chortled deviously. Dan floored it. He shaved *one and a half hours* off the journey. We arrived in New York City just as I was about to enter the washroom.

Before Dan set the throttle to full, while still back at the cafeteria, choking on rubbery cheese, I stated: *Wouldn't it be funny if she recited the ingredients of her soda can?*

It wasn't.

Fructose, glucose, asorbate acid—

A murder of French kids joined her encore. They rapped freestyle. I wanted another pill.

THE BIG APPLE

If that's the Empire State Building, I'm not impressed. I disappointingly said to Dave.

I was wrong. I was impressed. I snapped a shot to capture the moment. The window flashed back at me with a lovely picture of my camera.

I asked Dave if he would have fucked grandma.

I flicked my tongue in his direction. I suggested I could see the lust in his eyes. I asked him if he'd like to fuck my camera.

He asked me what was wrong with me.

Dan dropped us off at Penn Station. We'd only slept *six* out of the *last ninety-six hours*. We had plied our bodies with a variety of toxins. Somehow; we still looked astral. We had even developed the ability to shoot lasers out of our eyes.

Reflecting back to a trip photo: Dave looks cosmically intense →

In the picture, an EVIL woman in red is pursuing him. She looks poised to pounce with her fiery eyes. She looks as if she is about to erase Dave from the planet.

Behind her, slightly to her right, you can see the *Penn Station Carnivorous Gnome*, disguised as an overweight gender non-specific baseball-cap-wearing creature, probably named: Pat.

His sole purpose was to protect tourists from wickedness. He looked hungry. He was salivating. He was preparing to lash out.

Much like I willed Dave before, I willed him again, this time, to run for his life.

He continued meandering.

I looked back moments later. *The Gnome* was tearing shreds of flesh from *Evil's* broken carcas. Penn Station returned to safeness.

We stepped outside. We queued for a taxi. The evening was smashing. We looked at each other, grinning from ear-to-ear.

We were in fucking NYC baby!

NEXT STOP: The *Hotel Martinique.*

Dave checked the room service menu for downtime.

I sped across the street to *Speedy's Deli* to buy beer.

Our adventure was about to begin, minus downtime.

VANITY CHECK: The depression of the pre-trip months brought with it a kicking body.

With this keystroke I have to say: one day I hope to find my trip body again. After all, pardon my ego, it was smoking hot.

GREENWICH VILLAGE

NYC, BALLPARK POPULATION GUESS = FIFTEEN MILLION

I asked Dave if he thought a map would come in handy.

Being male—we headed that-a-way.

Healthy eating was in order. We set forth to *The Village.*

Does every city have a Village?

Walking was worrisome. I hovered instead. Hovering was a product of—anyway, lights in the distance screamed: *Village.*

The lights were wrong. We dragged our mangled beings forward. My recommendation to all: Don't sleep—drink to the level of copious—ingest—ride, I don't want to relive the bus—stumbleupon *Times Square* at night.

Without the ability to blink—a billion lights—

I began vanishing; Food was beckoning. We gobbled pizza slices, then hit the *Village* by cab.

Like Montreal, we found Creole—this time a restaurant instead of a pharmacist. We moulded into our chairs. We drank in a moment of calm.

Winding down our first night: We strolled deeper into *The Village*—came to a clearing—passed by *a fighter by his trade*—and pulled up two stools at a bar called *The Boxer*. At 2 AM, we decided to pull up stakes and make our way home; it was either that or dying.

UP-TO-THE-MINUTE-SLEEP TOTAL = 6 HOURS

Tomorrow, I'll find my **IDENTITY**. I promise.

DAY 4: SATURDAY, OCTOBER 11TH, 2003

Start spreading—

Agenda free, it was time to take a big juicy bite out of the Big Apple.

In this blurb, I wanted to write more but writer's block, unfortunately, blocked me!

WTC

The morning welcomed us with glorious sunshine. We went that-a-way. We stopped at Maui Taco.

NYC escapes description if you avoid being a tourist. We did. We took a route encompassing thirty kilometres lockstep.

5th Avenue – Gramercy – Union Square – Soho – Greenwich Village (again) – Battery Park – Wall Street – and eventually, Tribeca.

We abstained from alcohol.

When we passed the site of World Trade Center my stomach dropped. My eyes watered. I wanted the innocence lost forever, to return.

I came to a loss for words.

I collected several pieces of my lost soul at the WTC.

I think humanity lost some of its core at this tragically historic location.

SHAG

The tube was on: Pedro Martinez was beating Don Zimmer during the ALCS.

It was a treat to sip beers and ciders at the *Tribeca Tavern* during this historic event. I'm a Red Sox fan—I kept my cheers on the down-low.

We gleefully switched venues, finding *Shag*, which happened to be the only place in NYC—I deemed a must go during a pre-trip online search.

The flow—flowed at *Shag*. Dave and I alternated between beer and martinis. A couple sat to our left. Steve sat to our right. We hit it off.

The bartenders answered our nightlife suggestions by handing us a list of gay bars. WTF

The lovely couple to the left closely resembled *Comic Book Man* from *The Simpson's* and his perfect match.

We turned back to the bar to find another beer and martini.

Mr Comic Book asked about our trip.

On March 3—four days after—eight days after (insert car chase)—that's why—

At story's end, I asked: *True or False?*

Unanimously, they agreed: *TRUE.*

Stephen looked at me disjointedly. He asked if I was okay, followed by a series of OMGs.

Mr Comic Book suggested he'd be shaking in a corner, shattered, if he faced my reality.

Stephen was directing a play at a local theatre.

I attempted to convince him I'd be an excellent leading man, a ridiculously handsome leading man.

He laughed.

CBM encouraged us to screw acting—there were better things to fry in the *Meat Packing District*. On a stage, combatants were going to compete against each other fiercely. Frenzied spectators would cheer every soul-sapping jolt of electricity. The combatants were to be wired with electrical charges as they played the video game *Mortal Combat*. They asked us to join them.

There will be a food pyramid! Stephen said.

We joined them.

We drank more.

I hailed a huge martini glass to transport me back to the *Hotel Martini*que.

Dave was already there—

DEATH LASERS OF DEATH

Dave begged for downtime.

I sped to *Speedy's.*

The stands resembled those of a Coliseum. Electrodes dangled from vital parts of contestants' bodies. The players selected their characters on a large video screen for all to see. The battle commenced. Cheers erupted with each zap. The victims winced in agony. Another zap, a squirm, another zap, and the smell of burning flesh filled the air. Veins began bulging. The losers would keel over defeated; yet, vascular.

The amperage increased with each round.

Another zap—more burning flesh; I dreamt of past loves.

We said our goodbyes to our oddly pleasant new friends. Debauchery was calling.

HELL

Hell [hel] noun (plural hells) place of punishment after death: according to many religions, the place where the souls of people who are damned suffer eternal punishment after death.

SOHO's version was slightly different. The ambience was heated, the walls slathered in red. I think *Satan* shops at *Benjamin Moore*.

The beer was $9. When I put on my glasses, the price dropped to $5.

Ben – Cal – Jeremy – Cindy – Rico—approached us one-by-one offering to buy refreshments, we accepted.

Like Montreal, avoidance was bringing a smile to my face and booze to my belly.

Gay Chicano Gang Bangers approached us. They wore bandanas. They spoke a unique hard dialect.

We moved toward the exit, sharing pleasantries along the way with our collection of new friends when Jeremy noticed the half-tuck. He claimed it belonged to him. He urged me to stop half-tucking. I let him know in no uncertain terms it was now mine.

We burst toward the exits. David needed to start exploring the night. Before we made it out into the evening sky, Robby, a sweet young man, grabbed me, pulling me close. He began to caress my chest.

David went back to the bar.

Robby introduced me to his friend Karen. Karen was an actor on a popular Space related TV series. Robby queried my sexual orientation.

Before I could—he planted one on me, a deep, soul-searching kiss.

Karen wanted a piece of me—sticking her tongue down my throat. She said, *definitely, not.*

A lip war started. My jeans tightened.

I suggested: Robbie check to see what team David is on.

Two guys dropped from the sky. One of them implied I was fucking hot. He invited me home with him, for some unbeknownst reason—upsetting his boyfriend.

We had become chocolate in a room full of—

David escaped.

I looked downward to find Robby's hands inside my pants. I was flattered by his thrusting of affection. I pried his hands from my loins and attempted another getaway.

The exit turned into a washroom stall. Karen was with me. We shared niceties. Shortly after that, let's just say: My ship was docking!

AFTER HOURS NYC STYLE

Slightly drained I gathered my composure, lip wrestled with Robby and Karen for a moment longer—and then, bid them farewell. I bellowed for my martini glass; it was time for liftoff.

My new cabbie, quickly deduced: I needed more night because I was glowing and hovering in the back of his cab.

He drew my attention to men dressed in polyester leisure suits hanging on street corners. He told me in NYC, Mayor Giuliani did such a stellar job cleaning up the city—get this—the hookers circle in cars.

After fifteen minutes of my NYC indoctrination, my cabbie dropped me at an *AFTER HOURS CLUB*.

I quickly blended into the VIP line. The doorman gestured for five VIPs to enter. At the top of the stairs I felt a tap on my shoulder. Apparently, I wasn't a VIP.

The imposing doorman granted me entrance, just because, I'm smoking hot—SMILE.

Time for a security check:

X-RAY MACHINE – METAL DETECTOR – PAT-DOWN

The x-ray zapped my boys. The metal detector set off my knee. The pat-down felt fantastic.

I flashbacked to Calgary, to the harmonica and—

The club consisted of four rooms filled with white sofas. It was sexy-quaint. Four different genres of music were playing. The bar bellied up to me—I ordered drinks, several, more made sense?

There was a glut of snorting going on all around me. Fortunately, most drinks come with straws.

A handsome man sat next to me. We engaged in an interesting conversation about, something, and then—something more—

Wow! New York is fantastic, fast-paced, friendly people. You're devilishly handsome. Do you come here often? My cat purrs. Do you have a kitty? Buildings are tall.

My new friend rudely mimicked me. I challenged him. I asked him if he was drunk or high.

I'd shake my head right. He'd shake his head to the left. I'd frown. His frown was identical. I walked away from the window I was looking into—he disappeared.

I reflected on what I just saw?

I reflected on who I might have been talking to?

Blips passed. I spun in a circle. As I turned, I noticed every girl resembled J. Lo and every guy looked like he'd just walked off the set of the Sopranos.

I went back to the window. I asked my new friend to join me elsewhere for more liquids.

He mimicked the same question.

I left without him. I went searching for a new friend to grab a bite to eat with, just not Mr Reflection, he's a *dink.*

WHITE TOWER

Welcome to *White Tower Burgers*.

May I please have beef fat and lard injected directly into my stomach, with extra fat, and a diet coke?

My meal came to $4.50. For $1 more, *WT* offers a *Will* writing service.

White Tower may provide a small glimpse into the girthing-up of America.

I went for the straight injection. My other options ranged from a two burger combo to a twenty burger combo, all coming with boxes of fries and drinks, and defibrillators.

The only other person in the restaurant was a scary looking homeless man. The grease began to enter my intestines, warming me. I looked at the homeless man. A second man joined him. He was mirroring his words. They were equally dilapidated.

When I finally arrived back at the *Martinique*, I fell forcefully onto my bed. I drifted into a burger comma. My hovering ceased.

Sixteen hours sleep *one hundred thirty hours* into our journey, sounded, sufficient.

DAY 5: SATURDAY – 12 OCTOBER 2003

NEW YORK CITY – LONDON – Pay it Forward

Sleeping for *four hours* was a tad excessive.

I shook David. I asked if he enjoyed last night. I asked him if he enjoyed his downtime.

He looked at me and said *JASFLAHWEH.*

Noon was upon us. It was time to explore NYC, periodically, checking our vital signs along the way. Before we could embark on our adventure, I checked my fucking luggage into storage; it had ordered the twenty burger combo last night.

We stepped out into the crisp city air and began to head *that-a-way.*

Nine hours of directionless exploring lay ahead before we were to fly to Jolly Old London.

FIRST STOP: THE EMPIRE STATE BUILDING.

The line was *three hours*. I held up nine fingers. I folded three of them downward. I asked Dave how many were left.

JASFLAHWEH—he said.

We crossed the Empire off our list. We walked away frowning.

We strolled precisely forty-two steps straight into *Jack Demsey's Restaurant Pub.*

Jimmy, the bartender, was hardcore traditional Irish, fresh off the boat. He was a gifted conversationalist. We ordered a Strongbow and a Guinness.

Jimmy's voice wavered Irish when he asked if we'd done the Empire. He called us lovely young lads!

We told him about the line.

He handed us a card. The card would allow us to skip the line. The only catch was if he was to let us use it we needed to promise we'd try to bring four other people with us because the pass was good for six.

We said *yes* in a heavily bastardised Irish accent.

It was time to pay-it-forward. We approached strangers out on the street, first, hot women—no takers. Then couples, and families, we were repeatedly shunned.

We circled the building in a rectangular fashion.

Maybe the half-tuck was—

We rounded the last corner disappointed in our lack of success. A family of four approached. We asked them to come with us.

The patriarch sternly declined.

We turned the corner.

I looked back. The man was jogging toward us. He was yelling at us in New England accent: *Hey guys. Is the offer still available?*

He told us they were from Boston.

I suggested he go fuck himself.

In reality, I said: *Of course*

He apologised for his abruptness saying he was trying to teach his kids not to talk to strangers.

I hinted showing them common sense and street smarts may be a more valuable lesson. I said strangers wouldn't likely be the problem—Uncle Stan lurking in the corner, more likely, would.

First and last stop on the way to the top was security. Dave brought with him an all-in-one gizmo. His gizmo was similar to a Swiss Army Knife, only, with one thousand options. They made him check it.

My ears popped the entire ascent continuously to FLOOR 88. We then climbed to the top deck where we set our Bostonian friends free to enjoy at their own pace.

Uncle Stan was standing in the corner, ogling—

TOP OF THE WORLD

I found it mind blowing that big burly David was petrified of heights. He clasped the guardrail tightly, holding on for dear life. Easterly winds stroked his fear raising the hair on his arms. The sky baked overcast.

I too am afraid of heights. David's fear trumped mine.

A handsome young couple were attempting to locate where the WTC would've been. They were peering through coin-operated binoculars. I offered to assist.

I extended my arm, pointing with my index finger. Follow the point of my finger, I said. Imagine a laser is shooting out of it for approximately four miles. Look at the tall buildings, directly to their right are lower buildings. I asked if they could see the mural where my laser was hitting. *There,* I said, excitedly.

I looked back at Dave; he was crumpled into the foetal position, shuddering. I laughed internally. As I did, my fear of heights vanished. I reached up scooping chunks out of the clouds.

At the exact moment, I touched a cloud. A jet flew directly overhead. The roar of the engines amplified the clouds. It stopped the hearts of many on the deck. David collapsed again. He cried out for his mother. I LOL'd.

We returned to our seats at *Jack Demsey's* to thank Jimmy.

After quenching our thirsts once more, we hit the streets of New York. We weren't thirty minutes into our walk when Dave realised he forgot his all-in-one gizmo with Security at the Empire State Building. He ventured back to retrieve it. I decided to stay put and wait. I stressed inwardly. I began walking around the block to look for my REFLECTION. I found David Letterman's Theatre instead!

CENTRAL PARK

Forty minutes had passed before Dave returned. I was hungry and outside.

Hungry and outside was the only thing I could think to type, sorry.

I asked Dave if he thought it was convenient Central Park was in the Center of the City.

Once again, that was the only thing I could think of—I promise, I will kick-start the creative storytelling again soon.

It was time to eat. We had passed *fifty-six restaurants* before we settled for a restaurant called: *GOOD CHOICE…*

Loreena, the bartender, was a transplant from Ireland. She told us we must go to go to Galway. She produced a list of must go places for our trip.

We ate. We drank. We moved on.

We visited the *Rockefeller Center*.

I bought soft-soled shoes.

We drank some more. Drinking led to peeing.

We drank more, which resulted in more drink—which led to more drink—until we found a new place to drink, and pee.

We stopped by *Ms Keens Bar* at the corner of Sixty-Fourth & Sixth, a real gem, serving the finest cigars and scotch, minus the cigars due to the NYC smoking ban.

We fantasised about cigars.

James, from Ireland, the bartender, shared stories of the big dollars he makes serving the local elite.

We drank more.

I struck a conversation with a bus driver sitting at the bar. He was bitter. His bitterness stemmed from no New Yorkers, other than police and firefighters, dying on 9/11. Or so he said.

A New York Minute

BIG BOLD BRASH BEAUTIFUL

New York swallowed me, taking me deep into its belly. It immediately recognised I was carrying vulnerability. It opened its heart and began to caress me back to health.

New York is fast-and-furious—but somehow comforting—soulful. Fast quickly turned to slow motion—bringing clarity.

The more of the cities buzz I embraced, the calmer I became. It soothed me.

This feeling is rare, fleeting at best.

I've only encountered this kind of comfort once before—in Jamaica.

New York epitomises opportunity with commerce and culture colliding. The result is a vibrant tapestry full of diversity.

If you bring an attitude to New York, the city will quash you. It will chew you up and spit you out.

Some of the brightest most creative people from around the globe live in New York.

I believe it embraced us because we put aside our perceptions and realised it is full of vibrant neighbourhoods. New Yorkers try their best daily. They bring the city to life.

When terrorists lashed out at NYC, they missed the boat—in my opinion.

New Yorkers are everyone: every culture, every race; every religion. New Yorkers teach the world how to interact with one another in a quest to make every day glorious. New York is about acceptance. By striking NYC, New Yorker's resolve strengthened.

New York offered escape when I needed it the most. Escaping brought a twinge of happiness back into my heart. It helped me realise my core is solid.

While in New York I collected several pieces of my shattered life, placing them back where they belong.

New York, you've made a new friend.

THANK YOU!

So Long Big Apple—

You're ripping us off—no I don't want to get out. You are an evil man.

The going rate for transportation from Manhattan to JFK was $35. Our bellman-arranged-driver informed us one-quarter of the way into the trip; he was charging $50.

JFK is a dump. It reminded me of Albany.

In the airports waiting lounge we met a gorgeous blonde from Boston. She hit on us. In a seductive tone she said she was flying to London, alone. She whispered she'd like to get to know us, better.

Mustard looks yellow on bread. I said.

She looked at me confused.

We boarded the plane.

We were seated back row—middle seats. Back row—middle seats = upright seats—no view—with fully reclining seats directly in front of us.

I watched Charlie's Angels. Dave watched the Matrix. There is no reason for sharing our movie selections with you—no reason.

I became engrossed in the GPS system on the video screen.

We ate. We abstained from alcohol.

Jimmy, the third Jimmy of the day, a flight attendant from New York, was enthralled with us. He was taken aback by our devilish beauty.

I enjoyed describing myself as devilishly beautiful.

London was approaching. In reality, the plane was approaching London. We were on our final descent.

A sultry FA began freaking out while staring out the window.

Oh my God, isn't that Flight 123 out of Boston? God, I think we're a little too close. I think that's Mary in the window. I like her hair. Yeah, it is Mary; I can read her nametag—not—am I scaring you guys?

YES

TODAY + THAT PLACE

Writing love into my story in real time—

Before I fly from New York to London, I need to take pause. Love was missing from my life. So, I decided as I merrily typed away, I would write it in. After all, I truly believe if you write it, it will come.

If I walked along with the crowd—I'd have never come to this place.

Our eyes met across a crowded room. We knew in that instant. A smile, a wink, a nod—I found you standing next to me. Your presence consumed me as I fell deep into your being. We kissed. Sparks flew. My knees weakened. Yours did as well.

We ventured forth. A touch of your hand and a caress of your silky smooth skin brought life to my world. Each day we learn from each other. The more I learn about you—the more I become lost in your beauty. Every wrinkle, every frown line, every imperfection—perfects you. You're beautiful. I love you.

We both like to please. We do without order. The intensity grows. We climax together. Each time we make love—the music sounds sweeter. I sleep in your arms. You hold me without restraint. You bring safety to my heart.

I'm the luckiest man alive—I found my tomorrows.

One day when I wake—I'll go to that place.

When our eyes finally meet—the world will make sense. As I said once before—I'll say it once more: I love you, my dear, with every ounce of my heart.

Today I met my true love. Today my world became brighter. Today I became complete.

Is my true love real?

It has to be my dear. It is now part of this story.

I stepped out into the world, once again alone. I walked away from the crowd and entered *That Place*. As written, our eyes met, and I knew in that instant. I found my love. Fiction turned into reality.

We hugged. We kissed. Chills shot down my spine. You swept me away. I became vulnerable. Next—was no longer in my control, as the night progressed the passion intensified. The music truly did become sweeter.

In the morning you slept in my arms. I held onto you without restraint. I couldn't sleep; yet, peacefulness embraced me. My eyes transfixed on your beautiful body, consuming every inch—I became captured in your essence. You truly are beautiful my dear. I'm grateful to have met you.

Sadness fills my soul as it struggles to hold onto this happiness. You've entered my life, and the visit will be fleeting. I long for you to feel the same way as me. I understand you may not. I don't want you to leave—you've helped me to replace my frowns with smiles. I can't thank you enough.

I'll miss you deeply—I can't explain why. I hope one day our paths cross again. When they do, I hope we become lost in each other.

Thank you for brightening my world. Thank you for being real. Thank you for being part of my story.

Next time I write you into my life—I'll make sure you stay.

I hope wherever destiny takes you happiness fills your heart and you continue to share your beautiful smile with the world. In the brief moments I've shared with you—your smile warmed my heart.

Thank you. I love you.

LONDON CALLING

IMPORTANT READING INSTRUCTIONS

Please read this letters dialogue with a *meaty* English *accent*.

My story is entirely true. *One million pieces*—I have no need to embellish.

People have at times commented on the size of my brain. Some have suggested: LARGE.

I know it functions reasonably well despite my attempts to sabotage it chemically.

Shall we talk about the dialogue of the book, of course, yes is the answer?

Even with my large cranium, I must admit: it's impossible to remember every snippet, verbatim.

I promise: I've recreated the dialogue to the best of my recollection, especially the intense moments because they're etched deeply in my memory.

HEATHROW

DATELINE: 13 October 2003

I lay naked, exhausted from the previous night of passion. Beads of moisture formed on my brow, the taste of her sweet lips were fresh on mine. The throes of passion we'd experienced left me wanting more; more of her silky smooth legs, more of her flavourful skin. Her arousal completed me.

Now, the only thing covering my well-muscled loins was her essence. I longed for a repeat of the night—maybe one day. I'll keep a spot open for her in my heart, for now—

—Welcome to London. The current London time is 11:30 AM. We hope you've enjoyed your flight. The current London temperature is a haughty +15 (C).

LONDON CABBIE

WELCOME TO JOLLY OLD ENGLAND: THE USA OF EUROPE.

We were only *six days* into our living like rock stars experiment, like so many rock stars before us, at this pace: we were marching toward early graves.

Our caskets opened ever so slightly. We wanted to crawl in; life pummeled our bodies. The proverbial ghost was peeking at us from behind a pole.

David was sporting a new nickname: he was now *Yummy David*. I never coined it.

I'm not taking the piss—

Heathrow, much like JFK, was a dump.

The hardwiring in our brains was malfunctioning rendering our only decipherable mode of communicating to be Braille.

The luggage carousel begged me to remove my luggage. It was now tipping the scales at a whopping two hundred pounds.

The beautiful blonde from JFK approached. In a tantalisingly soothing voice, she whispered: *Why don't you hot, virile, sexy men, cum join me for a night of bliss at the place I am staying in Paddington? It has always been my fantasy to be fulfilled by two powerful young gods at once. You two would suffice nicely.*

We proceeded to drop the ball in a nearly impossible fashion. Dave said something about kangaroos. I spun in a circle four times. I tried to speak. I only managed beeping sounds.

David and I had arrived at the *Land of Idiots*—where we lived happily ever after!

THE END

Before the end came, we climbed over the fence of happiness and escaped. It was time to storm London, and once the storm fizzled, maybe, find a way to Amsterdam.

I suggested we head to Paddington. Dave looked confused. I suggested we head to Paddington. Dave looked confused. I suggested—

I screamed: *BOSTON.*

A blip blipped passed. We mused how big could London possibly be?

We considered finding a cab, for thirty minutes.

We began moving, stepping outside into London's energy-infused air, which happens to be similar to Bellingham.

I dragged my thirteen-hundred pounds of luggage to the line for taxis. London was calling our names.

FOLLOW READING INSTRUCTIONS NOW

Breathe in. Exhale. Gruff it up, lower an octave or two. Now imagine, a mouth full of scotch and tobacco. Be pleasant at first. Up the intensity; now, speak British.

Cabbie: *Where to lads?*

Me: *Take us to a hotel or a pub. Either would be fantastic.*

Apparently, my words were evil in England, maybe a sign of the Antichrist.

The cabbie looked crazed, performing brain crunches in front of us—squeezing and releasing until the veins began to protrude out of his skull.

His face was now beet red. He didn't withhold his vile disgust for our words. Seventeen veins were blasting out of his cranium. His head was on the verge of exploding. Here was a man responsible for our first impression of London—and he wanted no part of welcoming us. He rasped up his voice and barked.

Cabbie: *You have to be fucking kidding? Don't you know where you're fucking going?*

Me: *We'll pay you*—I said sheepishly.

He vanquished us from his *ride.*

We *squirreled* out of his cab.

In the waiting area, the next man in queue mentioned to us our cab didn't move. He asked if the fare was expensive.

I kicked him in the nuts.

FIRST IMPRESSION of LONDON: You suck.

I screamed *BOSTON* again, hoping the gorgeous blonde from Heathrow would come to our rescue.

Vacant comes to mind. I mean VACANT was our minds. We needed sweet slumber to arrest us in its purple cloak.

LOGIC, unfortunately, was lagging *three time zones* behind. We'd have to make our own decisions.

We came to a sign offering a possible solution:

HOTELS – ALL PRICES – ALL SHAPES – ALL SIZES – ALL—

The clerks behind the counter seemed sincere in their desire to help. They asked us what our budget was.

Three blocks later we hopped off the bus at the Airport Sheraton; 20£ lighter—

SHERATON = FOUR STARS = MUST BE NICE

Dave fell asleep while checking in. I set out looking for adventure.

The fucking airport was only fifteen miles shy of London. Airport Hotel = No Exploring. It was noon.

Dave hibernated. I searched for a pool, a gym, a pub, fuck—no luck. I gave up. I thought I was maybe too spent to think straight. I decided I would try again after a nap.

I woke up at 10 PM —in the past year I'd spent time as a habitual insomniac. Frustrated, I searched again for entertainment. My initial discoveries were confirmed.

I lay down again trying not to think about life. Life stormed back attempting to annihilate me. *It succeeded.* For four consecutive hours, I lay still, crying, as my past tortured me.

I needed a distraction. I stepped into the hallway. The fucking hotel didn't even have a coke machine. Were we trapped in a concentration camp?

I hated concentrating.

I spent fifteen minutes knocking on hotel room doors then running and hiding. I quickly bored of my juvenility.

I lay down once more. Sleep came fast. I dreamt of damsels in distress. Their bodies were naked, perfect. I threw my arms around them to protect them from predators threatening their survival.

I took off my clothing; they began to—

MY TRIP STATS TO DATE: DAY 6

Distance Travelled: 11,055.1 KMS – MEALS ATE: 8 – DIFFERENT TOILET FLUSHES: 2
DISTANCE WALKED: 104 KM – PHARMACEUTICALS INGESTED: 4
DRINKS CONSUMED: 75 (approximate) – HOURS SLEPT: 24

A death pace, slow pace, or somewhere in between: will be determined by stories end?

I invite you to flip the pages with me to find out!

In the meantime, I needed to lie down to look for the damsels. At least the hotel had towels!

DAY 7: TUESDAY, OCTOBER 14TH, 2003

Dave slept for twenty-four consecutive hours.

I woke him by wringing his neck.

We spent 13£ for shuttle tickets to London. Fifteen minutes later we arrived at Paddington Station.

Which begs the question: How can a shuttle ride of only a few blocks to a Four Star Hotel cost about the same as a sixteen-mile train ride to the city?

We bounded off the train. Paddington has coke machines!

We were famished.

Dave wanted a nap. I explained how close he was to finding death.

It was time to deposit my two-thousand pounds of luggage.

Midday was upon us. We had no place to stay. We were barely seventeen steps into London when we glimpsed two ninjas and a zombie. They were carrying banjos; alive in the daytime, created by oversleeping.

We blinked. When we opened our eyes, a *Strongbow* and *Guinness* were in our hands.

Farewell sobriety, your visit was painful.

I took a sip, and my reflection was once again, reflecting.

I said... *Eat.*

David asked me if I was stupid.

Liquids were providing clarity, we drank in two more, then headed that-a-way.

One hundred fifty paces – internet café – ten minutes later – hotel for the night + Amsterdam flights—were booked.

A *soft cuddly bear* brushed my left arm. We guessed a direction. One hundred paces the other side of the *Fountains Abbey* we found our hotel, the *Hotel Ascot*.

They'd overbooked; we looked at the desk clerk dumfounded. We booked the room a *five-fucking-minute* walk ago—

We were set up in a sister hotel. Three Stars dropped to two. We didn't care.

Wicked, Dave, the shower curtain touches your bed!

OXFORD STREET

On the edge of Hyde Park we took a deep breath and realised: We were in London, Baby!

Left foot – right foot – left foot – right foot – I'd stumble. We took my imbalance as a sign we needed beverages. I said... *Eat.*

At the *3 TONS PUB*, we met a couple from *Budapest*. I said *goulash tasty*—in my best Hungarian accent. We drank, fast.

Booze took London from a sad two to a whimsical playful five.

Our Hungarian friends handed me a *few pieces* from my life they found in their stew.

A denizen of shoppers packed world famous *Oxford Street*. Dave and I glanced knowingly at each other. We knew because our new friend British booze was waking up our old friend American booze, the day was going to be splendid.

Oxford Street shares threads with Bellingham—I mean Vancouver's Robson Street, only with more character—and oldness.

I paused.

Like Robson, Oxford Street it is one large commercial circus. The difference is when in a foreign land the same *crap* becomes *fascinatingly different*.

Back to pressing life issues: I found a chunk of shag carpeting. Mauve, I might add. I stole a broom from a janitor. I sprinkled my issues on the next room's linoleum. I lifted the corner of the shag and swept *them* merrily underneath.

It was time to avoid, have more booze, and hopefully: do some shagging.

Dave and I popped in and popped out, *carrying on*. We loved the architecture. We enjoyed the heavenly sounds of accented voices brilliantly seducing the crisp air. The voices made my pants happy.

LARGEST SELECTION OF STUFF

We must go in, I said to Dave. They have the largest selection of—stuff.

We rode an escalator down where a strikingly beautiful sales clerk greeted us. I pressed flesh with her, locking our hands together—it was a pleasure to meet her.

She said the pleasure was hers.

I came in my pants. The half-tuck drew her to me.

The half-tuck screams: Originality, saucy sexiness, and as many experts have debated long and hard: an **OVERSIZED** dick. At least that's what my brain was attempting to sell me.

Hands still clamped, I asked her to rub me—bad brain. I asked her what we should do that evening in her royally enchanting city as I gazed deeply into her magical eyes.

She was unquestionably thinking: DO ME as she politely suggested we'd have a brilliant time in Leicester Square.

Our hands parted. My pants, though sticky, dried.

Back on the street we walked a block, looked left down a laneway, NEON beckoned—it was time to chase.

BRADLEY'S SPANISH BAR

The warmth of the flickering lights from *Bradley's Spanish Bar* bagged us.

We bellied up to the bar. I confessed my sticky sins to an unsuspecting bartender.

A fetching thing about *Bradley's* is if you have an ample belly, you could almost belly-up by just setting foot inside. You see, *Bradley's* is infinitely charming, two levels—on this night—only one seat sat vacant.

From door to bar was only five steps; with the heart on both levels accommodating a maximum of fifteen patrons. The atmosphere is wicked. A perfect selection of tunes filled the air. Their jukebox was voted one of the five-best-things about London in Time Out Magazine.

Natalia, the bartender, and her friend Benito greeted us—they were both from Spain. They barely spoke English. We discounted barriers by solely sharing *Hola*, *beer*, and *Vancouver*, and smiling.

That was enough, and perhaps a foreshadowing of what we'd find in Spain.

Hello, Robert, Helen, and Andy.

We had just introduced ourselves to a gaggle of sophisticated Londoners. The artistry of language flowed freely between them. I needed them to fall in love with Canadians. I attempted to conquer sophistication.

My madness worked. Our globetrotting rock star ways, along with a smattering of depth and our obliterating charm, enthralled them. They became friends.

Dave and I became obliterated as Andy plied us with drink.

They invited us to join them at their next stop: a wine bar with *a one-billion-year-old tree* growing right through the bar.

A billion-years-old is old.

What's that dirt?

Dave and I looked at each other to discuss their kind offer. We looked back, only to have a time vortex swallow us. Our surroundings changed. *Bradley's* turned into a much larger establishment. We were chatting with a bartender from Ontario. We looked at each other again and shrugged.

Apparently, we took a wrong turn leaving *Bradley's* washroom and presto, new surroundings.

Where are you from fair maiden?

Ontario explained the missing accent.

As pleasant as our vixen bartender was, Ontario depressed us. We never came all this way to talk to someone from—talking to people from—can be painful at the best of times.

A QUICK BURST TO THE READING PRESENT: Ontarians before you get your panties in a bunch, I'm from Vancouver, half of Ontario, and all-of-the Quebec squeegee kids eventually tire of the east, and end up setting up shop on the left coast. Therefore, cut me some slack.

Hey, aren't you from Saskatchewan?

We drank up and decided to return to the hotel to ready ourselves for the night. After fifteen kilometres of walking and drinking, we didn't have a clue where the hotel was. So, we picked that-a-way.

Dave could still walk. Me, on the other hand, lay down and started to roll along the sidewalk like a log.

REMOTE TRIBE

Imagine being the only person that spoke English. Whom would you teach the language?

I rolled fifteen blocks that-a-way when we came to the *Cambridge Pub*.

It was a good thing since I was 'staring' agony down, I needed liquids or misery would prevail.

A beautiful woman stood outside the pub; *talk to her now*, I did. English was no longer my first language. I discovered a dialect of my own shared only with a remote tribe in the recesses of my brain.

She politely nodded.

I fell to the ground; jumped back to my feet, and slurred: *I'm okay.*

Once inside: *Hello, Rachel, Garth, and Jessie (Manager), meet the Seed and Dave.*

Garth and Dave looked as if they shared the same tribal roots.

Rachel was smashing.

Me drunk—

One would think after rolling fifteen blocks; *ONE* wouldn't require more alcohol. *One* would be wrong. We did not appreciate the asinine opinion of— *ONE*. We wisely decided to ignore *ONE* —instead; we partook in witty banter with our new friends.

Garth's inner ear was funky; it restricted his movement. He'd never been out of his neighbourhood. Garth is nearly 30.

Rachel draped herself over Dave's manly being. She was fascinated by his ability to understand me.

By this time my tribe excommunicated me sending me forth to a tribe of one.

Flying solo rendered my newfound dialect pointless.

If a tree falls in a—

Jesse took our vitals, which prompted a parade of shooters.

I said *Djojojfojjdjkhuiuu...*

We shot the shots; I became eyes openly blind—my retinas gave up the ghost.

Dave asked Rachel to join us later in our journey. He called her *Lovee.*

She called him a strapping, virile, young bloke. What's a bloke?

London managed to crawl, roll, and shoot, to a spirited &$#—in English: eight-point-five.

ROCK PAPER SCISSORS

Take us to the hotel, Rusty.

Our cab driver asked an interesting question: *Which hotel, lads?*

In Paddington, we think?

We then proceeded to work backwards through the alphabet—eventually, settling on the letter A.

You've got to be—

Before he could implode, I said: *Ascot, Rusty.*

He informed us his name wasn't Rusty—it was Ace.

Freshly drunk and showered, it was time for *Heaven*. Before we departed, Dave tried to give me a tongue bath.

I refused his offer.

Rusty #2 picked us up. During the ride I peeked out the window to find the guy I was talking to in the NYC AFTER HOURS, following me.

Bewildered, I asked him what, why—and why?

I asked him to leave me alone.

We arrived at *Heaven* to sadly find it closed, much to our vexation.

Dave suggested we go to the River Thames to watch David Blaine hover off a bridge.

English returned to me; I said *I've seen a river before.*

We'd prefer more drink.

We met Sarah. She was waiting for a bus. She asked if she could join us. She toiled with us riding the bus with her closer to her neighbourhood so we could—

We saw *NEON*, signalling us to come toward its buzz. We refused her offer.

Instead, we played: ALCOHOL – BEAUTIFUL GIRL - FOOD

ALCOHOL wins every time!

LET DOWN

GORGEOUS BOSTONIAN – HOT ONTARIAN – STUNNING LONDONER

We chose to pay 5£ to enter a cheesy bar modelled after an eighties TV series.

Cheers sucked pickled-goat-testicles. It was tacky—imagine—every bad hip-hop playing nightclub in American suburbia, add accents—and stir. Stir some more. Throw in the odd testosterone-fuelled conflict. Sprinkle in the odour of rancid puke. Welcome to *Cheers Trafalgar Square*.

We hated it. We only choked down three drinks—we had drunk ourselves sober.

The curtain on our first glorious night in London was drawing shut. Only twenty blocks separated us from *Dreamland*. Somehow, in London taxi math, twenty blocks = 30£—or roughly, $60 Canadian.

I checked the mirror in our room. My head had **LOSER** tattooed on it—Dave's, **SUCKER.**

I pledged to kill the next cab driver I saw—and then drifted off to sleep.

DAY 8: WEDNESDAY – 15 OCTOBER 2003

GESTALT

Woe is me; it took me eight days to comprehend Yummy David's role on this trip.

It wasn't the non-existent tongue bath. He was destined to join me as my chaperone. He was sanctioned by (?) to keep me alive.

Eight days provided pause.

Serious needed a moment on the stage. I needed to face it, unless a rice wine and crack induced comatose state was my resting place, like the tongue bath—I don't—

My dad died. My wife left me. And, I developed an affinity for Crack & Down.

The combination was never an option.

As I continue to share you may think avoidance is nothing more than denial.

Without avoiding, I may have never been able to start healing. I needed to experience life removed from trauma. I needed to realise life isn't all bad.

My life was never a cakewalk. It was full of adventure. It transcended definable realities. I loved the group; yet, I prefer to interact with the individual. I love the performance; yet, I fear the stage.

It was glaringly obvious it was time to take the stage. Dealing with my past was to be part of the performance.

It was time to combine fantasy with reality.

I was a storyteller craving the happy ending.

However, at this moment, I wanted to crawl into a cave and hibernate. On this trip, the caves turned into Pubs.

It was time for me to set new standards, higher standards. Facing the untimely death of the aged, and the all too early death of the young, plus debilitating infidelities, I felt my existence was no longer necessary.

Seed, a little over dramatic don't—

Drama free does not exist; so: NO.

It was time to define what to allow in—and to sort through the emotional baggage of the past; I needed to set it aside, then kick-start ME into achieving greatness.

To this point of the journey, alcohol and avoidance seemed to be vital parts of the pursuit.

YUMMY DAVID

It's time to shout out thank you to David!

David passionately desires knowledge.

Although different, our upbringings share parallel lines.

I was searching for something lost. David wanted to expand his horizons. He wanted to see if what he left behind was meant to be.

Like said, he came to keep me alive. He may not have understood that which he signed up.

Wise beyond his years, he asked: permission to come.

As we jumped from place-to-place, each time my world turned upside down, he oozed compassion. He found positive in my collapse.

He struggled with my winging-it pace. He did so gracefully.

He considered every stop to be a possible place to say farewell.

Fortunately, for me, indecision kept pushing us forward.

Our fucked up planet needs more Davids to help fix some of the shit transpiring daily.

I know that may sound a tad pessimistic, it's not all bad, I'm individually optimistic; however, globally, not so much.

ENGLISH BREAKFAST

The FERRIS WHEEL turned once more. It hit bottom. Each time it did the occupants dropped into the tray below. Not satisfied with the outcome they'd swiftly be placed back in place for another round. Every rotation the blazing British sun would bronze them ever so slightly.

Before I press on, why don't you grab your favourite beverage, and position yourself in a comfy chair?

David and I are sampling refreshments from several countries. One day we'll share our favourites with you. I hope our travels inspire you to globetrot, without the drama of course.

Now, where was I?

At 8 AM I rose. It was time to add shine. Rising was the only action needed as I was still glowing from arriving home at 6 AM.

The revolutions continued—fifteen thus far with little tan taking to the skin.

The sun was failing.

Thirty-seven turns later, and finally, my bread started resembling toast.

FLASHBACK TO CHECK-IN

Your room comes with a splendid hearty English breakfast.

Have they not heard of toasters?

Breakfast time was to allow downtime for Dave, and time for me to rediscover food.

Eggs, bacon, sausage, and hash browns excited me. The *English Breakfast Aficionados* would surely provide a feast to absorb the copious amounts of alcohol swishing around in my gullet.

When I entered the food area, tragically—Feast turned to famine. A murder of annoying kids filled the breakfast café, shooter-sized glasses of juice, and the fucking FERRIS WHEEL bread toaster.

Disillusioned, I exited the area, went outside, approached the first cab, and furiously snuffed out the driver's life.

LONDON ROUND 1: Took us down—then slowly upward—layered pompous and disappointment, on top of us, repeating the cycle, seemingly, endlessly.

London, you're allowed to hang onto your eight-point-five, but can you do us a solid or two?

1. Could you please fix your teeth?
2. While you're at it; could you get over yourself?

Amsterdam, please don't let me down.

I won't.

Who typed that?

UNTIL WE MEET AGAIN

I was dizzy from breakfast when I tried to wake David.

Dave looked at me dazed; turned on the shower, and fell back to sleep.

I did a workout in the communal washroom doing still-tipsy push-ups—

Ninety-nine… one hundred—

Alcohol was somehow stoking my metabolic rate. My body was turning solid. Food avoidance could very well be a good thing.

For a brief snippet, I thought about joining Mr Blaine on the bridge.

Go away sad—

At 10 AM, we set out to embrace London one last time. Intense hunger meant: we'd eat soon.

We had walked for three *fucking* hours before the next place was the only option. We crossed the street and once again were drawn to a PUB. A car u-turned in front of a bus, in front of us, we jumped out of the way.

I ordered three cokes, one orange juice, an apple juice, one tomato juice, three more cokes; and, a traditional English breakfast, with double of every side.

Dave ordered breakfast, and a Strongbow.

Our lovely server called us *Love(eees)* every time she passed our table.

Our server's accent was infectious. London was rising once more.

TIME FOR GATWICK: We went to retrieve our luggage.

We were twenty minutes over the twenty-hour storage limit.

I attempted to express it wasn't our fault: blaming locusts, rats—an earthquake. I noticed the chap retrieving our luggage didn't sport an accent.

He was from Ontario.

We love Ontarians.

We told him we were from Vancouver.

He waived the charges.

My luggage was now weighing two tons.

It had eaten all of the bags stored next to it.

AMSTERDAM

Life is joyful. Life is emotional. Life is fucking hard. Life is many splendid things!

Does it have to be?

Fragile, emotional, and fucking hard that is?

Lived to the fullest there is no avoidance of this ragged collection of realities; they're inevitably coming our way. I'm not certain we have a say in the outcome.

You may think darkness engulfs us as we cast our plotlines.

I think dark is part of the journey. Manipulating life toward happy while suppressing misery is what lifts us to fulfilment before the inescapability of death. Manipulation may help us feel we did the best we could.

We must come to a point in life where we define the things which matter.

This trip represents my journey to empty my tank full of dank, dark, depressing misery and then refill it to recapture the joy within.

My journey is self-exploratory. It is endless until of course, death. Every act works delicately toward critically exorcising my demons to bring me to a celestial blissful state.

Montreal, New York, and London offered: a taste of escape. They acted as band-aids. They inspired me. They let me ignore pain.

What's next on the EVENT HORIZON is about to drop some valuable insight into what, in my opinion: LIFE is all about.

My discovery may be visible, if it is, allow me some leeway, remember: I'm blind in one eye; therefore, it may take me a little longer to see the whole picture.

HIGH FLYING

DATELINE 15 October 2003 – continued—

The boarding announcement for *Easy Jet Airlines Flight 123* to Amsterdam blared over the airport's loudspeakers.

EJ Airlines doesn't assign seats. Boarding commenced stadium style, get out of the way granny, that seat is *mine, elbows flying.*

Slightly bored of the battle we gave in letting a Dutch chap take the window seat in our row. I introduced myself.

He ignored me by pulling out a BIBLE and pretending to read.

EJ developed a magical formula for success during a time when the airline industry is reeling in bankruptcies.

FORMULA PART 1: FLYING EJ = NO FRILLS

Except for the souvenir *In-Flight Magazine* advertising every destination EJ flies to, you pay for everything.

I liked the magazine. I didn't like the pages being stuck together because someone didn't want to pay for a barf bag on the previous flight.

I asked for a replacement.

FORMULA PART 2: THE FURTHER YOU BOOK IN ADVANCE = THE FLIGHTS BECOMING CLOSER TO FREE!

We booked one day in advance. Our flights came in around $100 Canadian. If we knew our itinerary earlier, we could have landed the flights for around $15 Canadian, or the equivalent of two super-sized Big Mac meals.

I snuck into the cockpit where I heard the co-pilot say: *I don't care how many chicks you've banged; you're still a monkey. Just fly the plane.*

Hmm, I wondered—maybe that's how they keep costs down?

The FAs worked the aisles in shocking orange uniforms which blended with the shocking orange interior of the plane, reminding us of, Burger King.

The man next to me began reciting bible verses. The safety instructions were full of the hard **Hs** and **Ks** of the Dutch language.

*T**H**e **K**urrent. Amsterdam time is 8 PM. T**H**an**K** you for flying Flig**H**t 100 t**H**is evening. T**H**e temperature is 16 degrees. Every tourist in Amsterdam is currently **H**alf-ba**K**ed and watc**H**ing porn. **H**ave an enjoyable stay. If you t**H**ink our language is **H**ard (?)—wait till Germany. Sc**H**metterlings*

WELCOME TO AMSTERDAM

We touched down at Schipol Airport in Amsterdam.

For the first time on the trip a home was booked; the *Hotel Victoria*. If my memory serves me correctly, it cost in the vicinity of 1 billion €.

We slid effortlessly into the customs line. In a separate line, frequent fliers were pressing their faces against a machine. A light would flash, welcome to the Netherlands, entry granted.

We glided to the luggage carousel. My luggage needed Jenny Craig; Dave's was in rough shape.

Perhaps, the pilots thought, Dave was transporting bananas.

We patched his luggage together with duct tape.

LONDON CABBIE: PART 2

Dutch cracked in the air all around as we walked in concentric circles.

We wanted to go our hotel but we'd forgotten how to move. A cataract of confusion came over us. A cab to the hotel was to relieve our puzzlement.

Our bags were secured in the trunk of the cab when the battle ensued. Dutch profanity flew by. We ducked hard **Hs** and hard **Ks.** The words pierced our near virgin Dutch exposed ears.

Schipol is a shiny happy airport. Out on the street the happiness ceased as our taxi driver was engaged in a drag-it-out battle with another driver over our business. Veins were exploding from his skull. When he was finally defeated, he transferred our luggage into a second cab.

As we pulled away from the curb, I glanced back: a *Gnome* was ripping into the flesh of our first almost-driver as he desperately tried to protect himself armed with only language and a bong.

Hotel Victoria, please.

The language barrier eliminated small talk.

The radio played: *Papi, papi, papi chulo. Papi, papi, papi, chulo.*

An infectious tune we never understood a single word of—the first song blended into a second: *Is this the Odyssey. It's here for you. For me. Just listen for the magic key—Just listen, let your love be free.*

Amsterdam was greeting us with songs.

We paid 50€ for the fare. Later we found out the train from the airport to our hotel was 10€, for the two of us.

Just listen, let your love be free.

We weren't going to allow money to bring us down. We were in Amsterdam after all. Rumour has it—the only way to go is up↑

LEVELS 109

Elevator ride up one flight—15 paces forward—Down 3 steps—Turn 75 degrees left—4 paces sideways—Up 4 steps—Turn 45 degrees right—Up 3 steps—Down 2 steps—7 paces forward—Down 2 steps—5 paces forward— Up 5 steps—16 paces straight – Turn 90 degrees right—Room 109—Insert key—We're home!.

I looked out the window. We were on the first floor.

UP TURNED INTO DOWN—UP—UP—DOWN—DOWN—AND FINALLY—UP.

We were excited about what we might find next?

INNER EAR

Dave grabbed the remote and turned the tube to a sports channel. The Dutch speaking announcers were bantering back and forth a theory on how Dave looked finished. They continued to opine that although my life was in the shambles, I was putting up a classic fight.

They questioned if I was living in denial.

The announcers flashed to the future envisioning beautiful Italian leather and lesbians.

I let Dave lie down.

I hit the *Orange Tree Bar*. I think that was the name. It was just around the corner from our hotel. After *Google Street View*, I believe it may have been called *Jupiter*.

Anyway, it's irrelevant. I was going to be drinking in a different dialect.

I sat at the bar. I pointed at a draught tap, pint one arrived.

I attempted to strike a conversation with my Barman, Garth. He spoke little English. He tried gallantly.

I, on the other hand, speak zero Dutch. So, I choose to speak loudly in painfully broken English.

Two men from Ireland sitting on my left laughed at my efforts.

Garth tilted his head to the right and started panting.

Two hours passed. I successfully pointed at the draught taps four times by the time Dave joined me.

I introduced Dave to Patrick O'Malley and Patrick O'Callaghan.

I whispered into Dave's ear: *Listen carefully. The Irish speak English, right? Do you understand what they're saying?*

Garth refreshed our drinks; he'd never left his neighbourhood, something to do with his inner ear.

We asked him directions to the *Red Light District*. He pointed behind us, then without lifting a muscle, or leaving our stools, the environs began changing. We floated through the walls of Jupiter. The world was *shape shifting*. The bar transformed into the hotel. We became holograms soaring effortlessly through the air. We were transparent in shape, unseen to those around us. However, the physicality of the surroundings was real. We melted through walls, bending down the hotel's hallways. We came across Anne Frank and Van Gogh sipping on *Orange Whips*, flipping through porn, eating chips. Anne was coyly whispering into Vincent's detached ear, too quietly for us to hear. Vincent's *Whip*, spiked with Absinthe, he reached for a knife and screeched: *Damn plastic.*

All too real, they turned, smiled; and gave us a knowing wink. In a flash, we landed outside in the crisp, clear, fragrant Dutch air, right at the end, or the start, depending on how you swizzle your stick, of the infamous: *Red Light District.*

FOUR PACES FORWARD —1 STEP UP!

LOGISTICS

Finally, my area of expertise—

Amsterdam brims quaintly with history. It's a colourful treasure trove for lovers of architecture. Historical yet innovative, it has *six hundred fifty* gable stones and one skinny bridge.

Digging into the recesses of my brain, historically; founded by two anglers and their seasick,dog. Legend has it the dog jumped ship to empty its upset stomach and Amsterdam was born.

Does anybody know what a gable stone is?

We decided upon food before the red lights.

FIRST STOP: *Lord Mike's Bar.* Mike greeted us at the door and then rushed to the bar to make drinks. We were too late for food, so he ordered a pizza for us.

We met a delightful quartet from Farnborough, England; Martin, Andy, Richard, and Fat Tony.

I whispered to Dave: *Listen carefully. The English speak English, right? Do you—*

Martin asked me what I do for a living.

I said something like a bartender and bar manager.

He was chronically glazed over, including his hearing. He smiled brilliantly and said: *No shite.*

Bartender and bar manager transformed into Boeing—he too worked at Boeing. He asked if I'd been to the plant in Farnborough.

Not wanting to disappoint him, I decided I work at Boeing, and Jack from corporate had given me a tour of the Farnborough facilities.

In the meantime, Andy and Richard interjected: *When I hold my right hand on the left side of my body, does it become my left hand?*

Fat Tony sat transfixed on a spec floating in the distance.

Martin beamed with joy because he was meeting brethren from afar. He promised to one day visit Seattle. His excitement peaked when he found out I worked in logistics.

Fat Tony's head swayed from side to side.

The pizza arrived. Pieces magically flew through the air to be inhaled wholly by our friends.

Fat Tony suddenly grew sunglasses, which baffled me because I hadn't smoked anything.

Lord Mike asked us the reason for our trip.

It all started March 3—

Upon stories completion, he asked if I was okay. Then, for some reason, he guessed our ages. He guessed I was 32—Dave 27.

I looked back at Fat Tony—*sunglasses*—I don't think our pizza was a regular pizza.

SEVEN PACES OUT THE DOOR—TURN 90 DEGREES LEFT—6 PACES FORWARD—UP THREE STEPS!

PORN

We came across windows filled with sluttily dressed mannequins; one moved, I asked Dave to hold me.

We had entered the *Red Light District.*

The mannequins were alive.

Window after window we were tempted to taste. Guilt and stigma were absent.

Dave gleefully strutted past the myriad of canals. I walked at his side.

The scent of cannabis filled the night air.

I began hallucinating. Families donning only wooden shoes were navigating the waterways using their shoes for floatation.

Dave suggested I was drunky.

Dave wanted to pursue sexual satisfaction.

We popped into a pleasure shop. Dave queried the breathtaking shop attendant: *How much for a blowjob, hand job, a threesome, a six-some, two clowns a donkey and an albino midget?*

For a bizarre reason, unbeknownst to me, I felt uneasy. Maybe there is something creepy about shopping for porn with a friend?

Maybe without guilt and stigma, it is no longer porn?

I'm not anti-porn. I enjoy sex. For some reason I've reached a state of porn abstinence.

Flashback to when I bought my first digital camera: first picture: A flower. The second picture: Full bloom.

While we continue venturing backwards I invite you to hop into the WAYBACK MACHINE with me. I was maybe 12 or 13. I was rifling through one of my brother's book collections when I discovered: *The Joy of Sex.*

I flipped the pages nervously. I found a section entitled *Slow Masturbation.*

The author suggested having your partner straddle your chest—naked—I started to rise—Once comfortably straddled they were to manipulate—slowly at first—back and forth—

I couldn't wait to find a partner. I glanced at my hands. I drew a lustful happy face on one of them. I gave it a seductive name: Kitten.

Have I shared too much?

Do you remember your first time?

I practised extensively. I became proficient. I started buying sexy hand teddies. I wanted more. I lifted my mattress and to my joy, found: Playboy, Penthouse; and Swank.

Slow turned to fast and then back to slow. I became more excited by the stories than the pictures.

I never thought this would happen to me—

One word, in particular, filled my loins with desire. I wouldn't allow my sexed-up digits to contact my—until it appeared, for penis's sake—it came up often.

Solo adventures continued. There were even ones involving warm summer nights, neighbourhood nudity, and running. I've repressed my recollection of most of these to avoid the need for extensive counselling.

One day my porn experiments took a drastic turn. Solo found company.

I never thought—began happing to me, all the friggen time.

Day – Night – Afternoon – Morning - In a Car – In the—*with*—right up to today (insert today's date); and a couple of days ago.

Once I put the magazines back under the mattress, I've been living a life full of porn with me being the principle player.

How much for slow—fast—slow—fast—oh—while running naked on a hot summer night?

FYI: I wrote this last little bit naked while sipping on a Mojito. Both of my hands were on the table most of the time—

NIGHTCAP

With porn freshly stroked off our agenda, we returned to crisscrossing canals.

We rounded a corner stumbling into *Crack Land*. Scores of lost souls lined the street. Crack defies boundaries. It defies logic. It disgusts. It doesn't discriminate. In a foreign tongue, it sounds more hostile.

We were surrounded by the lifeless faces of the living dead. Individual spirit washed away with each hit. All became one. Black hoods covered forlorn faces hiding sad stories sharing common threads. Further into the street, the carnage multiplied. One turned into two turned into—

Ghouls darted out from darkened storefronts.

Give me money—money—money—

With our arms together palms facing outward, we extended and parted in a breaststroke-like fashion, pushing the heartache aside with each stroke. The gloom was stifling. Liberal became bankrupt of morality. Amsterdam was no longer quaint. It was toxic. It was ugly.

We continued pushing forth.

Money—money—help me—

Bright reddish-orange flashes of light flickered. Plumes of smoke rose around us. I wanted to escape.

We crossed a bridge to retreat to the outskirts of doom. The multiplication continued. Young girls were frothing at the mouth close to overdose. Injections were taking place—visible to even the blind.

Hundreds of corpses were standing in FORMATION across the canals bridge—decked out in black, hooded, in unison, they collectively made the popping sound of lips pursing together as they drew on their pipes, embers would flash, the whites of their eyes would intensify, the once crisp fragrant night air filled with waste. Satan's Choir continued its toxic symphony, pop, purse, flash, smoulder—repeat, to the beat of a slow death groove.

Occasionally an ember would flicker out, expire, fading into the star filled sky.

With each life extinguished—two willing replacements carried the tragedy forward with unbreakable fervour.

This symphony plays out daily, worldwide.

We sadly sauntered away. We passed a line behind a velvet rope. The line was long. Compassion left me; CRACK vs. ALCOHOL—ALCOHOL—not so bad.

Money, money—gives me your money. A young girl pressed relentlessly.

Dave took her into a store, bought two chocolate bars—passed them to the girl—chocolate, a staple food of Crack?

He then said *Please, turn away. Sweetie, if you cross that bridge, you'll likely never see this side again.*

She took her place in line.

We staggered into a bar outside of *Crack Land*, filled with Londoners. We quickly deduced *Amsterdam's Red Light District* is geared to entice tourists into thinking they're having a genuine Dutch experience. It tricks you into believing you're living on the edge rebelliously—pushing the envelope.

If you want to stand out in *The Red Light District*, and be a rebel, don't get fucked-up, have tea instead.

Absinthe in front of us then consumed, the Londoners accosted us—trying to talk us out of our clothing. They wanted us to join other Londoners on the bar, dancing.

SEED AMSTERDAM RED LIGHT DISTRICT AFTER THE FACT TRAVEL TIP

Stay away from the *Red Light District* after midnight. It can become scary. Go figure, tourists fuelled-up on booze, porn, and illicit substances, which are illegal in their homelands, who'd-of-thunk: scary, could be an option.

AQUA MAN

DAY 9: 16 October 2003

The next morning, when I woke from my dreamless forty winks, David was deeply in REM. Not to disturb him, I decided to hit the gym. UP—DOWN—UP—DOWN—

Nine—ten—ripped—it was time to refresh in the pool. I can't swim. I can only tread water, violently. Bystanders usually feared for my safety; occasionally, tossing me a life jacket. Little did they know my swimming burns more calories than when swimmers swim?

Once in Jamaica while snorkelling a guide called out to me: *Come back to the boat 'mon'. 'Mon', do you have a family? No. Boi, do you want to have a family? Don't be such a Ras clot.*

He tossed me a life jacket.

I'm not afraid of water.

Let's go WAYBACK again. Our family was on vacation in Banff. The hotel pool was thirty feet in length, shaped like a football. I can't swim, but I love swimming, not the best pairing.

My parents watched from a balcony overlooking the pool. There was nary a lifeguard on duty. I swam showing off to my parents. I had trudged umpteen laps—painfully—before they noticed me.

With my parents' eyes upon me, I started again. LAP 1—LAP 2—LAP 3—I began to struggle—LAP 4, part way through the deep end my body shifted from horizontal to vertical. I sank. I'd hit bottom, eight feet. I was five foot two. I'd spring back to the surface; mouth agape, filling with chlorinated water. Each time I'd surface my arms flailed frantically, my parents were calmly waving back.

It took seven *bobs* before my brother Brian jumped to my rescue. I grabbed his head. I pushed him down. I climbed onto his shoulders kicking him in the face. I used him as leverage lunging myself out of the pool. I lay on the edge of the pool gasping, spitting water out of my mouth.

Brian saved my life.

I eventually expelled enough water to fill the shallow end. I looked at Brian, still gasping, and said: *Why did you get in my way? I was okay.*

I glanced up to Mum and Dad; they were still waving.

Taking the WAYBACK MACHINE seven years forward—I was at a High School Graduation after party in a friend's backyard. In seven years I managed to pack on a few pounds of muscle. I still couldn't swim.

Completely sober, I jumped into my friend's pool. I began swimming laps; my friends were the opposite of sober, completely. During LAP 4, I shifted to vertical. John Reynolds and Bill Wallace put down their beers and came to my rescue. I kicked them both in the head and lunged to safety.

When I regained my ability to breathe, I looked at them, and casually asked: *How does chlorinated beer taste?*

LAUNDRY DAY

Weather wise the summer of destruction was perfect. The fall of escape was following suit; brilliant sunshine greeted us once more. I shook Dave awake. It was time for a hearty Danish breakfast.

Dave needed to do laundry. If only he hadn't deigned* to accept my suggestion to pack more, he could have escaped this necessity.

Dave gently set is luggage in the chair beside him as we ordered breakfast at *Ristorante Tivoli*.

MONTREAL: BURGER KING. NYC: MAUI TACO. LONDON: CRAP. AMSTERDAM: ITALIAN.

Our stunning server delivered our feasts. I told Dave, I thought I was in love.

Dave suggested: I tell her.

We took Dave's laundry sightseeing. Amsterdam in the daytime on a crisp day is spectacular. We ventured down maze-like cobblestone streets. The architecture is fantastic. We crossed what seemed to be an infinite number of bridges. We snapped a photo at a sign emblazoned with: HOMO MONUMENT

Dave decided he wanted to live in Amsterdam. I told him to give it more time. He cursed his luggage. I snickered.

That-a-way was successfully suppressing the past. The canals waters represented pathways to endless possibilities.

The waterways allowed us to find a further escape.

With luggage dragged behind, Dave neared defeat.

I laughed because I could change three times per day and still not wear the same thing.

Before we made it back to the hotel we needed to find the train station to inquire how much it would be to travel to Munich. We were going to meet Greg there for Chinese food.

Two men walked toward us hand-in-hand.

Do you guys know where the train station is? I asked.

They paused, and then one of them replied: *It is back there one block.*

They turned around and began pointing. They hastily stopped. They called us *fuckers*. They walked away.

The train station was directly in front of us in plain view. It was also directly across the street from our hotel.

*The word deign in the past participle form was provided by JC at an After Party. An After Party is simply: A Party, after, A Party.

MISTER COCO'S

Dave opted for downtime.

I chose to solve our travel conundrum with movement.

The internet café basked in bright orange.

The EJ pilot behind the counter offered to help me turn my computer from Dutch to English.

He told me my voice was erotically charged and tantalising.

His gracious effort was futile.

I gave up on the information SUPER HIGHWAY, beaten—but not defeated. I believed the travel solutions would fall from the delicious night, sky.

MISTER COCO'S LOUSY FOOD AND WARM BEER: mostly the warm beer would certainly unlock the puzzle. Andrea, the lovely bartender, pitted beer against me with small talk.

She was from Montreal. She made a stop in Vancouver to get hitched. She came to Amsterdam to experience new. She *slagged* Vancouver and Amsterdam, calling them: marginal at best.

I gallantly defended home for one—two—three—four beers—shift to horizontal and—it was time for Dave to get up and meet Andrea!

BULLDOG

Did someone say bong?

When we exited *Mr Coco's*, thanks to Andrea, I floated at a forty-five-degree angle. It was time for a genuine, Amsterdam experience.

20 PACES FORWARD—CROSS A BRIDGE—90 DEGREES LEFT—12 STEPS FORWARD—8 UP—

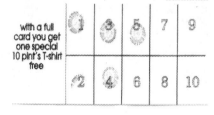

I was about to lose my bong virginity, Dave selected the hardware, along with pliable ingredients. I bought pints.

If I pounded ten, I'd win a Bulldog t-shirt.

Sounded doable, and not to mention, healthy.

Gurgle—gurgle—percolate—suck in.

I asked Dave if we had become *Crack-Heads*. The walls grew tentacles. I guzzled pint number one.

Gay Willie Nelson dropped by our table to say hello. He gave my camera the finger.

The bong gurgled and percolated more. I sucked in.

Pint four flew straight from the draught tap into my mouth.

A Dutch man was flying through the air. He told me Tiesto was the greatest DJ ever. I laughed uncontrollably. I don't know why. I then pressed my thumb and forefinger together trying to squish his head.

Another suck, and five beers short of winning a shirt, my night was done. The hamster driving the wheel in my brain was having trouble.

BACK STEP TO THE HOTEL—RETRACE THE ENTRY—INSERT KEY—FALL INTO DREAMLAND.

David, on the other hand, wasn't done.

16 STEPS FORWARD—2 STEPS UP INTO A BAR—EXIT—14 STEPS FORWARD—6-STEPS UP INTO ANOTHER BAR—EXIT—20 STEPS FORWARD—12 STEPS UP INTO—

DAVE'S NIGHT

—A WRINKLE IN TIME.

Clothing discarded, Dave immersed himself into a hot tub, greeted by a devastatingly beautiful blonde Dutch Goddess. Vibrant colours and scents tickled his senses. Red – blue - yellow and green flashed around him. Lavender and the sweet smell of exotic spices tantalised his sense of smell. He began to caress—she stroked his face with the soft blades of her hands. His arousal intensified. She ran her mouth gingerly across every inch of his body teasing him as she ever so gently brushed over—

They engaged in a seemingly endless kiss, their tongues melted together. David ran his tongue over her neck; it tasted like chocolate. They kissed again. When their lips parted—a donkey and albino midget whisked by—not before stroking Dave's now glistening body with their tongues. He kissed beauty again and again and again—this time the intensity of their arousal was greater. He pulled away. She was gone. In her place was a bearded man.

The bearded man *poked* David by suggesting David wanted his hot daughter.

Dave sat mystified.

The bearded man kept taunting. He dared David to kiss him, saying, if he did, she'd return.

David kissed.

The bearded man laughed.

Dave kissed again.

The bearded man said *one more time*.

David did.

Beauty remained absent.

Dave jumped out of the hot tub. He attempted to hide his arousal with his hand. Six steps from the tub he looked back, the bearded man was gone. Beauty had returned. She motioned for him to come back into her arms. He stepped forward and tripped. He fell violently to the ground—with his arousal about to smash into the asphalted floor—magically, a small (large) hole appeared in the pavement, his fathering future, saved. David lay on the ground, his face masked in puzzlement, sweat dripping from his brow. He felt a tongue from beneath the hole stroke his—*please let it be the donkey*, he thought.

A moment later, a second tongue joined the first; Dave gave in.

Dave—

AMSTERDAM – MUNICH: BLINK

DAY 10: 17 October 2003

—it's time to get up. You've been sleeping for six minutes.

It was time to move on to Munich. It was 9 AM. We still hadn't decided upon a mode of transportation.

David requested a *morning after pill*. I could see strands of a grey beard stuck to his chin.

Baked and half-laughing, I suggested renting a car.

We called *European Car Rentals*. I asked them if they had anything available for twenty-one days. David, I'm fucked—I mouthed. He *knew*.

I placed an order. I hung up.

Dave asked how the call went.

Was I just on the phone? I asked.

We bellied up to the *ERC* counter several hours later.

We need a CD player. I brought, a whack, of CDs, I said.

I tried to remember how to blink. Thankfully the bong hits erased the scent of booze, I thought. I screamed inside my head: **BLINK NOW!**

I asked Dave to *poke* me in my eyes.

He did.

I didn't blink; I punched him in the face for *poking* my eye(s).

I turned to my imagination. I imagined balls, rocks, and darts, flying toward my eyes.

I still didn't blink.

There was a sign behind the counter. My imagination told me to read it.

WE WILL NOT RENT CARS TO PEOPLE WHO CAN'T BLINK—ZERO EXCEPTIONS

I pleaded for Dave to do the talking.

Dave pulled out his credit card. He told the clerk I'd be the driver.

The clerk handed me the keys to a Citroen.

I asked if it had a CD player.

I brought a whack of CDs, I said.

I yelled inside my head for my outer voice to shut it and for my eyes to blink.

The clerk pulled our car to the front of the rental shop.

Great, a CD player! Did I tell you, I brought a whack of CDs?

The Citroen was a standard. I hadn't driven *stick* in years.

We pulled away from ERC. We glanced at each other. We smiled. They rented us a car.

Suddenly, I couldn't stop blinking.

Relearning how to drive *stick* in Europe, at speed, was going to be—

NAVIGATE

With our luggage securely stowed in the trunk, steering wheel in hand, it was time to hit the open road.

If we only knew where Munich was?

My shutter-less mind wasn't assisting one iota.

We asked a bellman at our hotel for directions.

He smiled. Then without speaking a single word, grabbed a piece of paper, and wrote (look right→→→):

He handed me the paper. He then pointed at each word. Finally, he stopped on Munich. He looked up at me and smiled.

Dave asked me if we could stop somewhere to do laundry.

I blinked: NO.

AUTOBAHN

Van Gogh and Anne Frank stood arm-in-arm sipping *Orange Whips* as they guided us out of Amsterdam.

At least I thought it was Vincent and Anne. When I reflect back: it could've as easily been two anglers and a seasick dog.

I found several lost pieces of me in Amsterdam. Escape clutched me—while I was in its grasp it reminded me the most tragic thing in life is quitting.

Experimentation in moderation adds spice—excess must never replace compassion—*Mister Coco's* beers don't count toward a Bulldog t-shirt—And, Europe, is different—and refreshing.

The highway was waiting.

Most countries in Europe suggest a speed for travel on the highway. Most drivers ignore the recommended speed and travel at their own pace.

Gridlock greeted us for the first two hours. We stopped for petrol and snacks. Dave bought a map. I showed a man at the pumps our note. He extended his arm and pointed ninety degrees to the left.

Back on the highway, the gridlock eased.

Amsterdam to Munich is slightly more than eight hundred kilometres. In America, around nine hours if you push the posted speed limit of one hundred kilometres per hour.

On the German Autobahn I cranked the Citroen *to two-hundred-fifteen-fear-stroking-kilometers-per-hour*. I had only driven that speed once before. On this day my emotional crap was escaping my body. I refused to slow down.

I believed the Autobahn was going to be a super speedway with banked corners. I was wrong. It was no different than highways back home. With a few exceptions:

LANE 1: Transport trucks travelling around one hundred.

LANE 2: (the slow lane) Cars and trucks cruising between one sixty and one eighty.

LANE 3: two hundred+++ which was where we belonged—

—of course it was. I was sleep deprived and still altered. I floored it to the point where the pedal couldn't go further. I clamped the steering wheel tightly. My knuckles turned white. Sweat formed on my forehead only to be instantly cooled by terror. My soundtrack was our only salvation. David Usher was leading us down the highway in song.

Cause this is my way out of it tonight. This is my last chance to ease the fire, and this is my way out of here tonight; how about you, how about you? Far off from a dream, that I used to know. All my friends are there to watch the world unfurl.

There was a bearded man rolled into a ball in the back seat.

I couldn't slow. Porsches, Audis, Volkswagens, and Mercedes, would blast up on our French ass. They'd flash their lights. I was forced to merge into LANE 2 without stumbling to death in LANE 1. Once passed, I'd whip back into LANE 3; relax, check the mirror; only to be flashed once more. I'd merge into the middle fracas once more.

Toll booths sprouted upon us out of nowhere. I'd drop from speed in a flash. After assimilating to the frantic pace stopping proved to be a significant challenge. I'd panic when we'd drop below fifty.

Released from zero, I cranked up the pace again, re-entering the race.

Standing at the edge, the edge of it all, standing at the edge, the edge of it all. Cause this is my way out of it tonight. And this is my last chance to ease the fire—

David's fear rendered him on the verge of desperation. His fraying nerves were leading us to peril, to the edge of it all, to our way out of here. He was gripping the handle above his head so firmly his knuckles were melting into his palm. My fear fed off his fear. Doom was pending.

I asked him what he was doing.

On the verge of tears Dave confessed his *fear* to me.

I told him I understood. I stressed his fear was making me nervous. I said to him while feigning confidence; today we were going to die in a horrific high-speed crash. It was going to be quick and painless, so there was no need for worry. I strongly emphasised if he didn't relax the chances of death were going to increase dramatically. I told him to recline his car seat; listen to the music, and fake sleep.

The music stopped. The car shouted at us in hard German.

VORSICHT AUF DER A9 RICHTUNG MÜNCHEN ZWISCHEN DREIECK HOLLEDAU UND KREUZ NEUFAHRN 10 KM STAU!!! FAHREN SIE VORSICHTIG

Dave freaked out.

I freaked out, a tad bit less.

The bearded man was still sleeping.

The music returned.

Took another pill to find my way, I hope that you'll be there. Cause this is my way—

Exasperated, David calmly pulled his harmonica and a revolver out of his bag. He mirrored a few notes of the song, raised the gun to his head, and pulled the trigger: **BANG.** His body slumped then fell into his seat. Blood spattered against the window drawing legs against the fast-passing German backsplash. He lay limp—his knuckled palm a permanent reminder of the terror that befell him. He looked peaceful. Bloody, but peaceful.

My grip loosened as I continued toward Munich, super-charged sedans were flying by, much like the shooting stars above.

Munich was nearing and—

NEWS **BAR**

—David opened his eyes. The revolver was an illusion. He only suffered a flesh wound created by fear. He navigated our way to Munich's centre.

We sipped on German gold and phoned Greg. I excused myself for a washroom break, when I returned my brilliant friend and brother at heart, greeted me. A smile graced his face. Dave stood behind him to the right, smiling radiantly. Our reunion cooled Dave's fear.

Greg's arms were wide open.

WELCOME BROTHER!

16

REBIRTH

re·birth noun Definition: the action of reappearing or starting to flourish or increase after a decline; revival.

A meta-memoir

CHOCOLATE LABRADOR

DATELINE: 21 October 2003 – Munich, Germany

Munich's *Vanilla Lounge* is chic. It fills nightly with beautiful young people, with their dogs in tow. Dogs in tow, foreign to most North Americans, in Europe, it brings civility.

The *Vanilla Lounge* is how would one say; Vanilla. Its lines are crisp, with a cleansed white décor. The servers are beautiful. The ambience is alluring.

The canine entourages add perspective. They are a constant reminder of responsibility. They comfort the spirit and soothe the soul.

Our last night in the care of Greg and Silvia, Greg's girlfriend, had arrived.

Dave and I had spent four days with them in Munich. We took a day trip to Salzburg Austria. Our time together was a wonderful break from my new realities, a time to regroup, to feel loved.

3:45 PM

Greg and Dave sat with me along the sidewall facing the bar. Two hours prior Wayne called. The GREAT REVEAL was upon me. I was going to find the identities of my birth parents. An incredible number of my life pieces were about to be shattered with, a greater number to be found, with one phone call.

I was emotionally fucked up.

Wayne tried to reach me the night before.

Seed, I picked up your mail. There's an official document from Alberta Vital Stats. Call me.

Three beautiful girls entered the lounge. They sat in a cushioned section to our left. Four tables separated us. A Chocolate Labrador settled at the base of their table. It drifted into doggie dreamland.

A chain of men approached the women. They'd attempt small talk. They'd crouch down to pet the Lab. Each one would turn and walk away, shot down. The Lab never opened his eyes or lifted its head.

I ordered a Melon Martini and asked our server the time.

My nerves were frazzled.

4 PM - 7 AM VANCOUVER TIME

It was time to phone Wayne. Avoidance was no longer part of the menu.

The previous hour, I tried to deflect my feelings, pondering if my father could be Mick Jagger, Richard Branson, a clown—

Greg called me a fool. He said for Branson to be my father he'd have been 11 when I was born.

Fiona answered my call. She said Wayne was walking the dog. She'd have him call when he came back.

I pondered more. I hoped my mother was going to be a 16-year-old girl. I wanted to move on, unknowing.

Tears began cascading from my eyes. My life was about to change—be ripped apart.

As the tears flowed, I intuitively knew the mystery I hoped for was not going to become my reality. It couldn't be. If it were, there would have been no reason for the decades of lying by my family. I came to the forgone conclusion I was going to become privy to a dark family secret. And, I was the main character.

I couldn't stop crying.

Ring - Ring - Ring

Greg answered. He told Wayne, I seemed okay. He said they'd take care of me.

The tears were blasting from my eyes. I began to whimper. I was shaking. The world around me disappeared. I can't describe what it feels like to sit waiting to hear the truth about your life. A fact withheld from me for 40+ years.

There are no words that can depict what it is like to watch your parents succumb to *THE BIG C,* only to find out they weren't your actual parents.

Why did they fucking lie for all of these years?

I was drowning in my misery, crushed by anxiety and uncertainty.

I looked at Dave; his face was flush, he too was crying.

Greg passed me the phone. I told Wayne, I was okay, *sort of*—my tear-stained voice cracked.

Wayne read my father's name. He said Kirk Bliner—a mechanic from Picture Butte Alberta. He said he wasn't sure because it was scratched out.

I felt momentary relief.

Your mother's name—

Before he could spit out her name, *Bernice* rushed into my mind. My heart stopped. Anybody but her, I thought. My tears escalated to critical. I dropped the phone onto my lap.

Greg reached over and grabbed it from me. He was crying. He softly told Wayne they would take care of me.

Dave hugged me. I continued to weep freely.

Greg assured the staff of the *Vanilla Lounge* I would be okay.

I cupped my hands over my face. I peered from the corner of my right eye. The Chocolate Lab lifted his head slowly. He leisurely rose and then sauntered across the packed lounge toward me.

I uncupped my hands—the Labrador was directly in front of me, I looked through my blurry eyes at him. He tilted his head, forlornly glared at me, and then with the utmost of tenderness, licked my face and sat down in front of me.

On this day, he took care of me. I wasn't sure who was going to take care of me, every tomorrow, after that?

BIRTH

FLASHBACK: 16 July 1960

A historical (speculative) account of the birth of Lindsay Wincherauk

The sun shone brightly on the Alberta prairie on this beautiful July day. However, something wasn't quite right in the Wincherauk home.

Nicholas whispered to Rebekah no one could ever know the truth.

Rebekah's eyes filled with tears. She cried out to Nicholas: *It's not fair. Life is not fair. Who will care for the child?*

There was to be no celebration. Rebekah knew what they were doing was wrong.

The pregnancy was kept secret for ten months; when Bernice began to show, seclusion became her new home, away from the judgement of others. She didn't want the child; however, there were no alternatives. Abortion was an unthinkable sin.

Questions circled the Wincherauk household like vultures about who the birth father might be?

Bernice wasn't sure herself. Or perhaps, she was so distraught by the identity; she was blanking it out.

With absolute certainty, Bernice was rebelling. She was a first born daughter. Shamefully, during these times, first born sons were revered.

She wanted her father to pay for his lack of love. She was 23. She should've known better. Getting pregnant wasn't payback. In reality, it shone an intensely bright light on the fact she would never be good enough.

Her pain became more excruciating when James was born, the fourth child, a boy, finally.

Nicholas loved his daughters. He just didn't know how to express it. His exuberance at the birth of James painted pain onto the faces of, Bernice, Sadie, and Beverly. The exuberance ate away their esteem. Rebekah tried gallantly to hold them together.

By birthing a child, Bernice was highlighting her failure in the eyes of her father. Bernice's soul wept—the baby's destiny—transferred to Nick.

Rebekah's responsibility was to hold the family together. The secrecy rendered her broken.

She wanted to rejoice; instead, she participated in the lie.

This day resembled a funeral. It wasn't the start of a brilliant life. It was the end of a family.

From this day forward we will tell no one. I will figure out what we are going to do with the baby. Once I do, we will never speak another word, EVER. Bernice has shamed us. I won't allow it to fester. Nicholas said with sternness, his voice cracking.

The doctor informed him a baby boy had been born. He was sombre. Darkness engulfed this bright July day.

Complications may have been a blessing.

Mere minutes after giving birth, the baby was ripped from Bernice's opened arms and whisked to another room. Giving birth did not bring with it validation.

For the child, the decisions made that day were going to create unexplainable vagueness in his life. It was going to instil a feeling of never belonging.

The baby rested in a room with three other newborns. No eyes looked in on them. The nightmare of birth was just beginning.

From this brilliant July day forward, everyone in the family agreed to participate in a lifelong lie. They were to divorce themselves from reality. Ultimately, the lie was going to impact only one person, the baby boy.

Life for him was starting behind the largest obstacles possible.

For those participating in the lie, they choose to give up their souls that day.

As for the baby—

TURN

WAYBACK: 4 August 1963 – Location Unknown – Western Canada

I vaguely remember our first family meeting; I was zero, actually, two weeks old, fifty weeks shy of one. We met in an open field. The prairie sun was blazing down upon us. Brian and Don may have been too young to understand what was transpiring.

The rest of our clan knew what was going down. Between a tractor and a baler my blanket lay. The family huddled a few feet away. Dad cranked the engine of a tractor to drown out their words, keeping our family secret from the ears of the nosey neighbours a section away. Storm clouds were forming to the east.

Rex, our family dog; a German Sheppard, guarded me.

I cried for someone to take care of me, protect me; to feed me. My cries fell on deaf ears.

Rex looked hungry.

The huddle broke. My family dispersed. The only words I made out were—*then it's settled, you'll care for the child.*

You'll take care—what a fucking lie.

The clouds became ominous. Darkness fell. I shook in fear, the tractor's engine clamouring, drowned out my squeals.

I couldn't fall asleep. In the morning, I was encircled by beavers. The tractors hum lowered. It started to spit, eventually, sputtering out.

The Beavers, Nelly & Millie, along with their two rambunctious boys: Todd and Rafe, and their daughter, Sue; adopted me. They transported me to their den by the river. They taught me how to crawl. They taught me how to swim. They taught me how to fend for myself.

My family remained absent.

I longed for them to return to me. Nelly & Millie knew that day was never coming. My human family failed.

They left me solo to figure out life.

At six months of age it became apparent that I wasn't a beaver, I lacked an overbite. It was time to press on. I crawled down from my twig bed and left the family nest. As I swam away from my first family home—my adopted family banged their beaver tails loudly.

Strangely, swimming never stuck with me.

I do recall at a much later date my mother and father telling me I used to be able to swim with the fishes.

It was time to find my flesh family.

Although some of these details are a tad vague, this is my closest recollection of the first six months of life. All these years later, 46+—nobody has refuted this picture of reality.

FACT OR FICTION: I'm not sure, the one thing I'm dead certain of—the humans failed. They forgot to come back, despite never truly leaving.

VENICE - FLORENCE

DAY 15: 22 October 2003

BYE BYE—

One—two—three—one hundred—you better look out 'cause here I come.

I hope my hiding place is good enough. Escaping reality provided a pleasant break. This place looks great; they'll never find me in here.

They did.

My reality burst to the forefront. I liked the escape better.

We were less than one hour away from my tearful goodbyes with Greg and Silvia. In that precise moment, I realised: I was the furthest I'd ever been from home. Home no longer existed. There was no place left for me to escape to—blood ties became diluted. With each click of the odometer and every beat of my heart, home became a distant blur.

Biff, Seed looks finished, defeated, his eyes seem vacant.

Driving away from Greg made me realise how lonely, I ~~was~~ am. My once endless string of friends was snipped, with actual friends now coming in at single digits. I had yet to process the previous day. I was only *one day* old.

Greg, Silvia, Wayne, Fiona and Dave provided hope where a family once was.

Without them in my life—well—I don't want to go there. With them, I have a chance.

I know, *Drama Police*, a tad dramatic, but c'mon, my fucking parents came back to life, and one of them hung around in the background assuming a different role—AND—she did a horrific job at it. Maybe it has been a phenomenal award winning performance.

Accepting the award for neglectful and harsh parenting—

With the Citroen cranked over *two hundred kilometres per hour* my hands no longer clasped the steering wheel. I was steering with only one finger. This upset Dave. His voice quivered.

I assured him one finger meant, comfortable.

He whined: *Seed; we're going two hundred.*

On July 19, 2003; after four months of relentless trauma, survival or destruction, became my challenge, I desperately needed a reboot.

Everything with meaning crashed. With each crash, my direction would change, and before I could attach significance to the trauma, another trauma would pay me a visit. The news about my parents paralysed me.

My father was a mystery—my mother—

Could you find somewhere else to stay? We need your room and the house, for the relatives—Lindsay who..?

One might think she would've overcompensated for giving me away; she didn't.

Fifteen days into our trip, for all intent and purpose, with the intensity cranked up, it was over for me.

I wanted to fucking die.

Maybe that's why Dave wasn't fond of my driving style.

I did owe it to him to try to keep it together. I just wasn't sure how?

Silence, alcohol, drugs, sex, all viable..?

Perhaps a combination: a quiet yet aggressive blowjob, performed by a vivacious blonde flight attendant, while I popped ecstasy like they were Gummy Bears, washing them down with swigs of Jack Daniels as a school bus full of *Catholic School Girls* wearing tartan skirts drove by. With the car hitting speeds of *two hundred fifty kilometres per hour*; did I mention: I was driving a convertible?

No.

Okay, I was driving a convertible—with the top down. Finally, as I came in the FA's mouth, a devious grin took over my face. I looked over at the bus, *Slow down, driver, haven't you seen high-speed fellatio before?*

The school girls were pressing their faces against the bus windows. When my friend raised her head from my lap, *cum* dripping from the corner of her mouth, I smirked with the devious grin still adorning my face—and waved. All the while, Dave sat silently, in the back seat

Reality: sort of, Monique did work for Air Canada.

I searched the skies for positives. I convinced myself the news couldn't have come at a better time. I became a liar to myself. Being part of a loving, caring family—would've been better.

I convinced myself travelling at excessive speeds through Europe while sleep deprived: was for the best.

I convinced myself if I found out back at home, the clock would have been ticking—

Both your parents came back to life, and they didn't want you? If that happened to me—I'd get over it in four days.

My thoughts raced back and fro between:

Wow, look at that castle.

(AND)

How could they do this to me? Dave, the mountains are amazing, watch how the villages blend into the countryside. History certainly lives here. If she didn't want me, why did she have me, bitch? Wow, lake, castle, villa, village, mountains—

Do I let them know, I know?

I was *infinitely* conflicted. This continuous loop kept tormenting me. Fortunately, I brought a whack of CDs to help alleviate the pain.

As the breathtaking beauty of the Austrian/Italian Alps, *very similar to Bellingham*, roared by, screaming out the realities of the past, my spirits bottomed out. In an instant, I understood: I may never be okay.

We passed castles. We drove through a never-ending string of villages. We climbed toward the heavens only to be greeted by an early fall blizzard. At the crest of the ascent, the mountains folded into long sweeping corners showcasing incredible vistas reaching out to the valleys below, only to climb back toward heaven again, soothing my soul. Europe, likely, saved my life.

Venice was only minutes away. As the sun set in the sky, Venice came alive. Pillowy-soft-clouds hung low in the night air, tempting us to reach up and grab them. The clouds danced in harmony. Their colours vibrant: a soft inviting white covered their edges blending into a soothing dusty rose, eventually, seducing us with vibrant intoxicating strawberry pink.

Venice was welcoming us—offering solace, providing a place to let my heartache drift away.

PARKING

If you're not part of the future—then get out of the way.

I placed my worries on hiatus. John Cougar sang our way into Venice.

I suggested we drive close to the hotels and find a home for the night.

Dave laughed *howlingly* at me.

I promptly parked the car at the bottom of a canal with Dave locked inside.

Once safely parked at the top of Venice's massive parking complex we crossed several bridges looking for a hotel. When we hit 75€ for the night; we took it.

It was time to retrieve the luggage. I hoped mine, read the *Jenny Craig Pamphlet*; I placed inside it.

VENICE AT NIGHT

Crossing the canals, we saw a collection of cafés inviting us for a taste of Italy. Lights from the cafés and parked boats beamed into the galaxies in a kaleidoscope of colours all dancing a slow seductive Venetian waltz.

In this land which is of 98% Catholic descent, we had *Hail Marys* on the tip of our tongues. We were ready to repent. Before repenting, I had to drag my bulging bags over water-soaked maze-like streets to our home for the night: the *Hotel Tivoli*.

Mr Cougar may be right. Venice may still be on her feet; however, she's obviously been dying for decades. The lagoon that has been her natural protection from invaders for centuries was now ironically beginning to swallow its mystically historic buildings, inflicting permanent damage; issuing tickets of disrepair.

It's pending demise for an instant helped me forget about the living death of my family. Like its twinkling night lights, I found my spirits starting to reach for the galaxies. Except for my excessively-obese luggage—for this evening, I was going to be okay. Venice is after all: the Divine Republic, and even with its pending doom, its beauty shines through. There truly is no place like it on earth. A collage of *one-hundred-sixteen-canals* dissected by *four-hundred-nine-bridges*, as grandiose buildings rise on each side transporting us back through the centuries.

As we casually sauntered to the hotel, my cares drifted through the sweet mist of the early evening air. I think it would be apropos to share astute words on Venice from one of its most famous patrons, Henry James:

Dear old Venice has lost her complexion, her figure, her reputation, her self-respect; and yet, with it all, has so puzzlingly not lost a shred of her distinction.

CURFEW

It was time to eat, drink, and find: a quiet relaxing speed reduced—

The desk clerk informed us we must be back to the hotel by 11 PM, or we'd be locked out. It was 6:30.

Rudimentary math meant we'd have a little more than four hours to eat, drink; and find—

75€ translated into a strict curfew?

We pushed forward, eating, drinking, and getting lost, in the maze that is Venice. I dropped Dave back at the hotel for downtime at 8 PM. I then headed out to unwind on wine and Italian beer. I found a smashing pub. I retrieved Dave at 10 PM.

We settled into a smashing pub full of young, saucy, hot exchange students. Curfew was upon us, just as we were heading into a speed reduced zone. I rushed back to the hotel. Curfew extended— at midnight, extended to 1 AM— at 1 AM it was—

Ah, that feels nice. Much better don't you think? There are no school buses in Venice; they're called school boats, and another thing, the tops are always—

ATKINS DIET

DAY 16: 23 October 2003

Morning sprang upon us with a sweet dewy mist decorating the air. We hit Venice's charming streets searching for sushi.

After clicking through an extensive list of criteria, we finally picked a restaurant because a girl in the window had hair similar to Corrie's.

We ate Italian!

The pasta melted in my mouth. Corrie's hair led us to a phantasmagorical dining experience.

At the table next to us sat a gathering of Americans. A lady similar to the one on the bus flagged down the server. Her fingernails scratched the chalkboard. She squealed that she was on the *Atkins Diet*. Her nails slashed more.

From behind the bookcase façade, Don Vito Corleone appeared; riddling granny with round-after-round of smoking-hot-lead. Once finished he reloaded, firing ten more rounds into her slumping body. Upon completion, he took a plate of rigatoni and, stuffed it down her throat.

Don't worry—she tripped, right?

Post lunch, we explored. Gondolas sat canal side, painted brilliant sky blue and vibrant candy apple red.

I told Dave, I loved him.

He refused to go on a boat ride with me.

Venice began weeping. I believed it was weeping for me.

Venice is one of the most remarkable places I've been. Venice is photogenic. It never takes a bad picture.

Dave wanted ice cream. I snapped a photo as he lapped it up. The photo captured him as a five-year-old boy on his first day of school, his mother at his side. She comforted him with gelato. With his first lick, David's face was covered by a grin from ear-to-ear.

It was time to say farewell. It was time to visit the birthplace of the Renaissance. I owed it to myself to find a way to enjoy what was next. My past needed to be my past, nothing more.

We were about to wind our way across mountain roads and penetrate long dark tunnels. I was about to discover, self.

With the speedometer hitting two hundred, the slow death of Venice lingered in the rear view mirror.

I don't want Venice to die— deep down I know— it won't.

DRIVING IN ITALY

Venice to Florence is two hundred sixty kilometres, in North American driving time: approximately three hours. In Europe: Eight-glances in the rear view mirror, one CD, Dave wetting himself, a stop for Panini, gas; and a leak— then, gridlock.

In North America, we are over freewayed. Motorists whisk from city-to-city bypassing undesirable areas by avoiding off-ramps. Shiny glass towers riddle city centres devoid of historical significance, at least not yet. They're products of progress— whereas, in Europe, every building seems historical.

One CD from Venice to Florence, two CDs while sitting parked on the highway on the city's edge, what's better: freeways or history?

Imagine little Timmy waking up in Rome. He looks at his father. He tells him he wants to create something amazing.

His father tells Timmy, *we already have the Coliseum.*

Back home, I get to be part of the history-making process.

While we sat parked on the highway, I decided to jot down a brief overview of Florence (Firenze).

It's known as the cradle of the Renaissance.

Florence's museums showcase over 30% of the world's famous artworks.

Its historical significance brings both rapture and frustration as people flock to glance at the masterpieces.

We'd soon discover the historical significance is the reason for the gridlock.

We asked David Usher to save us.

Standing at the edge, the edge of it all, standing at the edge, the edge of it all. Cause this is my way out of it tonight. This is my last chance to ease the fire—

Being stuck in traffic— licked— FINALLY— it began to flow. David navigated our way into the city. I'm blind in my oncoming traffic eye. Traffic started to on-come.

Four lanes suddenly turned into what seemed to be a gazillion. Cars zoomed by us from all sides; including from underneath our car. Speed was whatever was deemed okay. I closed my eyes. I opened my eyes. Dave was holding a revolver to his temple.

Suddenly, the horror intensified when we approached a roundabout. Every resident of Italy converged upon it at the same time. ~~Two~~ A gazillion lanes turned into lanes to the infinity. Cars, busses, trucks, salivating albino midgets & donkeys, a guy named Luigi, Pavarotti (he took up five lanes), scooters, *fucking scooters*; and several Hearses to pick up the carnage of tourists, filled them.

I turned my head, positioning my functioning patch-free eye in the centre of the windshield. It didn't help. I glanced at Dave; he was knitting a sweater. Three bikes passed through the cars back seat waking the bearded man. Roundabout navigated, we turned down the first calmed street; parked, and lay on the sidewalk, shaking; unscathed, the car that is.

I looked at David; he was shaking. I told him we couldn't go to Rome because there'd be too many Italian drivers there.

We decided to look for a hotel—a good thing, because Dave needed a nap.

Dave continued shaking. He asked me to hold him. I told him to hold himself.

We began to move. We found a row of hotels. The fourth one fit our budget. It was named the *Hotel Golf*. The room keys had a golf ball attached to them. They bounced.

Once checked in, I told Dave: he could let himself go.

I went to collect the car. We had parked eighty yards from the hotel.

Back in the room, Dave lay down. I, on the other hand, went searching for beer!

CATHEDRAL

Instead of finding beer, I stumbled upon *Brunelleschi's Cathedral Dome. I was in awe.* We had visited amazing houses of worship in NYC, Amsterdam, and Munich. Places meant to provide hope and solace. Each house of the Lord was beautiful with intricate details and an infinite number of hours of painstaking work by devoted artisans and masons seeking perfection. Firenze's Cathedral is unparalleled in depth, effort, and passion.

I questioned the idea of whether God needs palaces built in his honour for people to worship him.

I was conflicted, my emotions taxed to the max, my spirituality in question.

THINKING INSIDE THIS BOX: A SEED INTERPRETATION OF SPIRITUALITY

What is our purpose in life? What is God's message? Does God even exist?

About thirty people stood in front of the Cathedral snapping photo-after-photo as if they were gaining a deeper understanding of faith—this frustrated me.

God wouldn't have hired the artists and contractors to build his houses of worship, would he? God's message is kindness, love, and unity, isn't it?

Brunelleschi's Cathedral marked changing times: self-sufficiency, civic virtue, intelligence, and faith in man's abilities were replacing chivalry and nobility.

Do we need Palaces to worship?

I marvelled at the beauty and became lost in the opulence, my mind raced.

We're failing each other at alarming rates. Aren't we supposed to share the love, coming to the same definition of what's paramount in life—**KINDNESS?**

As I strolled away from the Cathedral I realised, I had been to a brilliant place. My religious ignorance—maybe my spiritual awakening, caused me to continue to question the course of man.

Surely, if God exists, opulence wouldn't be part of his message. Isn't excessive wealth, and weren't the magnificent houses of the Lord, built by the wealthy to control the commoners? Weren't the egos of nobility, placing riches above God's, if God exists—message?

For me, the message is simple: We don't need the houses of the Lord to find it. We just need to dig deep into our souls. I believe if you can come to a point in life where you accept we are all together, you might find the message:

BE KIND. Treat family like gold. Embrace friendship. Don't envy celebrity. Wealth can't be the sole goal of living. And, attempt to live by these simple rules. Bookended between: **BE KIND.**

I feel the Lord's Message has been lost in the ego of man and by the presence of greed.

I collected a few pieces of me in this historic place. More important: I accepted I might be walking down the right path.

If that makes me different—so be it.

FLORENCE - MONACO – MONTE CARLO - NICE

DAYS 17-20: 24-27 October 2003

CATHEDRAL FACE

In the morning, I retraced my steps, taking David to the Cathedral. The day was crisp, bright—beautiful.

The look on Dave's face when we rounded the last corner was a combination of DANCING FACE and ORGASM FACE, making CATHEDRAL FACE: unique in a sense.

Experts say your facial expression in these life-affirming moments will follow you for the rest of your life. Therefore, FACE, thoughtfully.

Dave's was a combination of a Macaulay Culkin's after-shave face from *Home Alone,* meets, constipation.
Dave, do you need a toilet?

After the Cathedral we visited the *Plazza Signoria* a virtual outdoor museum displaying some of the world's most significant works of art, all copies.

David struck a pose: *vogue, vogue,* in front of his namesake. I digitalized feverishly attempting to capture the similarities in character.

With everything behind me on a catastrophic collision course with everything ahead—life was playing a game of chicken. Every aspect of life was hitting warp speed. An explosive head on collision was an absolute certainty, rendering my future questionable at best.

That brings us back to David: somehow, he became the trips foundation.

Just as my worlds were about to collide and rip life into thousands of shredded pieces, he managed to flip a switch averting catastrophe, saving me from starting again at SQUARE ONE. His presence kept me from vanishing into myself.

My trip became his journey. He acted as my guardian. He assumed the role with dignity.

That concludes this instalment of *Dave's Love In.*
Dave, seriously dude, let's find you a toilet.

SHIRTS & BOOTS

We learned. We gorged on food and drink.
The houses of the Lord humbled us.
We bathed in the tap water of the Hotel Golf.

There was only one thing missing from our Florentine experience?

Mad passionate love making sessions with a gathering of intoxicating olive-skinned beauties as they took turns feeding you grapes, catering to your innermost desires, in a manner rivalling Caligula. Leaving both of your Herculean bodies exhausted and pleasurably spent?

That certainly would've been pleasant, but, no.

One rack kept drawing me back. The fabric across the midsection was silky smooth, tapering delicately in the rear. One shirt in a collection of hundreds pulled me in.

My fashion sense is keen. At least I think it is. I believe shirts are where personality lives. I have a collection of beautiful shirts, most of which were lying untouched in my gluttonous luggage.

This shirt was perfecto. I couldn't pass by—blue with a hint of shine, grey, patterned across the chest, breaking seductively toward the abdomen, sparks of light emanated from the torso, a one-of-a-kind. Personality exploded from its fabric, a work of art, worthy of display.

My traumatised body had become perfect for display.

I read the label. It was handmade by an Italian shirt maker from Tuscany. He used only the finest sun-drenched fabrics. His life purpose was to create a perfect garment. After he had created this one, he was retired to stud.

I exuded excitement when I asked Dave's opinion.

He flicked drool from the corner of his mouth while telling me it may be too much for me to pull off. He paused. When he continued, he said: *It may be too, you know, gay.*

A montage of Italian love songs played when I emerged from the change room. I asked Dave if he thought it hung beautifully on my taught body. He was still drooling.

The store's clerk suggested: I looked sizzling.

Dave channelled the clerk's lust by agreeing that I looked hot, maybe even: exquisite.

Seed, these boots, they're amazing. What do you think?

Dave slipped them on. Succulent Italian leather, bold red, black striped down the side, moulded to Dave's accepting feet.

Shirt & Boots set on the counter, it was decision time. I compared us to works of art.

I said we must buy.

How much? I asked the clerk

How much do you have? —Was his reply.

I SAID A LOT + A LOT MORE.

He calmly said: *perfect; the shirt costs a wee bit more than a lot.*

It was Dave's turn.

The clerk added several pluses.

As we walked out of the store, I commented on how lovely the store's bags were, adding *"eh"* to make it feel more Canadian—suffering a dose of buyer's remorse, I attempted to average out the amount of *a lot.* I purchased cologne and a shirt emblazoned with CLINK LONDON across the chest.

A lot x 3 STILL =

As we cat-walked back to the hotel, Dave began to float through the air, opening his deliciously coloured wings. He became a Papillion flying high in the artful Italian sky. I strutted alongside, fantasising about what kind of action my one-of-a-kind creation was going to bring my way in France?

TUNNELS

Florence to Monaco—tunnels every few kilometres, some exhilarating and curved, others straight and seemingly endless.

The music pulsed, beating down upon us, fuelling our emotions. Like a delicate opera, it weaved tales, built characters, created flow, inserted love, intensified, until it reached a crescendo of the perfectly choreographed beat. We drove on as excitement sparked in our veins as fast-charging bass lines swallowed our souls, only to break at tunnels end. The first beat of the next symphony would drop as the darkness of the tunnels turned to light once more.

The timing of the symphony was impeccable. It provided unforgettable memories. The clouds throbbed to the thump of the drums. As Italy turned into France, we were repeatedly elevated then returned to the sea for moments of tranquility during this six hundred kilometre stretch.

Sara McLachlan, Delirium, Dido, New Order, Sinatra, Sinead O'Conner, The Flaming Lips, Hybrid, continuously raised our spirits layering them toward the sky then dropping us quickly back to reality, allowing us to gasp for air. It was as if a Conductor was orchestrating our journey.

There could not have been a better manipulation of our auditory senses.

—it don't matter; it could be I was white or blacker. The fact in the matter: I drop some hip-hop—and progressed some message. the efforts don't stop—

The groove allowed our cares to drift away. We were left to simply enjoy the chills being brought our way by an Army of Sound.

The Gods of Song were shining brightly on this glorious day. I was ecstatic because: I had brought a whack of CDS!

MONA*CO* & MONTE CARLO

SMASH

I slammed into a wall in a Monaco parking garage, jarring Dave from his slumber. Dave bitched at me. He said *fuck* and threw his hands in the air in disgust. He questioned how I could drive fine at breakneck speeds, but between zero and one, I couldn't handle it.

I said *fuck*, loudly—I suggested: we eat.

I imagined a news report highlighting my ineptitude for driving at low speeds. Eyewitness accounts estimated my speed was topping out at less than *one kilometre per hour* when I nudged a bus bench.

Gloria, waiting for the bus, was the lone victim of my inability to drive.

I saw the car coming from a block away. I was reading my novel. I figured I could finish a chapter. Three pages into the next chapter I looked up. It was too late. He bumped into me. I said, ouch.

Monaco reeks of wealth. It is an old municipality steeped in a vibrant, colourful history. It is a proud Monarchy. It stands only *one square kilometr*e in area.

While we wandered past Monaco's opulence, we could almost hear *Robin Leach's* voice filling the air, something about champagne and caviar.

CARNIVAL

It was time for Carnival: MONTE CARLO STYLE!

NORTH AMERICAN STYLE: Shoot water pistol into a hole, racing your car to victory, WIN: A stuffed animal. WIN several times trade up for a larger stuffed animal.

MONTE CARLO STYLE: WIN ONCE: A DVD player. WIN several times trade up for a home stereo—eventually— I have pictures to prove it.

NICE HOTEL

Downtime for David became critical. I wanted to continue to escape.

I became a selfish DINK.

I'm trying to resurrect the use of the word dink.

We parked five kilometres from the heart of Nice. We searched for an internet café. The stop annoyed us. We glared at each other as we passed hotel-after-hotel, followed shortly after that, by passing restaurant-after-restaurant.

Our friendship was coming to a head. Our fuses were burning short. We sat down to eat. I sipped my beer and bitched.

It took a fucking hour to find food. What's wrong with you? All you want to do is fucking lay down. Fuck, Dave, we need to keep going. I don't want to waste the rest of this trip. I want to go home. I'm fucked up. I don't even know what home is anymore?

Tears fell from my chin.

Dave tried to calm me. He said, *fuck,* again. He told me to stop torturing myself. He said, we stop—we go. We hit a city—we leave. He asked me to let him take a minute to breathe. He asked me to relax. He said he hoped one day—I'd be okay.

Another tear dropped from my chin.

230

One hour later we found a hotel. I went to retrieve the car. We parked approximately seventy paces from our new home.

In Old Nice the first bar we hit was far too American—and beer was 9€.

Come to think of it, beer in Europe was always between 7€ and 9€.

Half a block later we entered *Le Club 6.*

Inside, every eye focused on us and on our $3000 worth of smashing fashion. I practised my French by saying *poutine*. The bartenders laughed.

Beautiful people surrounded us. Drinks in hand we climbed to the club's loft. A couple sitting on a couch to our right—were fucking.

We climbed down from the loft.

Then, we met Steph and Arno.

My story has come full circle.

We ventured to another club with them. Steph and Arno were visiting from Marseille. They used to be a couple. They spoke little English. I can say *poutine*.

I found an instant connection with Steph.

We danced.

We kissed.

The music gripped us.

With each song the passion intensified.

As we danced our tongues probed each other's mouths, embracing each other tightly; for a moment, I felt safe. Steph caressed my cock through my jeans. It stiffened. I sucked her nipples. We were oblivious to all around us. She slipped her hand into my jeans gripping my cock, stroking it. I was on the verge of exploding. I loosened her belt. I placed my hands on her midsection. I inserted a finger. She was moist. Our kisses intensified.

The music ended.

Outside the club, I hugged Arno. He held me tightly.

I embraced Steph one last time.

I imagined her beautiful naked body on top of me as I cupped my hands on her breasts looking deeply into her eyes.

I imagined our bodies coming together, with each thrust erasing memories of Trish.

We didn't want sex to spoil the moment. We broke our embrace and said farewell.

Dave was right; I needed to relax; we should've fucked.

DAY 19 REVISITED: SUNDAY - 26 OCTOBER 2003

My tears were continuing to flow when I told Dave I needed a few hours alone.

He asked me if I was okay.

No.

CASTLE HILL

Dave refused to leave me alone.

Every step of our stroll up Castle Hill, I cried, this burdened Dave. He listened as I showered him with a chorus of *why's*, concluding every verse with: *how could they?*

A beautiful sweeping waterfall wept with me. We came to an amazing Jewish cemetery steeped in history. I envied the families buried together. I felt sorry for my life.

Castle Hill represents a high point of fortification. Its history dates back to fifth century BC.

My tears stopped. I was ready to escape once more.

RED WINE

I ordered two beers.

They cost 15€.

We were engrossed in conversation with a Swiss couple from Zurich. They were travelling home the next day. They didn't like being away from their children. We loved them.

It was time to refresh our beverages. We decided upon red wine.

I ordered a litre. It cost 1€ (a slight exaggeration). I began to weep again.

We bid our Swiss friends farewell and headed back to *Le 6*. On this night we met Dominique, Martin, and George. George was from Beirut.

We moved to another club. I was staggering, profusely. Dave finally left me alone. I became slutty. Maybe slutty is too hard, easy; I became, easy.

I returned to our hotel spent, sans keys, at 6 AM. I decided to climb a tree to reach our second-floor room. I cracked my head on the bottom of the balcony. Blood painted my face.

Not to be deterred, I began to spark things off the window of our room.

I heard troublesome voices in my head. The voices told me to come around back. The voices turned solo. It was our hotel clerk. He asked about my face. I said I tripped upward.

He let me in.

LATER THAT AFTERNOON

Hold finger on the off button for five seconds—reboot.

I was angst-ridden when we woke at 3 PM. I screeched at Dave: *So much for going to St. Tropez—*

We reached Day 20. We were about to begin speeding for home. The pace had been relentless.

Today was our last day in Nice, Spain and Barcelona were beckoning tomorrow. Thank you for coming along for the ride. Escaping to Europe, as dramatic as this sounds, saved my life.

My story crosses the line between reality and fantasy. That said, the core of the story is real. Fantasy is part of the escape. Fantasy helps create new possibilities.

Now, where was I?

Oh yeah, won't you come along with me, I need to scream at Dave, we've skipped St. Tropez for a snack at McDonald's.

Dave, get the fuck up. We wasted the whole fucking day. Let's eat.

He asked me what was wrong with my head.

I glimpsed out the window; the sky was dark and grey. It was threatening to rain on our parade. Release heavens fury. Cry tears of pain.

Stop typing

Not a single drop fell.

I stepped onto the balcony searching for what I'd sparked off the window the night before. I had sparked twenty-two coins off our neighbour's window.

At the Golden Arches, David ordered a Mexican-feast-burger-combo and two draughts.

I considered vomiting.

I laughed at David and ordered a Big Mac Meal.

I paid with the coins.

When we sat down, I could only stare at my food.

The wine was free.

We went back to the internet café to search for accommodations in Barcelona.

A messenger conversation popped up.

STEVE SAYS: hey cupcake

LINDSAY SAYS: hey

STEVE SAYS: where are you now? …where to next? …Barcelona, if you're going to Barcelona, you must go to Sitges. it's fabulous.

LINDSAY SAYS: i just opened a Sitges website. it does look great.

STEVE SAYS: one thing, it is extremely gay friendly – predominately gay, but fabulous nonetheless.

SITGES, SPAIN

DAY 21: 28 October 2003

SPANISH BORDER CROSSING

After visiting the lavatory, I tugged on Dave's jacket; I was perplexed. I was basking in CATHEDRAL FACE. I explained to him; I think somebody stole the toilets. There was only a pipe sticking six inches out of the ground and cord hanging from the ceiling.

I needed to go.

SITGES

Hold a finger on the off button for five seconds—reboot—reboot again—and again.

We blasted past Barcelona fully intending to visit in a day or two.

I was holding my need-to-go since the border.

David navigated our way into Sitges. We passed its historic central quarter. We skirted past its brilliant clock tower. We parked the car on the edge of a cliff overlooking a bluff. We climbed down a flight of stairs looking for our hotel.

I attempted Spanish by saying *Hola*. I mentioned the name of our hotel.

We parked *one hundred yards* from the beautiful hotel; *the Port Sitges Resort*—two kilometres from town.

I rushed to our room. To my utmost joy, the room had a toilet.

When I exited the bathroom, Dave was already sleeping.

Sitges felt like a slice of heaven. I didn't care if we turned gay.

The thermometer was hitting mid-20s (C) when we strolled into town. Our cares drifted away. The ocean was lapping up against the city's pristine sand beaches.

Sitges dates back to the tenth century. It is a gem on the Mediterranean. Speaking of gems—

Marc, Vignette, and Maria took us in and embraced us. Marc, the bartender, did not speak a lick of English. He was a clown. Marc took the stage behind the bar putting on a delightful one-person show. He told joke-after-joke in an overtly animated style, laughing wildly at the end of each one. Marc pulled out a bag of tricks, match, card, coin; and trick—tricks. At the end of each trick, he'd point at something, taking on the persona of the Spanish bellman from *Faulty Towers*, and spewed laughter.

Maria, the owner, and Vignette, a server, best friends, lesbians, beautiful, English, about nine, maybe two dozen words. They hugged us, laughed with us (I think), kissed us, and welcomed us into their worlds, open armed.

Lovingly, they began to ply us with booze, loosening our inhibitions.

I slurred to Dave; I may be a lesbian.

Vignette asked us in eleven broken words the reason for our trip.

I shared my story once more: *On March 3*—

Vignette and Maria's jaws dropped. Vignette had tears in her eyes. She was trembling. The hairs on her arms were standing at attention.

I drew a tear. Vignette said I love you while embracing me tightly.

Marc continued his performance. He wrote our names on the mirror behind the bar. He started a small fire on top of the bar, unintentionally.

Vignette and Maria took us to a street called, *Sin Street*, full of clubs and bars. She took Dave away, leaving me alone. I sat and drank. Upon their return, she took us to a club; I can't remember the name, so, I'll call it, the *Cherry Bar*, a friend of hers bartended there. Dave fell in love.

Baylene was supermodel gorgeous. Better yet, approachable, her English, impeccable. She loved us. Drinks flowed freely. I shared the trip story. She hugged me. Dave danced. I danced. Vignette danced. We all danced. We drank feverishly. NIGHT 1 in Sitges was drawing to a close with me trying to decide between knee-walking, bile-puking, or floor-licking, as my preferred state of intoxication.

Pretty, pretty, pretty—

Dave asked me to stop stroking his hair.

We asked for our bill.

We didn't have one.

BOATS: BYE BYE REFLECTION

CLOSED

Maria's bar sat in darkness, empty—Maria, Marc, and Vignette, where nowhere to be found.

In Spain, you eat late. We ate late.

We missed our new friends.

Baylene was working at her bar. We glided up to her. Her eyes sparkled. Drinks began flowing.

She told us she never wanted us to leave. I whispered to Dave my pants were happy.

He cringed.

I suggested she loved us because we were like rock stars on a month long tour.

She then poured us a roster of this, and that's—this(s) and that(s) caught up with me.

I asked Dave if I was dead. I then decided the hotel would make a good resting place. I left. I stroked Dave's hair three times on my way out the door. I began walking.

Left foot, right foot, right foot, right foot, left foot; neat, sort of a circle. I think the hotel is by water, no, it is, by, boats. Try again. Right foot, right foot, right foot, forget it—if the hotel is by water, why am I, walking, uphill?

Strange, no beaches, houses instead, and funny looking mutilated trees. I'll keep going. Hey, I'm sitting down. Maybe I should—fly. *I believe I can fly.* Flap, flap, flap, I can't. Must come up with a solution, booze, makes me, drunk. Flap—

Car. Raxi. Chuckle, I said raxi. What's a raxi?

Cool, a cab.

I wonder if I can talk. Lindsay, use your words, *boats,* the cab began to move.

My mind raced.

The back seat belongs to me and me alone. Get out of here. Here comes the emotional train wreck. Why am I crying?

All the crap wasn't my fault. Remember, I didn't write the plot. Quit crying, Lindsay. Okay, forget it, let it out.

Hey, I know you, you're my reflection thingy. NYC, London, and—you're smiling at me, why? Look at me; I'm a drunken emotional mess. I'll be okay, are you drunk?

My core is—what is my core?

Where are you going, *be happy?*

The chemistry changed. My reflection began to fade away. It turned into a million brilliant lights, and in an instant, shot into the night sky, leaving behind a trail of—

My cab driver looked over his right shoulder, pointed to the left, smiled and said, *boats,* I paid the fare. He offered another smile and sent me on my way with—

Be happy.

HEAVEN FOUND IN A GAY PARADISE

DAY 22-24: 29-31 October 2003

I looked out the window to the Marina; the sun blasted through. I snapped a picture. The shutter only partially opened.

The calmness of Sitges led to immediate recovery.

Dave wanted to stay in Sitges.

I asked him if he wanted to go to Barcelona.

He said next trip.

He wanted to relax.

He wanted to eat.

He wanted to drink.

He wanted to have a gay old time.

THE RAIN IN SPAIN

Reboot Again

I asked David what I owed for last night's bill.

Zero, was his answer.

I gasped as I covered my mouth. I looked at Dave's boots, OMG, what were once shoes—were destroyed. I asked what happened.

He shared a painful tale full of long pauses.

He asked me how I made my way home.

I told him on the wings of an Angel.

He finished his story. It involved a lesbian, the beach, nudity, and rising tides.

I tried to calm him. I suggested three months' pay was washed away in a moment of dirty, sand-encrusted, sea lapping, lesbian—

He asked me to shut up.

On this early Thursday afternoon, the Spanish sky looked fierce. The darkest clouds I'd ever seen were surrounding Sitges. I had only seen clouds this ominous once before.

GOING WAY BACK (1985): Whitey and I were returning to Saskatoon from Edmonton. We spent a weekend looking for lesbians to have sex with—anyway, I looked out the window to the north and said: *Hey Whitey, those are the darkest clouds I've ever seen.*

He disagreed, so; I rolled his side of the car.

Back in Sitges, the sea was angry. The God of Fine Italian Footwear, Aldo, was showing his displeasure for Dave's carnal lesbian pursuits by slamming the sea violently into Sitges shoreline. It would slam into the break walls, spring upwards, at times flying forty feet in the air; spraying flecks of water in a fashion similar to fireworks. The rage-full display was astonishing. As the day progressed, the clouds thickened, threatening to release a deluge of water on the city below. Amazingly, not a single drop of rain fell.

TRAINS

What happened? Why weren't you open yesterday?

After a delicious late dinner, we went to Maria's again. This time our friends were there. Five candles lit the bar, providing an intimate glow.

The power had been shut off because of lack of payment. Maria decided they didn't need power. They used a cooler for beer. They cooked meals on a small barbeque. They concocted a scheme to borrow the power from a neighbouring business.

We hit Baylene's bar once more. She greeted us with her intoxicating smile. A Brit joined us at the bar.

He told us except Londoners; everyone else is a commoner: in the whole bleeping world.

I asked him how it felt to be the American's of Europe.

The beverage train began to chug down the tracks.

The conductor from the past chanted once more:

NEXT STOPS: Happy—followed by Funny, Charming, then Pretty, Pretty, Pretty. Further down the line, I Love You Guys, then, the town of Slur. Finally, the tragic city of I Can't Make Out a Word He's Saying Try Touching His Tongue I Think He May be Speaking in Braille; ICMOWHESTTHSITHMBSB—for short, all aboard.

I mouthed *I must go now* and *bye bye* to Dave. I walked away, *slurrily.*

Hmm, I don't remember seeing trains before. Trains don't go through water. Maybe I should walk across the tracks, no, me die if me do that. Flap, flap, flap, still can't fly. Singing will help. *Papi, papi, papa don't preach.* I suck. Great, an overpass, why am I crossing it, oh yeah, I'm going back to the hotel. Stop walking. Stop walking. Stop walking. STOP! Good. Now listen. Quit thinking brain. Turn everything blank and listen. *Chicken tastes good.* BLANK! I said. Swish, swish, lap, lap—ocean over there; if I make it to the sea, I'll find home—*excellent work brain and ears.*

DICKY - DICKY: HALLOWEEN

Hello, where did everybody go?

Four days walking in the same place was fantastic. David was right, downtime is good!

Dave had fallen for Baylene. Or perhaps, he needed rehab. Casting rehab to the side, it was time to explore.

KINDLY INSERT YOUR OWN CASTLE – BEACH – ARCHITECTURE – AND VACATION STORY HERE

We stopped for lunch at a sports bar named, *ESPECIALITATS*. I ordered eleven cokes.

Post lunch, Dave returned to the hotel. I continued to search for the answers to unanswerable questions.

The streets emptied. Sitges turned into a ghost town. I became panic-stricken.

I rushed into a hotel. I asked the clerk what was going on.

He said: *Siesta*

How Dave and I missed *Siesta* for four consecutive days is a mystery to me?

Seeing I was no longer concerned with alien abduction; I continued searching. *El Horno* is a hilarious name for a bar, I thought.

Suddenly, I was no longer alone. A Spanish woman appeared from nowhere swathing her arms across my shoulders. Two guys followed closely behind. She was snapping drunk. She grabbed my crotch. She began chanting: *dicky—dicky—dicky* while licking her lips.

I said to her, in amplified English, I don't speak Spanish.

I became semi-erect. My new street acquaintance grabbed my package. My *dicky—dicky*, was wanted—she licked her lips in a frantic circling motion, darting her tongue in and out of her mouth.

I looked to the skies hoping for aliens to take me away, now.

KITTY KITTY—

FLASH FORWARD: 12 October 2006 – Vancouver, British Columbia

Every day at precisely 5 PM, Fuzzy Nose & Toes rises from her catnap on my bed and heads to the sofa. She jumps up and glances toward the computer where I'm penning this story. I proceed to go over to the couch and turn on the TV. I usually watched Urban Rush, a local talk show that once teased me with the possibility being a guest.

I lie down. Every day Fuzzy sits directly in front of me. She meows between three to five times then gently licks my left cheek. She then turns, takes three cat steps, and lies down alongside my left thigh. I drape my hand across her back. She begins to purr loudly.

At exactly 5:25 television clock time, she rises and hops off the sofa, turns and meows. I get up and leave to go to my crap job. We have repeated this ritual Monday thru Thursday for five months.

If I did not get up at 5 PM and go directly to the sofa, Fuzzy would come over to me, swat my legs several times, and then head back to the sofa. She'd then glance my way and scream at me, in cat.

I've now shared this story with you as well as a few dear friends. While sharing I couldn't help but think I'm a grown man, full of potential; yet, I'm getting my tender moments of love and affection from my cat. After this realisation, I recoiled in the foetal position in my room weeping like a frightened schoolgirl. Later that night, I ordered a hooker*.

*No hooker was solicited by me on that night or any other night—that I can recall. Besides, you'd have to be fool to think hooker-sex would provide tender moments of love and affection, wouldn't you?

VIN DIESEL

Except for my shaved head, in no way do I resemble: Vin Diesel, some people think: I do.

Halloween was upon us with nothing to wear. So, I wore pants and a half-tucked shirt.

Sitges rocks—gay friendly might be part of the charm. After escaping with only a few grabs of my crotch, I returned to the empty streets of Siesta.

I rounded a corner. I gawked into a stores window. From behind me, I heard voices sharing a hint of Spanish. The voices were chanting *Vin* repeatedly, ending the chants with, *Diesel*.

I glanced over my left shoulder—a young couple was smiling at me.

Hola, Vin.

My costume was money.

I smiled back at them and casually sauntered away.

At 11 PM Dave and I sat at *Al Fresco* for a remarkable dinner. We met the manager earlier in the day when we stopped in for a drink. That night he spent a significant portion of the evening with us as we dined. He treated us like royalty.

The moments Dave and I shared alone, we retraced the last few days with incredible fondness. We cherish the love sent our way from everyone we met: Marc and his bagful of tricks, Baylene's intoxicating beauty, kindness, and expensive (free) drinks, the storm clouds that remained dry, downtime, and Siesta, all magnificent.

We spoke of Maria and Vignette, their graciousness, heartfelt wishes and their warm embraces. The night prior, before visiting Baylene, they joined us at a small bistro for drinks, where together, we watched German performers sing Credence Clearwater Revival and Simon & Garfunkel to perfection. The audience joined in song. Later we found out we were amongst several generations of the same family on a special night   a reunion of family.

Dave presented Maria and Vignette with Canadian flag pins.

They burst into tears holding the pins to their hearts.

Back at Baylene's bar, the party started once more.

Drink. Dance. Smile. Enjoy.

It was going to be sad leaving. Four days secured a lasting place in our hearts.

Once drunk, I slurred my goodbyes, hugged my new Spanish friends tightly, and exited stage left. Dave stayed with Baylene. I decided I wanted to go to a club—Vignette led me to product just before I vacated.

In the washroom, I asked the pharmacist *how much for two?*

He suggested four.

I accepted his suggestion. He charged me 4€.

Everything toxic we consumed in Sitges appeared to be free. Leaving may have been our only hope for survival.

Inside the club, the warmth of the chemicals began scorching through me. I became transfixed by the energy on the dance floor. Wave after wave of bliss and euphoria rushed over me sending me to a heavenly state. Dance entered my veins.

I danced.

I heard angelic voices serenading my name: *Vin – Vin, Vin Diesel.*

I looked to my right the couple from the street was dancing next to me, smiling.

We danced together.

They began caressing my body.

Our movements were in perfect synchronicity with the beat.

They kissed.

They stroked—

At ten the next morning, I told them I needed to leave.

They tried to encourage me otherwise as they continued calling me Vin.

I politely assured them I needed to leave as my hotel's checkout was in one hour and, I was driving to Paris, today.

They shoved a piece of paper in front of me.

They requested my autograph.

Once clothed, they snapped photos of me. They took a selfie of the three of us together.

One of them handed me a pen. I sat down. I searched for something to write.

Thank you for an incredible passion filled night. I had a remarkable time.
You helped to make Sitges a place that I'll never forget.
Wishing you all the best for the future—
With much love & many kisses,

Vin Diesel

Their names were Sonja and Samuel. For one night, Spain worshipped me like a celebrity.

The contents of the evening's activities will forever remain **VAULTED**.

BRIVE-LA-GAILLARDE

DAY 25: 1 November 2003

There was no need to REBOOT today—somebody left the computer on overnight.

What the heck—hold a finger on the off button for five second—REBOOT.

I didn't want to leave Sitges. For many reasons: not to exclude, I never slept, I wasn't worried though: Dave would certainly keep me awake during the drive.

Sitges to Barcelona took thirty minutes. The highway through Barcelona took two bleeping hours to navigate.

I asked Dave how much I owed for our last night with Baylene; once again, our bill came to almost nothing.

FOUR NIGHTS IN SITGES = 1€.

An *eleven hundred kilometre* drive lay ahead of us—*twelve hundred+* with our detour through Andorra. Andorra was added to the map to increase our trip country total to eleven.

Andorra is mountainous rugged and romantically beautiful, situated in the eastern Pyrenees; it is a skiing wonderland. Its scenery is breathtaking. The extreme topography vibrantly flashes a rich tapestry of colours that changes rapidly when fall begins to turn into winter. It's an artist/photographer's perfect palate.

We climbed the Pyrenees with almost a *thousand kilometres* left to Paris. The snow lapped across the windshield. My nerves were frayed. A pack of cattle, horned, were being herded down the mountainside by ranchers decked out in ancient garb, a real Kodak moment.

We climbed higher.

The snow began to intensify as we headed into the second blizzard of the trip. I glanced at Dave; he was fast asleep. We missed snapping a photo of the ranchers; instead, our only picture to remember Andorra was a sign at its entrance gate with a police car in the background.

Snow began blasting toward the windshield. It reminded me of the video game *Space Invaders.* Each flake represented fire from aliens. I turned on the high beams. The astral fire intensified. Dave kept sleeping. I whispered to him today was the day we were likely going to die, again.

For the next two hours, the roads reminded me of Amsterdam: Up—down—up—down to the melting line.

My eyes pained me.

Dave kept dreaming.

I thought about Steph when we passed Marseille.

Bellingham crossed my mind.

Each town we passed brought with it hallucinations.

My mind began to play games. I decided it was silly to try to make it all the way to Paris. I convinced myself if we were still alive when we reached the next town we could nestle down for the night. I managed to play this game for four hours.

Four-hundred-eighty-kilometers from Paris we finally hunkered down for the night in Brive-la-Gaillarde. Much to our delight: our hotel's desk clerk—was drunk.

BRIVE-LA-GAILLARDE TO PARIS

DAY 26: 2 November 2003

We REBOOTED again in the morning. The desk clerk was still jovially drunk. He cheerfully sent us solo into the bar for complimentary beverages while he prepared our bill.

We chose juice.

We'd only been at the hotel for about eight hours, how complicated could our bill be, I thought?

I'm not sure if he chose juice.

LAST TOLL BOOTH BEFORE PARIS

As we approached Gay Paris, the race became hectically hair-raising. Two lanes became—twenty. Every vehicle was shot violently from cannons into the fracas of the well-funnelled highway.

Oh, my, Biff, did you see that horrific crash; Jean Paul's Audi Quattro took out Michael's Ferrari flipping them both several times. OMG, an explosion, I can't make out the cars through the smoke. The carnage—this is awful. It's hard to believe Seed made it this far only to be taken out by—Biff; I don't believe it. Is that? It can't be—it is—he's unscathed. He looks at ease. And—his co-pilot, Dave, is knitting a sweater?

Released from the toll booth, I sieved my way between the other drivers, jockeying for position as two lanes turned into four. Weaving into the grid became effortless after *four thousand eighty kilometres* of driving.

DAVE'S DRIVING TOTAL THUS FAR = ZERO

GAY PARIS

PARIS ARRONDISSEMENTS

Dave navigated us through the bustle of Paris to the city centre, we thought. We parked the car in its resting place for the evening in ARRONDISSEMENT 14.

What's an arrondissement, you ask?

Arrondissement, Arrondissement, Arrondissement!

As I chanted the word three times—Michael Keaton and a man with a shrunken head appeared from nowhere.

I glared directly at Michael. He immediately vanished. The man with the minute' head ran out the door shouting, *I'm free*, in a squeaky midget-headed voice.

He ran into the street.

A passing taxi slammed into him.

I caught a glimpse of the driver. He was our first non-cabdriver in London. He spewed venom into the air about circus freaks running into traffic. When his last despicable word dropped from his foul mouth, his head exploded, spattering blood on every window of his cab, drawing legs against Paris's city backdrop.

We searched for a hotel at an internet café.

We failed at finding one.

We began canvassing the streets.

The Paris weather *bitch*-slapped us—the rain from the plain skipped Spain and was now drowning us. I leant into the wind. I was unable to fall forward.

I asked Dave to tie a string to me and run.

We walked miles passing *hotel-after-hotel* becoming more frustrated with each step. We finally settled for one in ARRONDISSEMENT 14. It was time to find our car.

Fortunately, we had parked forty yards away from the hotel, in ARRONDISSEMENT 14.

We asked the desk clerk what an arrondissement is.

Neighbourhood—was his answer.

We asked if we were in the centre of the city.

He said ARRONDISSEMENT 1, which strangely makes sense, marked the centre of Paris. He told us the neighbourhoods move in a clockwise motion up to twenty.

ARRONDISSEMENT 14 rivals the centre of most cities. We couldn't wait to experience ARRONDISSEMENT 1.

Wow! Paris just became gigantic. The rest of Europe seemed quaint compared to ARRONDISSEMENT 1.

CAR DROP

DAY 27: 3 November 2003

We decided it was time to return the Citroen. We checked our rental agreement for a European Car Rental Drop Zone. Fifteen blocks later, we were car-free.

After *five thousand+ kilometres* the weight of *one hundred poutine eating Frenchmen*, five if American, six if you're a pretentious Londoner, jumped from my shoulders, I was now free to drink more!

SENSORY OVERLOAD

After one hour of gawking at art in the Louvre, I could look no longer.

I drew the conclusion: I may be artistically, and historically, ignorant.

I contemplated: Was there a time where you were an aristocrat, a royal, a commander, or a philosopher, with your sculptor or artist commissioned to capture your ego, or; just a commoner.

I asked Dave to sculpt me.

I was happy we visited the Louvre near the end of our adventure because seeing one gazillion works of art at once may have lessened the awe for the rest of our journey.

I was awestruck, dumbfounded—the Louvre blew my fragile mind.

I asked Dave once more: *Shall I be sculpted nude or—naked?*

BEWARE OF CRAP

Pickpockets are part of the attraction, apparently—at the iconic Eiffel Tower.

It was time to face Dave's fear once more.

First, we had to dodge umpteen signs warning us our pockets were likely to be picked.

Dave asked me what a pickpocket looks like—

When we reached the summit, Dave latched onto the railing, shaking. I laughed. I picked his pocket. We shared another romantic moment with Paris glistening below. My eyes became filled with dreams of us riding Gondolas in Venice hand-in-hand; falling madly in love.

Dave called me delusional.

He questioned how I could've possibly typed the last line?

I wondered how he got into the book right at this moment?

I typed 'down' as we rode the elevator down *seventy-five stories* to the Tower's base.

I scanned the crowd for pickpockets to be accosted by vendors selling cheesy crap. To be sold later at a garage sale.

EIFFEL TOWER SIGNAGE SUGGESTION

TOURISTS: Keep Hands in Pockets.
Beware of Vendors selling Crap.

SVEN – SVEN - SVEN

First, we hit the Champs Elysèe, followed quickly by drinks in ARRONDISSEMENT 1—2—3—
We saw little.

We must go back one day to see what we didn't see this time.

Maybe next time, we will do Paris, on DAY 1.

We left our watering hole in ARRONDISSEMENT 4, breaking for home. Three Swedes approached us. They were all named Sven. They asked us to join them for the evening. They asked with a Swedish accent.

We entered a club. The nightclub consisted of four different bars: disco, sports, lounge, and karaoke.

The Sven's were an *Ikea* delight. Wow, *Ikea delight*; that was some lazy writing.

We loved them.

I asked the bartender directions to the lavatory. He pointed down a dark hallway.

I stumbled down the hall. When my ~~eyes~~ eye finally adjusted, I saw small rooms on each side.

I looked into the first room: a man was naked, on all fours, with his bare ass skyward.

In the next room, a man was performing a blowjob.

He gestured me to join.

I forgot to pee.

My senses became overloaded once more.

Dave stayed for Karaoke.

The Eiffel Tower is visited *seven million* times per year by people who didn't create it. If the visits are at the expense of the people who matter in our lives, we've failed each other.

LONDON – PART DEUX

Day 28: 4 November 2003

From Paris to London by train takes the blink of the eye via the Chunnel. I hated it. I hated the train.

We checked back into the *Hotel Ascot*. I checked the FERRIS WHEEL: my toast still wasn't tanned.

We stashed our bags, splashed water on our faces, and blasted to the *Fountains Abbey* to frolic.

Guinness's in front of us, we met Patrick and Tony, Patrick from Ireland, Tony from Brooklyn. Tony resembled Boston Rob of *Survivor* fame.

We engaged in conversation. This pair's gibberish bordered on offensive. Evolution had skipped them. However, they were still a wee bit entertaining.

Patrick told us going to Galway was a must. He said there were several schools there; the coastline is stunning, and the girls *git* themselves all liquored up nicely, his accent thick, Irish. He claimed women are complicated beasts, nothing more than a numbers game.

Swing often you'll score! He said.

Patty old pal, I think you complicate things. I replied.

He disagreed, telling us if you combine lines of blow, some liquor, and Galway's beauty, you're guaranteed to score.

He continued to boast he once fucked a hot chick over a balconies ledge in a nightclub as the rock band played below.

Sarcastically, Dave shot out: *Sure sounds classy—and not to mention; special.*

I added I would be proud of shining moments of that ilk—shareable during Christmas Grace.

Tony interjected he's money. He said he swings for the fences, never going home alone.

Dave asked for a copy of his formula. Dave said Lindsay'

s swing-free batting percentage is respectable.

Tony issued a challenge. He said he was in the big leagues and I was in the minors unable to ever climb into his league. Look at those two lovely ladies he said. They gave it THEIR A GAME—but were shot down in flames. He called them c--ts.

Seven minutes later, Sarah and Suzanne, left with Dave and me.

We shot playful winks toward Tony and Patrick as we walked out the door.

To be continued—

I STILL HAVEN'T FOUND...

Day 29: 5 November 2003

We toured London once more visiting: Piccadilly, Buckingham Palace, The Eye of London, a pub, Shakespeare's House, another pub, then a bar to eat, Salvador Dali, Big Ben—

I began to sink; anxiety was replacing go—

I wanted to go home.

I didn't want to go back to Vancouver.

Life was fucking clouded in the murk.

I struggled to breathe.

The second I typed 'breathe' U2 began playing on my computer.

Going home was going to bring more pain. I hadn't processed what I was supposed to do with my heartache when I return. I didn't want to burden friends at the risking of losing them. I was terrified of sharing the news with my already knowing ~~siblings~~, or they'd—

I imagined telling my mother: I knew she wasn't my sister.

Lindsay who..?

I was feeling despair. I was afraid to wear my emotions on my sleeve. If I did, I thought acquaintances would likely start to run, pass judgement, then leave.

Lots of people were adopted and come from fucked-up homes. Did you catch Survivor?

I began to fold my emotions into myself.

On this crisp sunny fall day, London took the reins by offering a brilliant backdrop. It did its best to distract me.

Dave was facing his trip ending anxieties. He wasn't supposed to be returning home.

My instincts tell me as tears enter my eyes as I write this part of the story: he stayed with me to watch over me.

The day was winding down—the decadence of night fast approaching. We stopped at Trafalgar Square. We stopped at a pub to toast London for its warm embrace.

Dave excused himself to hit the john.

Much like before when U2 graced these pages, in Dave's washroom break absence, U2 tickled my auditory senses via the Pubs sound system. I kid you not.

I have spoken with the tongue of angels. I have held the hand of a devil. It was warm in the night. I was cold as a stone. But I still haven't found what I'm looking for—

Like many times before, tears began cascading from my eyes, as I sat deep in thought.

But I still haven't found—

—took us into the London night sky—

POMP AND A BLOWJOB

Bradley's was once again calling our names. We bounced back up Oxford Street. I was half-tucked. A mannequin in a storefront was as well. Flashing back to Sitges: A mannequin there was too.

Mark, the manager, plied us with drinks while sharing anecdotes about life in London. Mark and David hit it off. He tried to convince David to stay behind to work at the pub.

We left the pub merrily making our way to Leicester Square. Two others in our party were now half-tucked. We sat down at—I'm sure you could guess: a pub.

A man dressed in black, with black hair, seated at the bar, asked the purpose of our trip.

On March 3—

With the introduction of each death, the stranger smiled. He began laughing.

I asked him what was so funny.

He told me he enjoyed death. He asked if he could buy me a shooter.

I left the bar and joined David in a booth at the back of the bar. Five of Mark's friends joined us.

Gerard delivered the Pomp. *Londoners are the masters of everything from driving to nobility. Everyone outside of London is nothing more than commoners; especially the backwards drivel that comes from America.*

Gerard finished the Pomp by saying we all must admit: *Londoners have PANACHE.*

I stood up, thanked Mark, whispering to him that his friends were *pompous fuckers*. I bit my lip.

He said he knew.

As a parting shot I muttered: *PANACHE; do you listen to the shit you say?*—and left.

The gates of *Heaven* were open, two distinct levels.

On the Main Floor, after I passed the pearly gates, they were handing out booklets on how to properly care for your COCK.

UPSTAIRS: The bump, grind, and booty of the revellers of Dancehall Reggae filled the club.

DOWNSTAIRS: It's Raining Men and ecstasy.

UPSTAIRS: Reggae equalled homophobic.

Somehow, the levels were coexisting.

As for me: I wasn't opposed to either. I wanted to enjoy my last night in *Heaven*. I spent my night in perfect balance between up and down.

My body shuddered with excitement when I felt a caress on my arm. Tiesto provided the backbeat. The man from the *Bulldog* flew by. An attractive brunette commanded my attention.

She kissed me.

I kissed back.

My shirt flew off.

She led me to the washroom.

We waited for a stall.

Once inside, she sat in front of me. She undid my pants. She lowered them. I pulled them back up. She lowered them again. I was hard. She took me in her mouth. I throbbed.

I don't want this.

My mind kicked into gear.

What are you, stupid?

Just enjoy the moment you fool, she's a—

What's wrong with you, it's just what it is.

I want more. I've seen this before—shut up.

Her mouth is around—she wants you.

I don't want this, anymore.

You're a fool.

I told *GUILT* to shut it.

I arched my back and moaned when my new friend licked—

I will make this my last time—

Enjoy Heaven, fool, who knows if you'll be back?

—last time, guaranteed.

Shut up.

There were three knocks on the door of the stall, followed by:

Hurry up in there.

Moments later I came all over her shirt. I felt empty inside.

> *we gotta make the most of our one night together*
> *when it's over you know*
> *we'll both be so alone—*

I flipped through the COCK book on the way back to the hotel—she passed—knees down.

Heaven in London, *Hell* in NYC, what's the difference: They both come with accents and emptiness inside.

Enjoy the moment!

DEFINING GIFT

Day 30: 6 November 2003

Aidan Patrick Edgar was born on April 19, 2004.

He was going to become my Godson. Wayne & Fiona are to be his loving parents.

Before I embarked on my journey they asked me to pick his first gift: the defining gift. Of course, they didn't know the birth date or gender at the time of the request.

NYC was far too early to haul the gift around. Europe was a high-speed blur. London became my last chance.

On the last day, we went to *Harrods*.

Borrowed directly from *Harrods* web page:

Noël Coward, Sigmund Freud, Oscar Wilde, Queen Mary, AA Milne and Pierce Brosnan have each added their mark to the store's rich patina–and as each year goes on, *Harrods* continues to grow, adapt, reassess and reinvent itself to create a new history.

Entering *Harrods*, it was evident we'd entered a place of distinction—as we strolled through the store, a *Harrods Bear* jumped into my arms.

Hoping into the WAYBACK machine and taking it forward to 2006: Aidan is now *two and a half years old*. He has a sister named Lauren. I love them dearly. I love his parents dearly. I see the love in their eyes for their children. Aidan and Lauren will never go without love.

I can't help but feel a little glum. I think life has bypassed my opportunity to be a father. I think this will become: my one regret.

At my age, I would never bring someone into the world only to have them watch me die when they are far too young.

As for Aidan: no one gift can define him. One day he will define himself. And, with love & support, the sky will be the only thing that limits him.

Much Love
Your, Godfather Lindsay

GALWAY

—continued

Back at the *Fountains Abbey*, we ran into Patrick and Tony.

Patrick in his classy way asked what happened to the chicks. He needed to know why they left with us.

We told him we treated them like humans, nothing more.

He didn't comprehend.

We shared a toast to life and departed for Heathrow.

Jokingly, I said to David: *Wouldn't it be great if we had the same flight crew we had on the flight from New York?*

JIMMY

Being that I was no longer Romanian, instead; I was British, I had no excuse for my eyebrows.

Are my teeth going to rot?

Was I going to become pompous?

Am I a Londoner or a commoner?

I'm now an only child, what does that mean?

How has the truth affected my life?

Fuck, I quit my job in the midst of my collapse. I wasn't sure what I was returning to, or whom I could tell about my life?

I was terrified. I started to cry a chorus of why's, once more.

We lifted off the Heathrow's tarmac soaring into the night sky. Europe saved my life—never ending change had trapped my life in a cycle of loss.

Thankfully, Europe let me know it was okay to be fucked up.

Oh My God, you two, we served you on the flight to London.

Jimmy called over his co-worker Craig. He asked him if he remembered us. They started bringing us a parade of gin and tonics.

Luckily, this time, we were seated in the row behind first class.

Our seats reclined.

Our legs stretched out.

Jimmy asked about our travels. He then mentioned we never told him the quest of our adventure.

On March 3—I'm scared of what's ahead.

I cried with each word I spoke.

Jimmy's eyes filled with tears. He placed his hand on my arm. He fired an array of questions my way.

He told me his father means the world to him. He said he doesn't know how he'd survive without him.

He told me I was amazing.

His voice quivered: *Tonight we'll treat you, first class. We'll treat you like gold. We'll make you smile. You deserve it.*

As tears rolled down my face, I smiled warmly at Jimmy.

We landed at JFK, took a taxi to Newark. David slept on top of his luggage. I strolled the airport reflecting. My head filled with pain.

GOING HOME→→→

Day 31: 7 November 2003

Newark - Toronto - Home – Uncertainty

GOODBYE 2003

Dr Saulnier was happy to see me because when I left, he thought that might be the last time—me snapping an all too real possibility.

Snap I did, I assured him.

I said if it weren't for Dave being with me I would have horrifyingly crashed the car, bringing my pain to an end.

I updated him on my family status. I updated him on my emotional state concerning my last love.

He asked me whom I blame.

Nobody, I said. I calmly stated: I wasn't sure if my family could be my family anymore. Unless of course: they acknowledge everything is different. I stressed it was messed up.

Brothers could no longer pretend to be brothers.

He called me amazing, absolutely amazing.

A painful cyst formed on my right hip on December 5. By December 10, it had doubled in size, grown a heart, and began talking, freaking me out.

I hobbled five blocks to St. Paul's Hospital.

My cyst took a taxi, stopping for coffee along the way—joining me twenty minutes later.

After my examination, the emergency room doctor asked if I had plans for the day.

My cyst attempted to answer.

Tests were taken

—a huge needle was displayed

—a surgical procedure performed.

The tests came back negative.

THE BIG C left, defeated.

UPDATED ADULT SURGERY COUNT

Left Knee 6 + Right Knee 1 + Appendix 1 + Eye 1 + Shoulder 1 + ~~Amateur Lobotomy 1.5~~ + ~~Dr. Bab's~~ + Exploratory Ass Surgery 1 + Cyst Removal Biopsy 1 + ~~1 Emotional Dismantling~~ + ~~1 Life Reconstruction~~ (ONGOING) = Grand Total 12 Surgeries Administered by Medical Professionals.

I figured that was enough?

I rarely think about these surgeries.

Dr Saulnier laughed when he found out I had surgery two days ago.

He asked if it was serious—as he was asking—he realised all surgeries are serious.

I asked him what's next.

He told me, I didn't need him. He was awed that my emotions were under control. He was impressed I didn't blame anyone. He said I was the right amount of messed up; my anger was in check. He then dumped me as a client.

I tried to convince him I was a great actor.

He wished me well and sent me on my way.

On December 17, I visited Dr Musial. I needed him to remove the surgery gauze.

I talk about you all of the time to my colleagues. Not about your chest hair. Your story is the most incredible story I've ever heard. It blows them away, don't worry—I never use your name.

I told him he could use my name. I asked him how I was doing.

He said remarkable. He couldn't understand how, but he thought I'd be okay in time.

I'm a terrible liar.

I felt like I fooled both Doctors, everyone else for that matter.

I escaped by writing.

I cranked page-after-page of my first book.

I avoided life.

On Christmas Day my life fell apart. I hadn't been part of a family for thirteen years, orphaned in a sense—being orphaned hurt me deeply, the baby of the family—what crock of shit.

I did my best to survive. Every year I'd cook a full meal, complete with all the fixings. The odd friend would drop by—I avoided the phone at all costs.

My ~~brother~~ Don usually came to town to spend Christmas with his wife's family. He'd call to say he was in Vancouver, returning home most times without seeing me—providing me motive to avoid the phone.

Not once did they extend an invitation for me to join them.

I became great at pretending to be okay. If I was invited to Christmas celebrations, all but twice, I declined.

In denial, my Christmases became stress-free. I began to love the day—mostly the visits from friends.

This year, darkness paid me a visit.

Christmas changed, forever.

I knew the truth. My family didn't know I did. I wasn't one of them.

Wayne and Fiona visited.

I pretended more.

They left.

They seemed concerned.

I was alone.

I slammed back every beer in my fridge. I drank bottles—bottles of wine. I reached out to Trish—Trish returned emptiness.

I punished myself with misery.

A thick blackness filled my home.

Out of all of the nights where Death had a chance, on a night where I would've given in—I passed out.

When I rose the next morning the sun was shining; I was still alive. I started the long climb once again—

17

THE TRUTH WILL SET YOU FREE

A meta-memoir

WHERE ARE YOU, FATHER?

DATELINE: January 2004 – Vancouver, British Columbia

With the arrival of the New Year, it was time to start once again climbing from the bottom of despair.

There was no way to go but up. I've collected most of my life's shattered pieces.

I was now facing the daunting task of putting them back together in hopes of reinventing me.

Where shall I start?

FINDING MY FATHER

Was confronting my family going to provide me with the path?

Hello, Mummy?

What am I, drunk, stupid—both?

I phoned the Leader School Board searching for information on Kirk Bliner. I told them he was the father of a boy born in 1960, a strikingly handsome boy.

I phoned the Picture Butte School Board, the Leader hospital, the Picture Butte hospital.

My voice cracked during each call. *He was a mechanic. He may be my father—about 66. My birth record says I was born—can you help me?*

I pleaded with the voice on the other end to search: *Can you check the medical, death, school records, in both towns—anywhere in the area.*

How could he have vanished?

I needed to know something; I cried: *It's a giant piece of the puzzle of me.*

The voices remained blank.

I cried more—I wanted my father to exist. The voices tried to comfort me.

My search was coming to a dead end, more of a mystery.

I told my story over and over again. *My parents came back to life. At first, I didn't think I would search – now it consumes me. I need to find something.*

No information was forthcoming.

I attempted one last plea. I understood it was likely futile. I asked: *If you heard anything; absolutely anything; please call, I need to know my father, I'm part of him.*

I hung up for the last time, defeated.

MADELINE

Foggy Night – 10 January 2004 – Vancouver, British Columbia

January in Vancouver often sends the depressed over the deep end.

The sun disappears. The rain inflicts its deluge. The combination brings most people to a depressive ledge. I was on that ledge.

The night was dismal. The rain had fallen for ten straight days and nights. I tried to keep myself company by watching *Law & Order*.

Dark clouds hung low in the sky with the mist from the ocean rising to meet them. It was nearly impossible to breathe.

The phone rang. The voice on the line was muffled, scratched out.

I think I may know who your father is—

A frail old woman entered the phone line. It was as if someone covered her mouth and blown smoke down her throat. The winter weather began creeping through my windows.

I found a single word: *What?*

She introduced herself as Madeline, from Scepter.

The phone line cleared, her voice smoothed. Madeline said *she might know my father. I will help yo*u.

I listened. I was confused.

She told me my father's name might be Elmer. She said she was sure of that.

The dead end—might have been ending.

Madeline told me Elmer was a good man, an honest man. She said Bliner confused her—but she kept digging.

I asked her why she was helping me.

Because you need it sweetie; I'm old, and besides; there's not much to do here.

She called me on a regular basis over the next several weeks. She contacted Elmer on my behalf. I sent her a photo of me. She began making arrangements for me to meet Elmer.

I thanked her.

She hung up.

The rain stopped.

Sleep escaped me—my file, reopened.

The *Cigarette Smoking Man* took a long pull on his—

PEN PAL

Throughout February and March, Madeline contacted me on a weekly basis.

She shared stories about the *period* of my birth. She told me how the community expected there was something fishy about it—my birth.

She shared farm stories. She offered recipes.

Her efforts confused me. Despite my confusion, I appreciated them.

Our relationship shared bizarre threads; yet, it was effective. It energised Madeline, by relieving boredom and loneliness.

> Sceptre, Sask,
> Tues. A.M.
>
> Dear Lindsay,
>
> Received your letter and will do what I can to help you solve all these unknowns.
>
> I will be in Calgary for a couple of days (will phone Elmer - we'll be staying in a hotel) so will be able to have a visit & no one will know what it is all about. My friend Elsa Hale will be flying in from London, Ont & I will go up from Med. Hat Easter Mon. on a Shuttle Bus (I don't drive) We will be in Calgary until Thurs. & then fly to Kelowna to surprise her brother for his 80th Birthday. He came to my 75th Birthday last Sept. so I am looking forward to getting away for a few days.
>
> We had very little snow here all winter and last week several very windy, dry weather - not looking good for us farmers as we need some April showers or whatever so the crops get a chance when we start spring seeding.
>
> Hoping all is well with you - I will be keeping in touch. Take care!
>
> Sincerely,
> Madeline Lecuyer

I waited patiently for her next contact. The mystery of ME—was slowly being unravelled.

A Little Nigger

DATELINE: 20 June 2004

Madeline didn't call again until Father's Day.

When she called, she informed me she'd shown Elmer my picture. He was confident we were related.

I sat speechlessly, conflicted between wanting, and the dead end.

Madeline told me a long story about the times. She shared tales of happy reunions and demoralising ones.

She weaved her way delicately through a story about a beautiful baby separated from his parents at birth. She lamented about the evils of raising a child as a single parent.

Ripping the child out of its mother's arms at birth and passing it to complete strangers—somehow, was okay.

She pressed on, saying the child, a beautiful boy, was reunited with her mother. Madeline's voice rose with excitement. The reunion was happy, extremely emotional. She said the mother desperately wanted to repair the past. She needed her boy to know he was loved.

I asked her why she was telling me.

She took a long deep breath and said to me because happy endings happen. They're possible. That's why she was helping. That's why she was telling me. She hoped Elmer and I experience the same joy.

I solemnly said: I wasn't expecting much.

Madeline continued sharing. She said the baby's father was in the military. He was different, not like the other boys. She said his father was black. A reality the town found out later.

I was at a loss for words.

Happy endings happen! She said.

That would have been a suitable ending for her story.

Madeline wasn't quite finished.

She had one more sentence she deemed necessary.

We all thought he had a little Nigger in him.

I hung up.

LET THE TRUTH SET YOU FREE

DATELINE: 30 June 2004

My brother Jim answered the phone. He tried to lead the call toward small talk about the Eskimos game.

I stopped him. I asked if he'd spoke with his daughter.

I no longer wanted to carry the burden of knowledge alone. It was time to reach out to the family.

Nearly one year had passed with me knowing the truth. I tried to contact Jim, my oldest and closest ~~brother~~, for weeks. My calls were unreturned.

Not to be denied, I called once more. Robyn answered.

I opened my lips—a waterfall of words poured out.

That's right; she's my mother. It's messed me up. I understand if you need to talk to someone about this. I don't expect you to keep the news secret. Have your dad call me."

Robyn said she wouldn't say a word. I knew she would.

When Jim finally called, he was aware that I wasn't calling about football. He tried to offer support, saying the news was devastating. He said he cried when he found out I knew.

He said Mum and Dad wanted to tell me. They just didn't know how. The rest of the family thought they would have.

I remained calm. I said I'm trying to understand. I don't blame anyone. I said the news shattered me. I said to Jim I found out at the end of a series of traumas—I was an emotional wreck.

I repeated the words of the civil servant.

Could you phone your parents and ask them who your real parents are?

I told him I cry every day.

I never flinched, letting Jim realise I was coping, but at the same time, a wreck inside.

I assured him I loved Priscilla. I told him she saved me with the inheritance. I bought furniture with it. I paid off debts. I went to Europe. I said I had to go or maybe die.

I asked him for help and support. I told him how diligently I worked trying to finish my first book. I said I needed help: financial help.

Without giving it a second thought he told me everything was tied up. *We can't help you.*

I told him the request wasn't the main reason for the call. I called because I was alone. I was scared, broken. I needed to make sense of something I was struggling to understand.

I told him my parents came back to life. I wanted it to be anybody but Bernice. I hoped it was a young girl who made a mistake.

I cried as I tried to come to terms—Bernice was twenty-three—what's wrong with her?

Jim dropped another bomb by telling me my mother had a baby girl four years later; she gave her away, he said.

The news didn't make me feel better.

Great, I'm not an only child. I thought.

He stressed again they couldn't help. He said sorry. He said I will always be his baby brother.

The call isn't about the money, I said, again. *I can't be your little brother anymore. Things have changed. I don't want to deal with this alone. I watched your parents die. I'm trying to understand.*

I repeated: *I'm trying to understand.* I said *everything was beginning to make sense. Lights were going on. I never understood growing up why ~~Dad~~ talked about Don after my football games and not me.*

Jim raised his voice.

I don't want to hear shit like that. We were all raised the same way.

I pleaded with him. I asked: *How could we have been? Before I arrived—you were gone. They didn't want another child. I'm just trying to understand. I hope we weren't all raised the same. Your parents were seventeen years younger when they raised you.*

I could hear the angst in his tone.

I don't want to hear one fucking bad thing about MY FATHER.

CLICK

My, ~~sister-in-law~~, Jim's wife, Charlotte, attempted to mend fences, a valiant effort; however, my fence, wasn't broken.

I remained alone.

I emailed my ~~sister~~, Beverly. Asking for help—explaining how I felt. As I write this—I think I was testing them—reducing things to a monetary level. I hope the associated thoughts are wrong, baby brother, priceless, until he needs help, then—well honestly—I was broke.

I TOOK THE LIBERTY OF EDITING PORTIONS OF THE FOLLOWING EMAILS TO PROTECT THE INNOCENT

DATELINE: 14 July 2004 – Email from Lindsay to Bev & G

HELLO BEV & G

I thought I would drop you a short letter about events which have taken place in my life over the last year. It has been one of the most challenging years of my life. Somehow, I made it through to this point not bitter and jaded. I'm reasonably happy. I have a bright future.

The following is an outline of the past year—

—here you have it—very confusing—incredibly emotional. Many things are going to take me a long time to come to terms with

—I can't explain how much the family stuff affected me. A civil servant broke the news.

—I do not ask you to understand what that would be like, because, quite honestly: I can't even tell you how I feel—

I know things like this happened in that period.

—this is my life. I think some people have forgotten that—very few people spend their childhood watching their parents die. ~~Dad~~ started getting sick when I was 15, earlier actually. I spent five to six years of my life going to the hospital to watch his sickness. I would not have done anything differently if I knew the truth. I still loved them regardless of circumstance. I know this period was tough on everyone—I do not deny that; however, for the most part, Brian and I were too young to witness the day-to-day sickness.

As for my upbringing: grandma & grandpa did the best they could, considering their ages and the fact they had to work right up until they got sick.—

—my upbringing was not all positive. Remember, I watched how ~~Dad~~ treated Brian.

I am not interested in hearing the reasons why this took place or how my upbringing was the same as everyone else.

I now have to deal with the fact my biological father would like to meet me. I also have to deal with knowing my mum and dad are still alive and did not want me. I have to also deal with the fact everyone in my life has changed. I know some may think nothing is different. That may be okay for them, but for me, everything changed.

I can't pretend. I feel like I have been lied to and betrayed. After all, it is **MY LIFE.** A civil servant should not have been the one telling me.

As for extremely positive changes: The news gave me an understanding of why things have been certain ways. Amazingly, through this, I have stayed focused and worked harder than ever—I used every ounce of energy and every cent of what Priscilla so kindly left me toward finding what I want to do with my life. I know with certainty I am doing the right thing, and I am very close to great success.

—I spoke with Jim; he said he was not in a position to assist. I have some friends...

...ask family first. I believe that is what you are supposed to do. I need to raise $4,000 - $5,000—funds are to be used to keep my project moving forward.

I have no expectations. You can help (even if it is only partially), or you can't—

—I want you to know it took courage to write this e-mail.

As for the family stuff: I need time to figure out my emotions; I could easily be screaming, yelling, stomping my feet, and feeling sorry for myself.

I am just trying to understand an incredibly confusing situation.

Much like, I was not there to watch Bernice - Sadie - You - Jim and Don's childhoods—I can't comment—

For the most part, you were not there for, so it is unfair to comment on— mine. Please understand, the seventh child, raised by older parents, who didn't want me—not the best. I am not saying they did not love me or I did not love them. I am saying: it was difficult.

Anyway, I hope you have read this with an open mind.

Hugs,

Nephew Lindsay

P.S My nickname is *The Seed.*

REPLY FROM BEV

DEAR BROTHER, LINDSAY,

YES BROTHER LINDSAY, THIS IS HOW I THINK OF YOU AND ALWAYS WILL, AND I HOPE YOU READ THIS WITH THE SAME OPEN MIND YOU ASKED OF ME.

FIRST, I WILL TELL YOU WHAT WENT ON IN MY LIFE DURING THE TIME FRAME OF YOURS AND A BIT LONGER SINCE WE HAVE NOT KEPT IN TOUCH THE WAY WE SHOULD OF THESE LAST YEARS.

WE MOVED TO—3 YEARS AGO WITH THE HOPES OF EARLY RETIREMENT SINCE *GARTH (HUSBAND)* IS NOT IN GREATEST HEALTH, HIGH BLOOD PRESSURE, HIGH CHOLESTEROL AND DIABETES.

I AM SURE YOU WILL BE HAPPY TO KNOW THAT HE QUIT… ABOUT 5 YEARS AGO AND LIFE IS MUCH MORE PLEASANT FOR BOTH OF US, LIVING WITH AN… WAS NOT PLEASANT BUT SOMEHOW I MANAGED. MOSTLY BY STICKING MY HEAD IN SAND AND PRETENDING.

THINGS HAVE BEEN TRYING WITH BOTH SHANNON AND AIMEE (daughters), BUT THEY ARE ON THEIR OWN, AND IT IS TIME FOR US TO LOOK AFTER US.

JUST AS YOU HAVE THE OPPORTUNITY TO START YOUR OWN COMPANY WITH THE INHERITANCE THAT PRISCILLA LEFT YOU WE HAD THE OPPORTUNITY TO CLOSE DOWN OUR BUSINESS AND ENJOY RETIREMENT HOPEFULLY.

NOW TO THE MORE SERIOUS MATTERS. I CAN'T IMAGINE HOW YOU FELT WHEN THAT CLERK TOLD YOU THE PARENTS YOU THOUGHT WERE YOURS WERE NOT. THIS IS SOMETHING THAT SHOULD NEVER HAVE HAPPENED, BUT IT DID. NOW AS A FAMILY WE HAVE TO DEAL WITH THE CONSEQUENCES.

FIRST, REMEMBER WHAT THINGS WERE LIKE 44 YEARS AGO, IT WAS NOT ACCEPTABLE TO BE AN UNWED MOTHER TO RAISE A CHILD ON HER OWN. I TRULY BELIEVE BERNICE TOOK THE ONLY CHOICE SHE HAD, AND THE CHOICE ALLOWED HER TO KEEP YOU IN HER LIFE. THE DECISION NOT TO TELL YOU WAS NOT HER'S BUT MOM AND DAD'S. I HAD ALWAYS HOPED THAT MOM HAD TOLD YOU BEFORE SHE PASSED AWAY, AGAIN THINGS WERE TAKEN FOR GRANTED, WITH HOPES THAT THEY WERE DONE WITH EVERYONE'S BEST INTEREST AT HEART.

I ALSO THOUGHT THAT BOTH BRIAN AND DONALD KNEW, BUT I NOW FIND OUT THAT THEY DIDN'T.

I HAVE SPOKEN TO BERNICE AND SADIE BY PHONE TO LET THEM KNOW THAT YOU KNOW THE TRUTH ABOUT YOUR BIRTH PARENTS. I REALLY HOPE YOU FIND THE STRENGTH TO AT LEAST TALK TO BERNICE ABOUT THIS AND GET HER SIDE OF THIS FOR SHE IS THE ONE THAT KNOWS EXACTLY WHAT HAPPENED.

LINDSAY, YOU WERE RAISED AS MY YOUNGEST BROTHER, AND THAT IS WHAT YOU ALWAYS WILL BE. MY FONDEST MEMORY OF MY WEDDING IS YOU AS RING BEARER, SAYING,

"ABE YOU DROPPED THE PIN!" BOY, YOU WERE CUTE.

I HOPE YOU FIND THE STRENGTH TO DEAL WITH THIS; LIFE JUST MAKES US STRONGER.

YOUR LOVING SISTER

BEV

P.S. PLEASE KEEP IN TOUCH, I WILL TRY AND DO THE SAME.

DATELINE: 18 July 2004 – My Reply

HELLO BEV

Thank you for responding. I like that you acknowledged you couldn't comprehend what I must be feeling. It shows you try to understand, or at least: understand it must be difficult.

I am also glad you shared your challenges of the past with me. I feel it shows how strong a person you are. Garth is fortunate to have you. Sticking your head in the sand may have been the only option. I'm glad Garth is doing better.

As for the decision, not to tell me—you are right, the decision was in the past. Nothing can change it—and right or wrong, it now has to be dealt with—ultimately—it is mine to deal come to terms with—in time I will make what I feel is the right decision.

As for me: everything changed, I cannot pretend it is the same. I cannot act like I don't have a different mother and father. I think I have a tremendous opportunity to gain understanding about who I am. I try to look for positives, and as mentioned before, I loved Mum & Dad (grandma & grandpa). I know they did the best they could in a trying, situation. It wasn't fair to them, or me. After all, it is **MY LIFE.**

Also as mentioned: some things about my life growing up were difficult. This information at least helps me to understand why. It was not a reflection on grandma & grandpa, but more on a difficult situation. I am sure they didn't want to work as late in life as they had too. On that note: no one in the family knows what it was like being the youngest of seven, raised by aged parents.

When I sent you the e-mail, I was illustrating the challenges that took place. I, in no way, feel sorry for myself. In general, my life is great. The fact I could come out of extreme situations caring and loving, without pointing fingers, or going poor me, is a real testament. I turned out pretty good. As for life making you stronger—I think you are a strong person deep down or you're not. Life doesn't build character it reveals it. I have a lot, as do you. Bev, your e-mail shows what a fantastic person you are. It shows you care. That means a lot to me.

As for Bernice—I am not sure how to handle it. I know your perception is different than mine. I have a tough decision to make, and in a way, I think the full responsibility of this should not be my burden. Some of the memories were not good, and with this knowledge, let's say: it is very disappointing; I will not give specifics—those are mine to find a way to come to terms with—probably mine alone.

As mentioned before, my life is fantastic. I have had bumps along the way; yet, I am happy, have a great attitude, and the best times are ahead. Despite these extreme situations, I would not change one thing about my life.

Like said, I have been a *best man six times*. I am the *godfather* to a good friend's child. And, I have made several personal accomplishments during the past year. I am very proud of these facts.

Anyway, that is all for now.

Thank you for being honest.

Many Hugs - All the Best

BABY ~~BROTHER~~

I haven't heard from a family member since (Two+ years and counting)—except for my ~~nieces~~/cousins who weren't part of the lie.

As for Brian and Don, I ask one question: How could brothers four and eight years older than me not have known?

The story has it my grandparents began raising me when I was 5—making them 9 and 13 at the time.

Brian, Don, Mum just had a baby; he's 5.

When I found out the truth was supposed to be my time to yell scream and stomp my feet. To let them know I was hurting inside. I know they lived a lie for a long time. I know for them the lie was the reality.

As for me; I'm yelling now.

MY LIFE HAS CHANGED. FUCK

Acknowledge that fact.

It wasn't time to tell me about your husband. It was time to take care of me, to hold me. It was time to tell me you love me.

PLEASE KEEP IN TOUCH. I WILL TRY AND DO THE SAME.

What a weak way of saying goodbye. If I'm wrong, I'm sorry, but honestly, I'm pissed. The anger will pass. I don't think it's worth wasting my time and effort on; life presses forward.

YOU'LL ALWAYS BE MY BABY BROTHER—

If I am, where the hell have you been?

I live less than one hour away by plane. I've been on my own since I watched *your* parents die twenty years ago. Family visits during those years don't even fill the fingers on one hand.

Does my mother still get to pretend, too?

That's what I thought.

You're right: I need to find the strength, but not the way everyone thinks; instead, I need the power not to think about this, to erase the memories from my mind, can you tell me how to do that?

Again, that's what I thought.

ON JUNE 30TH, 2004, MY FAMILY, THREE ~~BROTHERS~~, THREE ~~SISTERS~~, ~~AUNTS~~ AND ~~UNCLES~~ AND SO ON AND SO ON—DIED IN A CAR CRASH—REDUCING MY WORLD TO JUST ME.

That day marked the last conversation I had with family. The calendar has turned to July 2006.

From baby brother to alone—in a flash, with no time to grieve, I need to find the strength.

One last thing—

How do you think your REAL baby brother, Brian, feels?

HELLO FATHER

DATELINE: 1 August 2004

I spoke with my father for the first time today. I'm 44.

When I came home from the gym, I made the call, without rehearsal, I improvised. I was terrified. My heart thumped. It skipped beats with increasing frequency.

What if Elmer rejects me?

What if he doesn't?

Life can be fucking confusing.

Why was this burden falling on me?

Quit feeling sorry for yourself.

Fuck off, Drama Police.

Maybe, I stumbled upon the truth so that I could tell this story so I could let others know: they too can survive.

That has to be the case. I need to survive. If I don't, I risk becoming another sad boring story—serving little purpose. I once read that for a story to be worthy of an audience, it must be bigger than 'I'—without question: mine is—that's why 'I' will type the next words.

I picked up the number supplied by Madeline. 1-403 67—

—please let it be an answering machine, I hoped. That would provide an easy way out, dumping next on someone else's shoulders.

A man with a gravelly voice said hello. His voice sounded experienced. His voice seemed as if he's lived a hard life.

My hands were perspiring. I skipped hello and muttered: *I think there may be a chance that I am your son.*

Those words were the strangest I've ever said.

To be repeated to a man on a park bench in the future.

My heart dropped to the floor below.

I now understood surreal. I was speaking to my father for the first time nineteen years after I watched the man I thought was my dad die.

I must have paced six miles during our *one and half hour* conversation. The conversation was a blur.

He has two sons.

That means, I went from the youngest of seven to an only child to the eldest of two—and now, I'm one of four in birth order. These changes occurred in slightly more than one year.

Elmer told me his youngest son has a drug problem.

He said he was a womaniser.

His voice dropped as he talked about his wife. She had a problem with alcohol. They both did, he said. He couldn't help her. The addiction was going to kill them both.

He paused to collect his thoughts. He said his wife was his true love. Leaving her broke his heart. He couldn't help her. His demons were crippling him.

I could hear the relief in his voice as he shared.

He said he wanted to die. He poured himself into the bottle hoping to die. He thought booze would provide an answer; instead, it ripped everything apart, crumpled it up, and destroyed.

His voice cracked. He said he had to choose between leaving and dying?

He said he lives daily with the heartache of abandoning her. He will take it to the grave.

I felt connected. I thought Elmer was letting me know he understood my suffering. Here, his son, a son he was never sure of, calls out-of-the-blue, where do we start the conversation?

I think he started from the only place he knew.

My wife died on the day I left. That's what I said. That is the only way I could get by—she lived five more years before finally succumbing.

Fifteen years passed since her death. That brings us to today. He continued to tell his story.

He said he found clarity from the decisions of his past. He said he inflicted great pain on his life. He was forced to accept his shortcomings, doing so released him from the guilt.

I couldn't find anger. I simply listened.

He told me he tried to do the honourable thing with Bernice. She refused his efforts.

I began to cry.

I told him I didn't want anything, nor did I know what to expect. I said I wasn't sure if it was okay to call.

The flow of my tears intensified. My voice cracked.

I told him I'm messed up. I said I found out by accident one year ago.

I said—I didn't expect anyone to understand what I was feeling—I didn't.

I don't think there is a book, psychologist, or psychiatrist on the planet who could prepare you for a moment like this. I was talking to a man I thought I watched die decades before.

My spirit folded in half, emotions taxed. A short conversation couldn't undo or explain 44 years.

We were drunk the night you were—one night.

Reality bites.

He offered to take Bernice's hand in marriage, Bernice pressed him to take a test—that's the last he heard from her.

Our conversation was both pleasant and unpleasant. My father was a man of character. The more I listened to him the more I wanted to hate my mother. The more I listened, the more troubled I became by the fact I wasn't the most important part of the fucking equation.

I don't apologise for my anger.

After talking to my "birth father" for the first time in 44 years, three questions sprang to mind.

1. How do you end the conversation?
2. Will it ever start again?
3. What do we do now?

His words comforted me.

I said I guess we find out if you are my father. If you are, we'll take it from there.

If you're not—at least we had a pleasant conversation

We shared a moment of silence.

He agreed we need to find out if he is my father. He said it was time for the adults involved to deal with it. He stated that they treated me wrong.

He said, *sorry.*

August 1, 2004, I spoke with my dad for the first time. Our conversation was deeper than any I had with my father I watched die.

My heart breaks.

I need my family to understand my pain.

What if he's not my father?

HAPPY BIRTHDAY

FLASH FORWARD: 16 July 2006

The two-year anniversary of my first conversation with my birth father was fast approaching. The promise of continuing the conversation was nothing more than a fantasy. Today was my birthday. It was a happy day. It was a rough day. It kept repeating the cycle between happy and hard. Tomorrow was the day my ~~dad~~ died.

Elmer hasn't called. It was still being left up to me to piece my life together. Maybe my search was meant to end at the pleasant conversation shared years ago, maybe that should've been enough?

I couldn't let it be; I needed desperately to know the truth. With my life odometer rolling over another year my desire to finish the impossible became increasingly all-consuming.

I needed to meet my father. I wasn't sure what the meeting would bring.

It saddened me he hadn't made an effort. I understood that was the likely scenario. Sadness turned into madness the more I thought about it.

It's time for the adults—became lost in silence.

I overanalyzed.

1 403—GREAT—I reached Elmer's answering machine. I can leave a message and pass the responsibility on to him:

Elmer, it's Lindsay, I don't know why, but I think it would be good for us to meet. It would help me complete the puzzle and put things to rest. Please call.

LESLIE

Lindsay is often mistaken for Leslie.

To this date, when someone calls me Leslie, *I want to*—I'll leave it at that.

Leslie irks me. I already have a girl's name.

I returned from my birthday celebration. The message light was flashing on my phone

I picked up the phone and hit *98.

You have one new message. To listen to your new messages, press one.

I pressed one.

Leslie, this is Elmer Kirk—

I hoped our next conversation would come in less than 44 years.

I will call him tomorrow. I thought.

A Lot of People Were Adopted

DATELINE: DECEMBER 2004

A product of being the main character in a twisted story is that other people try to offer their two cents' worth.

Most people struggle with silence. We don't realise it is okay to remain silent.

Let me clarify, I mean: when someone is going through a tumultuous time, sometimes it is best to, just listen. Unfortunately, many people aren't skilled at listening.

At times, self-righteousness jumps to the forefront.

Your parents died in a car crash. Lots of people die in car accidents.

My story highlighted why listening without offering an opinion is vital. I don't want to wear my heart on my sleeve, but I need to talk. I don't want to appear weak; however, at times, I've been reduced to a shaking near suicidal mess.

Life can be fucking hard to come to terms with—I want to keep it private; yet, survival depends on dealing with, then coping with that said life.

Do you go home for Christmas?

A fair question—I no longer know how to answer.

Revealing leads to judgment.

If I answer vaguely, I find solitude.

If I reveal, solitude is often around the corner because *most* don't know how to react. I risk becoming labelled with baggage.

I don't expect anyone to understand.

I'd often be asked to tell my story.

On March 3—that's my life to date.

Most times, at story's end, opinions would begin to flow, unsolicited.

It wasn't acceptable to be a single mother. A lot of people were adopted. The people who raised you were— other people have it worse. Paul was adopted—you guys should talk.

And, the Crème de le Crème:

You watched your parents die? They came back to life, you're weird.

I kid you not. Opinions of others have become my reality. I wish I were embellishing. I'm not.

It is the unfortunate gift of my story.

It may be fortunate. It's inspired me to write about it screaming:

HEY PEOPLE: IF YOU HAVE FRIENDS WHO'VE GONE THROUGH A WHACK OF TRAUMA. IT'S OKAY TO LISTEN SILENTLY THAT IS ALL THEY LIKELY WANT. IF YOU CAN'T, ONLY LISTEN WHY ARE YOU PRETENDING TO BE A FRIEND?

Regardless of the pitfalls of my story, I think it is imperative, I tell it.

My realities made me grow silent when I needed to speak the most. Sad, when I desperately needed, a hug.

Comments without thought stifled me. They've made me ashamed of my reality. They've diminished me. For the most part, they are mean.

I wasn't adopted; yet: *A lot of people were adopted*—has become typical rhetoric.

My parents didn't raise me. Nobody I've shared my story with was there.

The people who raised you were your parents.

No, they weren't. Love was never present.

It wasn't acceptable to be a single mother at the time.

How could saying that possibly be comforting?

My struggle taught me a valuable lesson: Don't diminish others—remain silent—listen, and realise: understanding may not be part of the equation—and, your ears may provide all the comfort needed.

Oh yeah, as you've read to this point: I'm no longer going to remain silent!

CHRISTMAS CARD

7 DECEMBER 2004

Once upon a time, I owned a red convertible. When the sun was out the top was down, regardless of the temperature. If you rode up front with me you remained toasty warm. If you rode in the back, we'd chip you from the back seat when we arrived at our destination.

Before ownership, I never noticed red convertibles. The day I drove it off the lot, they were everywhere.

What does my car have to do with Christmas?

This Christmas Season was the first where Bernice knew I knew the truth. It was my second Christmas dealing with the pain. The first came close to being my last.

Last year when I received my annual card of obligation, it took on a different meaning: when it was from a sister—oh well. Now that the cards came from a knowing mother, I can't find the words to describe the feeling.

My TV was playing in the background. Gwyneth Paltrow was on a talk show. She was talking about the incredible bond she has with her mother, glowing when mentioning how much they love one another; without her mother, life would be empty she said.

Later that night, I flicked on the tube again, stopping on a crime show. The plotline involves a son seeking revenge on anyone that has done his mother wrong.

My friends and acquaintances begin their holiday travels. Many of them are stressed out. Most of them have somewhere they belong.

I travel to a dark place. The happiness of others adds to my sorrows. I feel guilty for these feelings. I punish myself more. I put on a false brave face. I feel like an outsider. My anger disgusts me.

Most holidays take on different meanings: especially Mother's Day, Father's Day, and Birthdays.

The bond between mother and son—father and son—the importance of the first five years of life—

Every so often a sad story was inserted displaying the tragic consequences created when the bond never forms.

I WANT TO SCREAM

Holidays, make me hypersensitive. They are my red convertible. I flip the channel, another convertible.

For children devoid of the bond: these days are constant reminders of the lost love.

If we fail to find the strength to rise above the cards dealt our way we risk repeating the cycle over and over again.

I found this portion of the book incredibly difficult to write.

I know I'm better off than if my mother raised me. I don't want to complain, too much. I don't want to blame anyone, for anything, even though, I may be entitled to—I like my life. I hate parts of it.

As much as what happened in the past is wrong, I wouldn't change it, not a single thing.

I am full of flaws and insecurities. I've made numerous mistakes. I may have to repair some fences. I know I'm a good man.

On December 7, I received my card from my ~~sister~~ mother:

Knowing the truth changed the meaning of the message. When it came from a sister, I could shrug. Being that it was from Mum, I cried.

Is she trying to punish me crossed my mind?

I was expecting an acknowledgement of the truth. It never came. The card devastated me. I felt isolated. I reached out to Wayne and Fiona.

As for others:

You're better off without her. If I were you, I'd phone her and confront her. Your parents that raised you are— Are you going home for Christmas? If I were you–if I was you–if I were you; he's got baggage—

I remained silent.

The card always comes with a gift. I don't care about gifts. I prefer, love.

When I was growing up the charade was in full flow. The gifts from my ~~sister~~ mum offered comedy filled moments amongst friends. When other kids were receiving, stereos, clothes, cameras, games, athletic gear—

Lindsay, what did you get from your sister this year? Tell me. Tell me—Yeah, I got a camera and hockey equipment—Sure, it's nice. We are talking about you now. What did you get?

One year, she gave me a cassette tape of the soundtrack of the movie Xanadu.

The next: a vest in a kaleidoscope of colours so abstract that when I returned it to the Department Store where she bought it, the clerk began laughing.

The list goes on: *"The 100 Year History of the Calgary Fire Department"* (a book), six consecutive years of shirts with wildlife on them: a bear, squirrel, chipmunk, fox, a bear chasing a chipmunk up a tree on the arm, and finally, a duck.

I became proficient at faking excitement.

Wow! I didn't know the Deerfoot Mall caught on fire during construction.

At least she gave you a gift.

Thanks for opening your mouth.

You may think I'm bitter. My mother and sister treated me like I was nothing more than an obligation. With me in her life, she had to pretend. Guilt seemed to have a reverse effect.

Lindsay, I'd hire Brian. He'd be more reliable.

I turned on the TV. Oprah was talking about the importance of mothers being the primary caregiver to ensure a happy life.

I turned silent again.

CHRISTMAS DAY

Wayne & Fiona stopped by early Christmas afternoon to make sure I was doing okay. I waited for them before opening my gift. I have lived twenty-sixth years on my own.

PRESENTS DON'T MATTER

I tore off the wrapping, throwing it to the floor.

A TEA TOWEL

I wish I were lying, an emotionless card and a tea towel—this year's gift from ~~brother~~ uncle, ~~sister~~ aunt, ~~sister~~ mother, and their dog.

The thought doesn't count.

Love counts.

Wayne and Fiona hugged me.

A mother is supposed to love her child.

A mother is supposed to take care of her child.

A mother is supposed to fight and protect her child.

A mother is supposed to hold her child.

A mother is supposed to let her child know he/she is loved.

DEAR FAMILY

DATELINE: 3 January 2005

You've destroyed my life. I'm so full of anger and resentment. I find it difficult to put my pain into words.

Collectively, you're responsible for the miserable failure I've become. I'm stupid. I lack ambition. I just take and take. I never give anything back except for my vile disgust.

I needed to alter myself to stomach the idea of writing this letter. ALTER = SELF-MEDICATE. I've used a combination of booze and illicit drugs. My life has filled with hallucinations. The illusions help me cope.

The world owes me. If I live long enough without becoming too *fucked up* my existence will be my payback.

I don't want to fight. I want the easy way, three ~~brothers~~ and three ~~sisters~~; I'm the baby, love and support was never to have been a question. It was supposed to be my birthright.

Our ~~parents~~ died, and the fucking equation turned upside down. We went our separate ways. My safe place no longer existed. Our family lost its glue. We were supposed to rise to the occasion and take care of each other. We didn't.

I'm full of hatred and blame. You've harmed me. Everything bad in my life rests on your marginal shoulders.

My failed relationships, work problems, financial problems, my troubles keeping a roof over my head, my lack of friends, my inability to love, everything, was taught to me, by you.

The result being: a miserable life that when it's over, you'll likely rejoice, hell, that's bullshit, you probably, won't notice.

I ramble. I want each of you to feel my debilitating pain. Hold on a second; I need to bang a needle into my arm. I need a swig of vodka. Once the juices enter my veins, I can finally escape, you.

The pain you caused runs fucking deep. I don't recall ever hearing *I love you*—from any of you—ever. I'm your baby ~~brother~~ for God's sake.

Every time we said bye, I cried. I showed each of you my love. Did you fucking miss it?

Dark thoughts enter my mind. I live in a dark place: DESPAIR. I don't think I'll escape. I will probably survive a few years subtracting from those around me until the day I die—most likely in a fucked up drug-fuelled comma.

My demise will alleviate your responsibilities. You can speak badly about the one bad egg of a baby ~~brother~~ you had, the one who neglected the grownups in his life, the one that stumbled down the wrong path.

Better yet: I could kill myself in front of you, a challenge because it would require having you get together in the same place to see ME. Twenty-six years on my own, I can count the number of visits on one hand.

I hope you take pride in what you've done. My misery should be divided out to all of you equally during the holiday season.

I'd like to cause you more pain—

—*but, you didn't destroy my life.*

There were even times where most of you provided joy.

Most of you, my lovely ~~sisters~~, left the nest before I arrived.

My memories are few. I never felt loved.

Beverly treated me the best.

Sadie, I've come to realise your place in the family tree was likely difficult.

Stepping back into my misery: I'm not miserable. I don't bang needles into my arm. I only occasionally drink copious amounts of alcohol. I'm full of ambition.

As for the boys: Brian, you get a free pass. We were close in age—yet we were the least, closest. I'm sorry.

I witnessed the family dynamic and decided: it was best to try to be like Don.

I want you all to know; I'm okay. You probably don't care. I think you've missed something special. You turned invisible when your presence was required most.

I loved your father and mother. I know they loved me. At least I think they did. I need to believe that.

I robbed your parents of their golden years.

I know some of you weren't my biggest fans. I took the energies of your parents, and you were forced to pretend I was one of you.

Do I blame you for anything?

Yes

But not for what you may think: one of you should have told me the truth. It was the right thing to do.

I don't blame you for that. I can't imagine how hard it would've been to decide which one.

I blame you for lack of direction. I blame you for not showering me with love, for not nurturing me or being there for my successes and failures. For not picking me up when I fell. For not raising me higher when I was up.

We were all raised the same.
Mum had a baby today. He's 5.
Wasn't Mum just in the kitchen?
I never knew she was pregnant.

I guess that explains: the lack of birthday celebrations.

Not being one of you has made me an individual. I learned to fend for myself. I'm funny my friends say; comedy is a product of pain.

I don't wish you heartache. 2003 was the most difficult time of my life. It was time for you to erase your past frustrations. It was time for you to step up to the plate and love me. Not a single one of you did. I needed you.

You're missing a special man. I'm beginning to rise. At times I wanted to die. Luckily, I'm wired never to give up.

I've now written two books. I write a column for a local newspaper. Pretty impressive for someone who never stepped inside a journalism school, don't you think?

I'm full of love. I treat people with kindness. Occasionally, I fuck up. When I do, I try to learn from my mistakes.

I've been a: Best Man 6 times – Pallbearer 2 times – Usher 1 time – MC 1 time – and, I'm a Godfather.

I have brilliant friends.

I've loved and lost on several occasions.

Sadly, I don't think I will ever be a father. I wouldn't want them to spend their youth watching me die.

It hurt to type the last sentence.

I know my future shines brightly. The best is ahead.

I've cried several rivers about the family I no longer have. My tears have run dry; your absences sadden me. I don't think I ever truly had a family.

When my life spiralled downward, friends, not family, picked me up, dusted me off, hugged me, told me they loved me and helped me wipe away the tears.

We were all raised the same way.

We couldn't have been—I never abandoned you. Remember: I'll always be your, baby ~~brother~~.

A WORD TO EACH OF YOU

BRIAN

We were left to pick up the pieces after ~~Mum~~ & ~~Dad~~ died.

You were the only one who probably didn't know the truth.

It must have been incredibly difficult following Don, the golden child. Living directly under his shadow must have been horrible. ~~Dad~~ wasn't unfair to you. I witnessed it firsthand.

We were forced to listen to the nightly fights, mostly about money. We didn't grow up in a loving environment; quite the opposite—it was filled with struggle.

I learned a lot from watching you. You're a good man, the baby of the family—taken away from you, without you knowing. I stole that from you.

We both struggled for the last energies and attention of our ~~parents~~. I had the unpleasantness of watching your treatment and decided survival required me to be more like Donald.

The pain of the hospital wore on us both. We took the burden—regardless of what others think. I will not diminish their heartache—I'll just say: the everyday grind on a young heart and soul is relentless.

I know at times, I wasn't good to you. I am sorry. I truly am. I do love you, Uncle Brian.

That was weird to type.

Thank you for easing my pain by being there with me through our journey through Hell. I know ~~Dad~~ wasn't good to you—but you never complained—and were there at his deathbed—~~Mum's~~ too when their times came—your presence gave me strength.

I wish you the best. I hope you find incredible happiness.

DONALD

I wanted to be just like you. I looked up to you. You were a star. ~~Dad~~ loved you. You brought the family pride.

We shared a common bond. I tried to emulate you. I came close. Coach Schneider even yelled at me using your name.

I know you visit Vancouver regularly. Each time you neglect me. I can't explain how much that hurts. Before 1996, I couldn't understand at all.

I know you were angry when I couldn't pay back the money you lent me.

I should've made a better effort. I'm sorry. I'm sorry we lost touch and never talked about it again. I will rest the responsibility my shoulders. I could've picked up the phone. I didn't.

What pains me the most, as I share this with you: Priscilla told me you are a remarkable, loving father. I knew you would be. Having said that, you must understand how fragile we are. How much we need the love of our parents. How much we need a family.

I needed you. Where were you at my low point when I found out the devastating news?

If your distance is about money, that's sad.

JAMES

For the most part, you treated me like your little brother.

We were the closest. You went to my games. You always welcomed me. In a sense, you were my father. Thank you.

Your daughters are beautiful kids. You and Charlotte are fantastic loving parents.

Like Don, how can you not understand the pain I'm feeling?

Look into your daughters' eyes. Think about how you feel about them. That feeling was missing for me.

I'm not mad at you. Maybe you are with me.

CLICK

BEV

Being the cutest at your wedding isn't enough.

SADIE

I'd guess ~~Dad~~ wasn't great to you, any of the girls for that matter—that's only a guess.

At one time, we were close, but as the years went by, the distance between us grew. I won't pretend to understand what it was like when you were born.

I wish you well. It's sad you didn't have the strength to be the voice of love.

The emotionless cards and presents of obligation hurt deeply. I want love. It's absent.

BERNICE

You're my FUCKING MOTHER.

Your demons must haunt you. Don't you feel the need to clear the air?

I want to scream. You stayed in my fucking life. You left me on my own to discover the truth. Didn't you think that day was going to come?

I don't hate you. Hate takes too much effort. I'm certain my words can't even inflict pain.

It was your responsibility to tell me the truth.

I don't know what spins in your head.

You had two children.

You've failed both of us.

COLLECTIVELY

A BIG FAT ZERO TIMES

That is the number of times my phone has rung since you found out I knew the truth.

I've heard for some of you; I'm still your baby ~~brother~~. That nothing has changed.

Am I bitter, at least a bit—my bitterness will eventually pass—I will never get over being left alone. When I need you the most, I was alone—alone when I needed to hear SORRY, nothing more.

I watched your parents die. It has become crystal clear as long as the weather is fair and the truth can be swept under the rug, then, and only then, I can be your little ~~brother~~. Your silence doesn't eliminate the lie.

Blood doesn't run deep. I've turned out okay. I've made mistakes. I've grown.

I'm desperately trying to find meaning.

You've all chosen not to participate in my life. I'm sad. I can't continue to be your little ~~brother~~ you never hugged or told me you loved. I can't.

You have your own families. I'm not part of them. My friends have become mine. That role was supposed to be yours.

Is it too much to ask for you to acknowledge my life has changed?

I'm sad we've missed each other's lives.

~~Love~~ Love
Lindsay

I hated writing this letter. I had to; it is part of the healing process. The emotions it evokes run deep. I drive crack heads and junkies to work, every day.

Remember the first part of the letter: most of them fall to where they are because of neglect. The deepest pain in life is when existence is not acknowledged. I exist.

Does my mother get to keep pretending she's my sister? –

That's what I thought.

18

HOME

A meta-memoir

SCREENWRITER MICHAEL

DATELINE: 10 September 2005 – Lolita's Restaurant – Vancouver, British Columbia

I met Michael at Lolita's Restaurant, on Davie Street, at the edge of Vancouver's vibrant Gay Village, just six blocks from the smashingly beautiful beach at English Bay.

When I met Michael, Lolita's had only been open a few months. It was an instant success, buzzing nightly with a hip, artsy, thirty-something crowd, drawn in by modern Mexican food in a trendy atmosphere. On any given night you might find yourself rubbing shoulders with an actor from Los Angeles in town working in Vancouver's Hollywood North, or an up and coming musician.

Michael just happened to be a screenwriter. We struck up a conversation which eventually led to the story of my past. Michael's interest grew with each word as I passionately described the events of my life in 2003. At story's end, for a brief moment, Michael sat speechless, mouth agape.

You have an incredible story. It's a testament to you that you've survived. You must share it, Michael said.

He told me my story has a movie written all over it. He believed it might help others.

He offered to send me writing information about a writer's boot camp out of LA.

He nudged me to press on.

You have passion and pain in your eyes; you must tell your story.

I nodded. *It's my life. It's all I know.*

He questioned me on how I envision the story ending: *Tragically—happily—a combination?*

He bubbled with excitement as he encouraged me to start thinking about who would play the part of me in the movie?

I was a smidgen overwhelmed. My mind raced between you must tell—and how does it end?

How does it end? I wasn't sure where to start!?!

BECOMING A WRITER

I'd like to ask you to bear with me as we hop into the WAYBACK MACHINE.

WAYBACK MACHINE SETTINGS: December 2001—at the beginning stages of my relationship with Trish—early into visiting the AFTER HOURS CLUB and my indoctrination into the world of drugs. Profession = bartender.

Every Sunday morning when I'd tire of the *sketch parties* filled with a collection of ephemeral sketched-out friends, at various, often dark places in Vancouver's underbelly, I would desperately search for something to help me ground my focus. I needed to strip my mind of the dirty thoughts spinning through it, thoughts that led directly into a cauldron of emptiness.

When Trish hosted the parties, with a rainbow of drug-induced colours shifting in my eyes, I would retreat to the computer—and I began to formulate what I believed to be honest, funny, and controversial theories on the male–female dynamic from a bartender's point of view.

I began to tell people I was writing a book. I asked Greg in Germany to be my co-author. Our pen names became SEED & EURO SEED.

I blasted out sixty pages. I never believed we would finish it. I figured the momentum would eventually die and then I'd put it aside allowing it to become another good idea with no finish.

We put it aside.

WAYBACK MACHINE: NEW SETTINGS: November 2003 – October 2004.

When I returned from Europe on November 8, 2003, I needed to escape from dealing with my realities of discovering my birth parents were now; a person who once played the role of my oldest sister, and a man I didn't know. I poured myself into writing the book I had started writing at the sketch parties two years prior.

By Wednesday of each week, when my mind would return to normal after the chemicals from the weekend finally abated, I would collaborate with Greg about my freshly written sections.

Eventually, Greg and I agreed on a title:

SEED'S SKETCHY RELATIONSHIP THEORIES

A GUIDE TO THE PERILS OF DATING

(HOW NOT TO BECOME A BAR REGULAR)

The message is simple. Don't rely on other people to make you happy. Expect the best from yourself. Never settle for anything less. Treat those who are important to you like gold. We are lucky if we go through our lives with a handful of good friends. You may meet quality individuals along the way that at any moment provide you with insight and perhaps enhance your life; remember, it is only at the moment. And, these moments should never be at the expense of the people in your life who matter.

Excerpt

Escaping my world by writing allowed my passion to flow. I was determined to become a writer. I felt an incredible force within me pushing me to finish. It was the first time I realised I might have a responsibility to try to make a difference by sharing my experience.

By focusing during my time away from bartending on writing, I was able to halt my downward spiral.

Maybe instead of writing the relationship book, the first book I needed to write was my story. I simply wasn't in a strong enough mental state to do so. I needed the spiritual and therapeutic experience of getting in touch with my TRUE IDENTITY to be able to move forward. In a nutshell, the pain was too fresh and intense to write my story; so Greg and I wrote a relationship book instead.

Like said, we had written 60 pages in two years. Upon returning from Europe, we wrote 320 pages in four months. We finished writing in March 2004—the release date arrived six months later.

The book had a modicum of success.

Wise, Wicked, Hilarious and Genuinely Sensitive Guide!
– Grady Harp (Amazon Hall of Fame Top 100 Reviewer)

THE SELL YOUR STORY FORUM

DATELINE: 24 April 2006 - Vancouver British Columbia

S unday at noon, Wes arrived at my door.

Wes travelled from Australia to Saskatoon to attend his mother Peggy's funeral. Peggy's husband George passed away two years earlier. Wes's family foundation was now gone.

On his return trip back to Down Under, Wes graced me with a visit. He had a one-day layover. I greeted him at my front door. We embraced. We came together as if we had never been apart.

While we strolled along Vancouver's seawall, we reminisced about the past and updated where we were both at in life now. With each word, we were updating our "Best of" album.

We recalled a story where Wes, while he was managing the *Planet Restaurant*, set a customer's hair on fire. Wes and one of his bartenders, named Ripper, set a pyramid of shot glasses ablaze, then blew the flames out from the bar, up to twenty feet. They called it a *BACK DRAFT*.

Wes promptly kicked the guest out of the restaurant for standing too close to the bar.

PIT STOP #1

THE ENGLISH BAY BOATHOUSE

We ordered lunch.

English Bay is a spectacular setting where the ocean caresses the mountains, reaching for the sky in harmony.

I asked Wes to read a section of a book I was writing about the oddities of life, entitled: *Poutine*.

He read with great interest. I sipped my beer and watched.

Wes was noticing.

This day belonged to Wes except for the *"Sell Your Story Forum"* at the *Fox & Fiddle Pub*. I heard about the forum by reading the local entertainment rag *The Georgia Straight*. Since I was an aspiring author—I decided I must attend.

PIT STOP #2

FOX & FIDDLE PUB

The lineup stretched for more than a block.

Aspiring authors from all walks of life were attempting to unlock the doors to the glamorous world of publishing.

The *Sell Your Story Forum* at the *Fox & Fiddle* was jam packed. Wes and I arrived fifteen minutes after the doors opened.

Admission is $20. A Doorperson said.

I'll get that, Seed. Wes responded.

I looked at the sky thinking. *Whoever is looking out for me, thank you*!

The sky looked back. It called me an idiot. It told me to thank Wes.

Inside the mob of eager authors turned into three hundred, all hoping for a chance to enter "the get rich quick" world of publishing.

Not wanting to sit dry, Wes picked us up a round of ales. We were the only ones in the crowd drinking. It struck me as odd. I was under the assumption most literary greats were either drunks or substance abusers; at the very least, deeply troubled.

I surmised that if many of our famous authors are troubled and prone to indulging in vices, then I must be the only author at this event on the right path.

I think of myself as a comic writer. Comedy comes from painful and even tragic experiences. Pain leads to *VICE*; therefore, I'm on the right path.

The lights dimmed. Lasers shot through the room; a thumping bass line filled the air. The judging elite sat at the front of the room, five in total; one with a thick British accent. They were to act as a sounding board. They possessed the keys to admittance into the kingdom of published authors.

A microphone dropped from the sky; the host began to speak.

Let's get ready to —is Jim Wilson in the room?

The over-exaggerated stage area disappeared in a flash—the lights grew brighter—the music lowered. Jim Wilson entered the spotlight. He stood on a podium directly in front of the panel.

ARRIVING LATE = NO SEATS LEFT = SITTING ON A TV STAND BESIDE THE PANELLISTS.

Wes and I were virtually part of the panel.

One by one the authors pitched their book ideas.

My book is a tale of drunken debauchery—
My book is about a Basque love triangle in 1947—
My book is about the mating rituals of the Brazilian frogs, their ejaculate, and ginger—

The panellists mercilessly critiqued the dreams of the sober literary whizzes.

Incidentally, the panellists bore a striking resemblance to the panellists on American Idol. Complete with a Brit; whom I could've sworn was related to Simon Cowell, the founder and one of the original hosts of American Idol.

When it was Simon's turn to critique, he tore the pitches to shreds.

You need to grab the readers' attention in the first sentences; you've failed miserably.
Why would you write about a Basque love triangle in 1947?
I like ginger. I'm not so sure about frog goo?

The remainder of the panel tried softening Simon's harsh criticisms by offering kinder advice.

I was thinking the authors needed to start drinking—heavily, for the next five years, maybe throw in the odd pill, and once life starts spinning out of control—start writing.

Wes asked if I wanted another beer. He said he'd only buy it if I would present something.

I told him, of course. I just wasn't sure what to pitch?

TICK – TICK – TICK

With the last pitch, pitched, it saved me from pitching the unknown.

The MC announced that there was time enough for two more authors.

West thrust my hand into the air. I was one of three hundred—hands—in the air, that is.

We have time for two more authors whose names start with L...

Wes raised my hand again.

With the MC's final selection he pointed to me, a mere three feet away.

The first L on stage said into the mike almost mumbling his words.

God—the Lord—and Oh God—

Simon used the words "festering" and "drivel" in his critique.

The first L author walked away, head hung down, weeping.

It was my turn.

My inner voice shouted three times: *TELL THE STORY!*

I shook my head from side to side violently. I asked my voice to boom. I spoke directly into the microphone. *HI I'M.*

I asked my voice to take it down a notch.

I haven't prepared anything, so, I'm going to share a short story that took place in my life in 2003. On March 3—Aunt Priscilla said she was going to cut my evil sisters out of her Will.

The impossibility of speaking in a whisper allowed everyone in the room to hear me.

The hands on the clock raced forward. My three minutes on the podium were nearing the end. The host asked me to wind down my presentation.

Okay, I guess this is what makes my story unique: Not every day do you meet someone who watched both of his parents die from THE BIG C *and laid them to rest, only to discover 16 years later that they weren't his parents after all!*

Simon called me an excellent storyteller and encouraged me to join the BC Storytellers. He told me I had left the audience wanting more! Simon mouthed the words *"evil sisters".* He snickered.

The next two judges said "great" and "fantastic".

I felt overwhelmed with a sense of pride, only to be replaced by the thought: *I suck, this was a fluke.*

SELF-DOUBT told me to enjoy the moment while it lasts. Then in a flash, he was gone.

I walked up to and shook the publisher's hands, thanking them.

Simon offered more kind words: *You blew everyone away. Stay focused.*

Next, Nancy, a prominent publisher, asked me to submit my manuscript to her attention using the exact words I used to end my presentation only a few moments earlier for the heading of my submission.

Not every day—

Before the kind words of the panellists, I spun in procrastination. My wheels rotated in a quagmire of denial.

My hope of writing this story was fading away. I was giving up.

When I look back at this part, I see that I wasn't procrastinating. My book project may have stalled; however, life kept rolling along. I continued weaving my days through pleasure—pain—happiness—and despair. And, although I was suffering from a dose of writer's self-doubt, each new day was adding to my ever-changing tale. My mind was full of material that would eventually find its way to the keyboard and onto the screen.

My moods would swing dramatically upward to the skies above and then down to the depths of despair.

One moment I would bask in the glow of self-confidence as I yearned to place my thoughts onto a fresh page. The next I would wallow in self-doubt thinking the whole process was pointless.

I know for certain I wasn't ready to write my story. I guess I needed a break from me.

I was flying solo. My family was gone. They had abandoned me after I told them I knew the truth. I was still in shock—reality had frozen the blade of my pen.

I became a bar regular.

I'd still occasionally trip into the AFTER HOURS.

I desperately needed to find work because Priscilla's blessing was dwindling.

Out of desperation, I took a series of menial jobs that I have practically erased from my memory bank.

The images of a dead Irishman sitting in a chair as one-by-one, mourners, came up to him with two tumblers of scotch, sit beside him, take a swig, toast him; and then dump the second glass of scotch on the floor sprang to mind. *I think I may have worked a stint for a catering company?*

In addition to the menial jobs, I somehow managed to land a semi-regular gig writing Opinion Editorials for 24 HOURS VANCOUVER (a commuter newspaper with a daily circulation of 220,000). Over the course of two years—my opinions were published fourteen times. I had something to say.

The topics ranged from dating to addiction to the gap between the wealth and poverty.

How did I land this gig?

Like many of the menial jobs, HOW—has been erased from my memory banks as well.

When Priscilla's money finally ran dry, Wayne & Fiona saved me from becoming a poor writer, without a home. Not only were they always there to offer me hugs, but they also offered financial support, they saved me on several occasions from eviction, until I was able to turn menial into something more substantive.

Despite my mixture of emotional turmoil and self-created challenges, most important of all: Thanks to Wes's visit and Nancy's request, this fateful day gave me the courage to write my story.

For the next two months, I cranked out my story. I thought I was penning a masterpiece. What I put together was crap.

SUBMISSION DATE: 15 JUNE 2006

PIT STOP #3

THE IRISH HEATHER

We stopped for two Guinness at the *Irish Heather.* Wes read more from *POUTINE.* I flirted with our bartender while he read. She seemed to take a shine to me.

Wes suggested I stay with her —we could meet up later he said.

I reminded him the day belonged to him.

PIT STOP #4

STEAMWORKS

At *Steamworks*, Lisa was our bartender. Lisa's hot. Hot seems to be a recurring theme in my story.

Lisa asked how we knew each other; she was curious about our stories.

We shared. Lisa shed a tear. She was sorry to hear about Wes's mother. She bought us shooters.

Tears formed in my eyes, Wes's as well. Wes told me he loved George & Peggy. He said this trip was likely the

last time he'd ever see Corrie or visit Vancouver.

Tears rolled down his cheeks. He emphasised his love for Libby, his partner.

His voice cracked.

He raised his glass.

We cried. Wes performed a toast.

To my loving parents George and Peggy.

284

Pit Stop #5

The Mill

At the Mill, we sat outside. Directly to our right were three generations of women from the same family; Grandma, Perry, and Shelby. They ranged from granny to eleven.

Refined with a thirst for "STUFF"—Shelby had no business being only eleven.

Her divorced parents vied for her love with the said material things.

Her voice rivalled Marilyn Monroe's. She shared sage advice her grandpa had given her. He didn't care whom she married—*just make sure you marry rich.*

Pit Stop #6 + 7

Cardero's & The Lift Bar & Grill

Next, we stopped briefly at Cardero's; followed by *The Lift Bar & Grill*—a stunningly beautiful establishment on Coal Harbour's waterfront.

At the *The Lift*, we became the centre of attention. Our bartender happened to be from Saskatoon; leading to more reminiscing.

Pit Stop #8

The Denman Freehouse

We'd come full-circle. We were back at English Bay; this time occupying stools at the *Denman Freehouse*; two doors from the days starting point.

I love Wes. If he lived in Vancouver, I might die. He lives life to the fullest. No obstacle is too large for him to conquer, whether that be drinking or climbing the highest mountain. He doesn't accept can't. I thank him for raising my arm!

Wes told the bartender he had a fantastic day with a great friend.

A raspy-voiced black man asked me what I thought of the Vancouver 2010 Olympic Logo.

I told him I liked it.

He then lowered his voice and said I was hot.

I laughed.

He said, *extremely hot*.

He called me Honey. He introduced himself. His name was Willie Taylor. He's a Drag Queen.

I mentioned his Adam's apple; he looked at me confused.

English, Willie's friend, and the bartender, joined our conversation. He said he'd seen my ad.

I asked him *for what?*

He said it's been running for years.

I assured him I wasn't running an ad for anything.

He disagreed. He said I provide a service, an Escort Service.
I told him he *ain't seen any ad of mine.*

Unfazed, he asked: how much I'd charge.

I asked for what?

With a straight face, he said for oral; for him to blow—

$500—I joked.

I felt his hand slip into my pocket. He told me he gave me his digits. If I was serious, give him a call.

I wonder if he would have gone for $550.

TIME TO LIE DOWN

Wes suggested going to *The Sandbar* on Granville Island. I thought about it. I decided to cross water while in a liquid state was a bad idea. Not to mention, I was one sip away from incoherent.

I told him I couldn't. I said my home was calling me—it asked me to pick up milk on the way. Of course, it was only the voices in my head.

The hill up Davie Street was steep. For part of the last two kilometres, the grade is thirty-two percent. Two percent when not liquefied.

We strolled to the corner of Davie & Burrard Streets together. I closed my eyes for only a moment. When I opened them, Wes was gone.

Alone with my thoughts: writing or hooking; either way, I'll have something to fall back on.

KAYAKING AND A TRUE FRIENDSHIP

Drunk-sleep turned into an early rise, 7 AM. Wes had made it back to my place to sleep, somehow, by 7—he was already in full flow. He was excited to return home to begin living the next chapters of his life.

I asked him how *The Sandbar* was.

He offered me their drink menu. He said he roamed around Granville Island. Wes used to work on the Island. He said the fond memories brought him to tears.

I asked him how he made it made it back to my place at the end of his night.

Well. I didn't feel like making the five-kilometre hike. I chose another option; one that cuts the distance in half, water! I decided to commandeer a water vessel. I quietly and politely borrowed a kayak.

I placed my right hand over my mouth. I asked Wes about it quietly and politely.

He said he didn't want to wake the owners who lived in the houseboat so—

I asked what he'd have done if they woke up.

Paddle faster, was his answer.

Wes wasn't a thief. He did have the courtesy to moor the boat to an Aqua Bus Stop with a note attached.

> *Please return this kayak for me.*
> *It belongs to the Brown Houseboat across the creek.*
> *Thanks*
> *Wes*

The inevitable was upon us. It was almost time for Wes to leave. Emotions began wafting over me.

I desperately tried to fight the tears. We ate our last, and what sadly might be; our last meal together at *The Elbow Room.*

After we had eaten, we returned to my place for him to gather his luggage. I called him a taxi.

When it arrived, he paused briefly at the taxi's back door.

We embraced tightly. Tears raced down my face.

I told him I loved him.

He said he loved me too.

He said he left something for me in the cutlery drawer. He said he never wanted to hear a word about it.

He got in the cab. It rounded the corner. Wes was gone, maybe forever?

I hate goodbyes.

Inside the cutlery drawer, I found cash: not $20 or $40, something much more substantial.

A note was attached→→→

Someone finally came to one of my games. Wes was noticing.

Wes moves on—and on—back to his family!

I will pause for a moment to send out a message to all of the establishments we visited. Please send me GIFT CARDS for the free advertising to—

12 kilometres +8 Establishments + 7 x ___ Adult Beverages = More Please + 1 Request for a Manuscript + Countless Interesting Conversations with Interesting and Deliciously Hot Individuals + Smile + Laughter + Tears + 1 Emotional Toast = Best Of—

→→→

WALKING PNEUMONIA

DATELINE: 30 April 2006 – Vancouver, British Columbia

I was burnt out, fading fast, struggling to breathe.

I began coughing in January. At first, I thought nothing of it, by April, it became intense; I was forced to go to my doctor.

COUGH - COUGH - COUGH - HEALTH - COUGH - COUGH

I tried to make light of the situation by humorously coughing the words: *HEALTH – SARS – BLACK LUNG.* Breathe in slowly, breathe out—

COUGH - COUGH - COUGH – BLACK PLAGUE - COUGH - COUGH

My doctor asked how long I'd been coughing.

I lied, saying five weeks. I had been hacking up junk from my lungs for ten weeks.

He told me I have walking pneumonia. He said I needed a major antibiotic. He compared me to a sick tree with infected leaves. *If we didn't treat the leaves, the whole tree would eventually fall and die.*

The medicine didn't work.

My ears plugged. I was close to deaf. Everybody began to sound like the parents from the *Charlie Brown and Snoopy* television show.

I returned to the doctor. I coughed up the chorus of a TOP 40 song for him. He offered a new diagnosis.

My pneumonia cleared; unfortunately, it took my *Superpowers* with it. The doctor told me I had caused permanent damage to my lungs.

I didn't like the sound of *permanent.*

The good doctor continued by telling me my lungs were severely inflamed. I would need a super-strong steroid inhaler to attempt to clear heal them.

She advised me to ignore the suggested directions and double the dosage.

My ears began to clearing in an incredibly painful fashion, one week later, *Mr & Mrs Brown* left.

The clearing was only a temporary respite from a new storm.

Venturing a conservative guess on the number of times I coughed over a five month period: 5 PER MINUTE X 60-MINUTES X 24 HOURS (ASSUMING I COUGHED DURING SLEEP) X 150 DAYS = APPROXIMATELY: 2 MILLION HACKS.

Financial obligations placed me in a situation where pressing issues needed immediate attention or they'd risk turning into even-more-pressing-issues.

Automobile insurance and rent came due on the same day. My cash flow had dropped to zero. My landlord wasn't interested. He wanted his money.

Kitty, I have bad news. Today we might lose our indoor home.

Marginal paying jobs suck. If you find yourself in the land of the *so-so*, no matter how hard you work the hole will grow deeper—mine had reached my neck.

Without car insurance, my driving job was about to end.

I needed help.

I asked friends.

When behind the eight ball; and *demoralised*, asking opens the door to judgement from those you ask.

Why don't you take a job delivering pizzas? You need the cash.

I reflected that was *fucking* helpful; did you hear the bit about no car—

COUGH - COUGH - COUGH – HERE'S YOUR PIZZA – COUGH

I told my friend: *I'm not a kid anymore, potential employers look at me differently. I said I'm not opposed to working marginal, I'm fucking driving construction workers to job sites already; but c'mon, for the most part, past a certain age—*

My friend didn't care. He told me to lie. He lied to get his job, he said.

He wasn't joking. He was serious. Fucking liar—

> *It's not a lie if you believe it yourself.*
> - George Costanza

I stopped talking.

I was in my forties—my career pursuits were typically two-year stints; get bored, quit or be fired, repeat. My resume reflected this pattern.

Wait for a second, recently, a career counsellor told me to—*Stay away from the Moors. If you stray from the road werewolves will devour you.* So, it's best to stay the course.

I've found my passions: writing, photography, activism, journalism, art, comedy, interpretive dance, dreaming.

One look at of my curriculum vitae and any interviewer would certainly see my diverse interests and talent.

Where do I see myself in five years—in Management!

It looked like bartending, and marginal, would be on the docket until I opened the right doors. I was committed to pushing and pulling until they opened. I pressed forward chasing my dreams with fierce determination.

Now, where do I find a place that wants a bartender in his forties?

INTERVIEW 1: I coughed three hundred times. The interviewer asked if I was okay; then handed me a *Halls* cough drop.

The inhaler wasn't working. My coughing was nearing a critical level. My chest felt like a bodybuilder was doing squats on it twenty-four hours a day—I *Googled* a diagnosis: I discovered, I was dying.

With the storm still raging, I longed to hear a loving voice. Instead of hearing love, I popped another *Halls*. In a non-lucid moment of weakness, I called a past love.

CLICK

That didn't go well. *Don't call again*; that wasn't nice. Nor was, *I'm entertaining someone.*

I'll try again tomorrow. I thought.

I had to face the facts: I was going to die alone.

THINKING INSIDE THE BOX: BREAKING THE FORMULA

If we don't follow the recipe as we trek through life, we sometimes find solace in solitude. If we don't marry by 25—have kids—get divorced by 35—work an uninspiring career—marry again—*have a second litter*—shampoo—rinse—repeat—we risk having to spend time alone. As painful as that can be, I think it delivers us to a place where we learn from life, and most important: We find out how to like ourselves.

GUILT piped in for me to quit mulling and get over myself. *GUILT* told me I'm afraid to succeed.

I asked him for my sweatshirt back; demanding him to quit borrowing my stuff.

I promise I'll never phone a past love in a moment of weakness, ever again—I hope I'm not lying.

A work friend picked up the insurance tab for my car.

Now, if only some magic money would fall out of the sky, I would be able to pay my rent and avoid being evicted.

Luckily for me, Wayne & Fiona, who love me, provided me with the magic money I desperately needed.

It was time to go back to my Doctor. He confirmed my lung damage. My Doctor gave me a new, more intense prescription.

The pharmacist filling my new script told me my medicine was *powerful, shit*.

His words, not mine.

He said it was *one hundred times* stronger than the last medicine, and my lung disease would be annihilated, swiftly—along with a*nything else in the medicines path. Don't stay on it for too long he said.*

One hundred times stronger more than *one hundred times* = *ten thousand times* stronger; I didn't want that to become my next reality. If it did, "side effects" would likely be replaced with "terminal effects".

I asked what the side-effects would be.

Man, there are way too many to list. If you stay on it for any length of time—anyway, this shit is powerful. Don't worry you will only be on it for twenty days.

I thought, great, technically I'll no longer be sick; yet, I may wish for death.

I GOOGLED the side-effects:

INSOMNIA—VOMITING—INCREASED APPETITE—HALLUCINATIONS—WEIGHT GAIN—EUPHORIA—GLOWING—HAIR LOSS IF YOU HAVE HAIR—HAIR GROWTH IF YOU DON'T—TEENAGE PREGNANCY—PREMATURE EJACULATION—DEVELOPING A SENSE OF HUMOUR—MENOPAUSE—GROWTH OF A SECOND TALKING HEAD.

THAT WAS PAGE 1.

Fantastic, my symptoms were going to disappear, but only after I became a pregnant, bulimic teenage girl with an obesity problem. It was no wonder I was going to get fat because my second head has an eating problem. And, to top it off, he never shuts up.

ENTER THE CONDUCTOR

DATELINE: 6 May 2006 - Vancouver, British Columbia

I was offered a job working as a security officer on a construction site. The hours were going to be excruciating: 6 PM to 6 AM—seven days per week.

I was burdened by financial hardship while also suffering from an attack of pneumonia.

I needed the cash.

It felt like the Grim Reaper was circling me, waiting for the right moment.

Who needs cash if he wins?

I accepted doing four nights, which frantically morphed into six.

With the unrelenting attack of pneumonia, it was as if I had one foot in the grave. Half buried is better than buried became my justification.

I strolled to the gate at the edge of the development. Billboards promising a *Hot Sexy Urban Lifestyle* hid the construction trailers at the site.

A rat scurried by, the first rat I'd ever seen.

Hidden, behind the billboards and the fenced trailers sat a frail desperate girl banging a needle into her arm—covered in track marks. I guessed she was 18 at the most. I imagined a conductor barking out town names as she travelled down this sad, lonely lifeline.

Next Stops: Loneliness—followed by Despair—and finally—Death. I will soon be back to check your tickets.

A friend of hers appeared from nowhere. He was maybe two years older; arms track marked as well. They saw me. A twinge of embarrassment shot through their lifeless faces.

She cried out *DAMN IT* as her syringe filled with blood. She couldn't find a vein. She relentlessly slammed the needle into her arm.

I heard the conductor once more: *Final Destination: Death.*

They rose from the ground and began staggering away; needles still dangling.

Their emaciated faces and rail-thin bodies etched into my mind. They shook my spirit to the core. I felt tremendous sorrow. I was certain they would die miserably and alone. I wanted to help. I didn't know how.

She was maybe 18—

STAY AWAY FROM THE MOORS—

Dateline: 29 May 2006 - Vancouver, British Columbia

The medicine wasn't working. I was sick. I was scared.

Despite the unrelenting nature of my illness, I was lucky. I had discovered my passion—writing and telling my story.

My two jobs weren't providing me with sufficient income for survival. I needed to find more work.

I solicited the assistance of an employment agency. I was asked to take an aptitude test. My results indicated I had discovered my calling. My counsellor advised me to never stray too far from it. She told me I belonged in the creative fields.

As the month of May came to a close, I was becoming increasingly frustrated, and alone.

I hit the streets looking for employment. I coughed each step of the way.

Doors to the wrong opportunities kept slamming shut in front of me.

Were the slamming doors a blessing?

Working seventeen hours a day for pennies became the norm.

I was working from 6 PM until 11 AM, six days per week. Between 6 PM and 6 AM, while I was working the security job, I would scratch out page-after-page of my story on sheets of paper. From 11 AM to 2 PM each day, my free time, I'd sit down at my computer and crank my notes onto the screen. I'd then sleep for three hours. I did this every day.

Burnout paid me a visit.

Pneumonia forced me to reduce hours.

My hours were cut more because of a shortage of work.

I began robbing Peter to pay Paul.

Paul wanted his money.

I was struggling

I needed love.

I needed money.

I wrote another page.

WHO'D PLAY ME?

DATELINE: 10 June 2006 – Vancouver British Columbia

After the conversation with the screenwriter Michael, ten months had passed without giving any thought about who'd play me?

On this beautiful June day, I took a portion of my manuscript with me on a stroll. I canvassed the friends I ran into on the street: *Chris, Christine, I'm writing the story of my life… Who'd you see playing me?*

They suggested Ed Norton Jr.

NEXT UP: my friend Robert. He suggested Ed Harris, though he thought Harris might be too old.

John Cusack on the other hand—

I'd stop, have a pint, read twenty pages, move on; quaff another pint, read twenty more pages.

I dropped into Lolita's Restaurant for a pop. I hadn't been there since I met Michael.

I plopped myself down at the bar and began reading. I picked two pages and asked the owner Lila if she'd mind taking the time to read them.

Four beautiful women sauntered in and sat down at the bar directly to my right.

My friend is celebrating her 40th birthday tonight! A demure brunette excitedly stated.

I replied with sincerity, looking directly at the birthday girl: *There's no way you're 40, maybe—28 max.*

Her face became flush. Lila finished reading.

The imagery, the flow—very powerful—almost brilliant; I'd love to read more. Who's the author?

Humbly, I said: *I am.*

Self-Doubt, in its petulant way, whispered: *I'm not good enough.*

The birthday girl queried me what I was writing about—I shared the events of 2003. Then I asked her: *Who'd play me?*

She suggested a Vancouver actor named Morris.

When I mentioned Cusack, she directed me toward Matthew Broderick of *Ferris Bueller's Day Off* fame.

He happened to be in town.

Maybe he could read a few chapters? I thought.

I asked if she knew of a way to get hold of him. *Through me, I'm directing the movie he's here shooting.*

I asked her if she'd be interested in reading some of my work.

She challenged me to sell her. I sold her with: *Not every day do you meet someone who watched both of his parents die from THE BIG C and laid them to rest, only to discover 16 years later that they weren't his parents after all! It's like being reborn as a whole different person.*

She jotted down her email address and handed it to me.

I Heard You Might Be My Father

DATELINE: 4 June 2006 – Vancouver, British Columbia

Are you my father? No. Would you like to be?

On a beautiful summer June day, I strolled along Vancouver's seawall. I passed two men chatting as they sat on a park bench. I overheard one of them say: *Yeah, you can be too close to those you date. Like, when I dated Bernice. We lived only five miles apart. She was a piece of work.*

My ears burst into flames. I walked on. I made it only one hundred paces when I turned around and walked back to where they were sitting.

Sir, this may sound weird. I overheard you as I walked by, are you my father?

He stared at me with a confused look.

After a short silent pause, I said, *never mind*, and walked away.

DATELINE: 8 June 2006

Much to the *disappointment* of my second talking head, on this day, I never coughed.

READING THE SIGNS

DATELINE: 16 June 2006 – Vancouver, British Columbia

FATHER'S DAY

I sat in the darkness of my home. I had averted a financial crisis. My increasing debt load ruined the possibility of approaching the bank to consolidate my debt.

Father's Day was in two days.

I'm drunk.

My dad died long ago. I now know he wasn't my father, but in my intoxicated state, I tricked my brain into believing I need him. I fucked up my life. He was supposed to show me the way.

I'll call him tomorrow, wait, on Sunday; Father's Day.

Will he answer?

Will he listen?

He's my dad. He has to talk to me. He'll show me the way.

I must fucking snap out of my inebriated state. My dad—the one I believed was my dad, has gone to heaven?

I must find out who my real dad is.

THREE AMAZING KIDS—

Dateline: 30 June – Vancouver, British Columbia

An old lady using a walker apologised to me for being in my path as I passed her on the sidewalk.

I calmly said *no problem; you're not in my way.*

It was a hot and steamy early summer night. We strolled together for two blocks. She told me she was going to die from an inoperable brain embolism. She was 83.

Do you have children I asked?

I have three amazing kids!

I asked if they were here to take care of her.

She said they lived in Toronto. She went on to tell me they have their own lives to live—and their absence doesn't make her sad—she knows she's loved—they're with her in spirit. She thanked me for the chat.

DATELINE: 8 JULY – VANCOUVER, BRITISH COLUMBIA

Stephen came on line hitting me up for an online chat.

He left Vancouver for a stint teaching ESL in Orlando Florida. He was one of my friends who pulled the magnifying glass away.

Stephen: u heard about dale?

Me: not really. what is going on?

Stephen: i called him Tuesday. he has been in the hospital for a week. they amputated his toes and part of his foot.

Words escaped me.

Me: geez, i'll go see him tomorrow. what? oh my god.

Stephen: i know. i started crying when he told me.

Me: man that is horrible.

Stephen: i guess something to do with diabetes. u know how feet are for him.

Me: oh boy. I feel so sad for him.

Stephen: he seems to be fine with it. on the surface at least. i don't know if he wanted me to tell people or not.

Me: that's okay. i won't let on. i'm sure he'd tell me.

Stephen: i suspect what will happen as he goes on, is that they will have to amputate his legs. down the road i am talking.

Me: oh my. Steve, well, we'll have to be great friends to him.

GUILT laid it on heavy; we battled. Dale was in the hospital for three weeks. I knew about it. I didn't realise the severity of his ailment—I thought he broke a toe—I hadn't visited. *GUILT* pressured me more; visiting was to be immediate.

I avoided going alone. I enlisted my friends Allan and Steve. Steve was a 21-year-old transplant from Taiwan. He was a veteran of the Club. He was orphaned from his parents while he pursued an education.

Our friendship grew as he was almost a casualty of the Club. He needed someone to listen to him while he was *high*. I listened. He flirted with illicit drugs. They almost consumed him.

Why is that tree looking at me? Why is it talking about me?

As *paranoia* embraced him, his friends vanished. I didn't.

Like Brandon, he's a good kid, gay.

We were incredibly different. Somehow, being outsiders and underdogs gave us an instant connection. It offered distinct perspectives.

When his father died a few months back, unlike Dale's amputation, I had a reference to relate to his pain.

Our birthdays fall one day apart. Steve's is July 15; mine is July 16; one week away if you'd like to send a gift. Of course, it would only be one week away if you're reading this on July 8 (insert any year here).

Anyway, Steve's afraid of clowns; he sees them as evil.

He once told me if he was stuck in an elevator for twenty-four hours with one other person, he'd like it to be: *Brad Pitt. I will spend the first ten seconds trying to convince him he is gay, the next five seconds trying to persuade him to have sex, and the rest to do (you-know-what).*

Steve has a bright future. We need more Steves in our lives. He dreams big. He kicked an evil demon out. He wants to stomp out poverty. Dancing and porn turn his crank. And besides, I didn't realise it at the time: he may have been taking care of me.

Dale's spirits were remarkably soaring. Visiting as a threesome may be a tad cowardly; *shut it, GUILT*; we visited.

I avoided bad humour about tiptoeing or going out on a limb. I tried my best not to look at Dale's foot.

As Dale continues forth, his pain becomes ours whether we look away unable to face his limitations or visit because we feel we must. It is people like Dale who moves through life with integrity who helps to teach us valuable lessons about the importance of valuing life regardless of the situation.

We hugged. Dale didn't care that we hadn't come to see him earlier. All he cared about was that we were there now.

As I weave my way through life, it has become abundantly clear life keeps moving forward, happiness and sadness lie around every corner. Regardless of where we begin, we are all connected. And that connection makes it paramount for us to reach out and be there for one another when we are needed the most—if we're not, evolving stops.

BRAKE LIGHTS

DATELINE: 8 AUGUST 2006 – VANCOUVER, BRITISH COLUMBIA

I contemplated suicide last night. The thought repetitively weaved through my mind.

I tricked it out of my soul by allowing fifteen minutes of *woe-is-me* time, in—and then no more.

My Demons smirked.

Early Saturday morning, I finished my never-ending, painfully unsatisfying security job. I shot home for downtime. I slept in; I felt I had wasted my day.

When I rose, a gloriously perfect day greeted me. I was alone.

I sat down to continue writing this story. Unfortunately, I've drawn a blank; words escaped me. A short while ago I was in a place of perfect clarity. I had important thoughts to share. Then poof!—lucidity got scorched and blasted its way out the window.

I'm in trouble. I'm not sure if I will be okay, ever. What I need most; well, I'm not sure exists. Maybe I don't allow it to,

I don't know if I want this life? It's too fucking hard. I'm tired of suffering. Maybe I'm just whining.

I internalise my rambling thoughts; therefore, I know, I'm not whining.

Unless of course, you're reading over my shoulder as I type.

Am I whining?

I finally found the gumption to get out of the house. I threw on my favourite shorts and flip flops. I must've walked twenty miles on this Saturday, alone. I stopped at a beer garden. I was told I look fantastic for my age, twice; while sipping ale.

I'm not old.

My feet are *sexy.*

I became the centre of an audience of American tourists from Georgia, Seattle, San Francisco; and New York. I dished out improvisational observational comedy.

The audience ate it up.

Lindsay, you are one funny man.

I wanted more about my feet.

I moved on.

I dropped by my friend Richard's place for an impromptu visit. Richard is a thespian. He's a great friend to many.

A few years back he was in trouble. We met at the Club. We fed off each other's *zest*—I'm not sure what the *zest* was for, I just know it never left a sticky soap feel.

When we met, he was masking inner turmoil. He was struggling with the demise of a relationship. And, he was facing pressing medical issues.

One night at the Club, when he was leaving, he stopped and said: *Goodbye. .*

Two days later he called from a hospital. He'd attempted suicide. I think he was searching for someone who wouldn't judge him.

I struggled to find words of wisdom. I tried to listen more than talk. I asked him never to try it again. I suggested his failure to end his life shows that he wanted to live; *WHAT A LOAD OF BS*—my words.

On this particular Saturday, far removed from his suicide attempt, his company was intoxicating. We shared life. We spoke of writing and acting pursuits. We laughed.

I left his place. I realised I forgot my keys 30 minutes later. I jaunted back to retrieve them. Strangers let me into his building. I let myself into his place. He wasn't home. I noticed a container of Frisks on the counter. I popped three of them into my mouth.

These are funny tasting Frisks, I thought.

I washed the taste away with water.

Richard returned.

Richard, the Frisks tasted funny. I said.

They weren't Frisks.

The night continued. I met a wonderful person from afar. The night turned into bliss.

Sunday morning was once again perfect; I wasn't alone. We sauntered to my friend's hotel. We engaged in a lengthy conversation about family and life.

He asked me how I cope.

We kissed. For a brief moment, I felt safe. We parted company.

I met with my friends Steve, Brad, and Saiah. We shared anecdotes about the past evening. We went to a sketch party together.

At the party a friend of theirs, Martin*—said to me, you are an epically funny man!

I thanked *Pain* for the gift of humour.

Sunday night I slept alone.

Monday was a repeat of the previous two days. I was alone once more.

I repeated my daily cycle of nearly endless walking. On this day, I had only one necessary errand. I needed new brake lights for my car.

I approached an auto parts store. A couple, both in wheelchairs, were blocking the entranceway.

The man shouted at his girlfriend: *You're a fucking bitch.*

He closed his fist and punched her in the face.

I looked around. No one else was in sight.

He closed his fist again.

I screamed: *Stop it! What you're doing isn't fucking cool!*

He paused. He flipped me the bird.

I positioned myself between them.

He yelled: *This is none of your fucking business! I will kill you!*

I told him to calm down.

How are you going to kill me; run over my toes?

He shut up.

His girlfriend trembled.

The police arrived.

My duty was over.

I find myself intervening in scenes like this on a regular basis.

I need someone to look out for me, to hold me; to tell me I'm going to be okay. I'm not sure if I've ever been all right.

Whining, feeling sorry—

I have no family, half of my time I spend at a job I hate. Before you advise me to change my situation—I am. I work hard at everything I do. I'm taking a risk by writing this story by potentially opening myself up to judgement.

My friends are either gone or married. A family of my own, likely, isn't in the cards—the window has closed because I wouldn't want to bring a child into the world at my age.

I look great for my age.

I'm funny.

Why the gloominess, you might ask?

Because it's all a fucking lie, I talk shit. I turn pain into laughter.

Thinking isn't—maybe it is my downfall?

I contemplated suicide last night.

Don't worry. I won't do it. It's funny typing, *don't worry.* I'm not sure who'd care—speaking specifically of my family.

Why won't I do it?

Because I've come to realise life comes filled with sad stories that can lead to desperation and loneliness.

Because I often run into someone who is struggling to find happiness, and when they share their sorrow with me, I gently tell them: *If the story ends with a tragedy—it will be just another sad story, sad stories blend with each other. Sad stories are boring. We are supposed to embrace each new day. Please don't let yours end in sadness, live life to the fullest.*

Finally, Brandon ended his life. His success devastated me.

Richard tried; his failure lifted my spirits and helped me realise life is precious, and even when we've reached our lowest point, we can always make another human being smile. We can always offer a glimmer of hope. And, as long as we're doing that, we're living a successful life—even if we can't see through the clouds.

Please don't let my story end sadly.

Hey, I told you to quit reading over my shoulder.

*An unfortunate side note: Martin overdosed on GHB. He is no longer with us.

ZOMBIES SIPPING MOJITOS

DATELINE: 19 August 2006 – Vancouver, British Columbia

The Dog Days of Summer were beginning to wane. I needed to drink in as much of its last few drops as possible. I threw on shorts and my summer 2006 shirt, a mid-August purchase, nature's thermostat was cranking up.

Back to my shirt: It made me look damn fine. AUSSIE BUM tattooed (in red) across my sculpted bronze chest of steel, it gripped my body tightly.

My EGO typed the previous paragraph.

Teams who'd built various contraptions were hurling their flying machines off a runway, forty feet above their chilly, watery graves in the waters of False Creek. One after another, busses, hockey skates, crabs, boom boxes, and even cars; some winged, others wingless, would prepare for launch. The aviators were fully costumed. Before attempting flight, they'd do a little dance and sing a little song. I stumbled upon *Red Bulls Flugtag*; German for flying day.

Not a single bird took to flight; instead, crews would pluck the pilots from the water while 40-thousand people looked on.

I stayed for ten non-flights. I then proceeded on a long walk along Vancouver's brilliant seawall which provides a divider between the concrete urban jungle of the city and the Pacific Ocean.

The temperature was approaching 30 (C).

As I rounded the last corner before English Bay, I was inundated by a horde of zombies—zombies times one thousand. It was 3 pm. These weren't amateur zombies but instead: serious mother-blanking zombies. And, as we all know: Zombies feast on human brains.

These particular Zombies looked famished.

I tripped my way back into civilisation. Zombie stragglers were coexisting harmoniously with the living.

Zombies Eating Sushi – Zombies Sipping Lattes – Zombies Furniture Shopping – Zombies—

I turned uphill toward home. I spotted two elegant women in the vicinity of 45 and 65 torpedoing toward me arm-in-arm.

The eldest one in a piercing fashion locked her eyes on my chest. As we passed each other on the sidewalk her head swivelled to maintain eye contact with my pectorals.

Once within earshot, her voice cracked in a sultry manner much like the late great sex kitten Bridget Bardot (for those of you that don't know who she is, Google her): *AUSSIE BUM! I want me some of that.*

We slipped behind nearby shrubbery for a little—

—Five blocks later, after my moment of fantasy, as I was about to pass a Starbucks Coffee; if you play Starbucks Coffee backwards on a turntable, it comes out as: *Eeffoc Skubrats.*

This particular coffee joint provides sixteen patio seats for watching people pass by, I paused. I looked left, right, left and right. It was a perfect summer day. I looked again. I was in a coffee free vortex. It was five pm. Not a single soul around.

I searched for meaning. I wondered if Zombies & Ninjas would get along.

Planes – Zombies – Women Past Cougar – Caffeine Losing its Grip

Could these be signs?

It was written: in the *BOOK OF REVELATION:

Before the world falls into a death spiral, we will begin to experience bizarreness. The more bizarre, the tighter the coils of the death spiral will become.

The final sign we've reached the abyss of doom: Zombies buying a Lazy Boy, sipping on a mojito; while listening to: "Brown Eyed Girl".

Luckily, not one of the shops stocked Lazy Boys.

*There is no evidence this particular BOOK OF REVELATIONS exists.

This story is true—with the exceptions: 1) there was no slipping behind the shrubbery; and 2) the revelation of the fictional BOOK OF REVELATIONS is fiction.

Mojito sipping Zombies are purely for entertainment purposes.

GREATNESS + THE THING + FOX MULDER

DATELINE: 8 September 2006

Nightly shifts on the edge of Vancouver's drug-fuelled war zone have scraped away my capacity for compassion. I started comparing the victims of substance abuse with rodents feeding on discarded waste.

Cracked out demons fight like rats for garbage and beg for money.

The sight of it disgusts me.

I found myself no longer caring about the individual's circumstances in life. I wanted these cretins to disappear. They no longer offered anything back to the world. They only take until they die. They believed they were bigger than the drug. They're stupid. Their struggles with substance glaringly highlight the difference between having and not having for all to see.

I turned the corner where the construction site opens to the trailers. A two-legged rodent with crack-pipe in hand had just drawn the heated drug from its chamber—at the same time, injecting heroin, showing zero regard for people passing by—I immediately gained an understanding of selfishness. What a fucking waste of life. His legacy will be a failure; his story is fucking annoying, not sad.

I walked across the street to Tinseltown, an upscale mall. It was supposed to revitalise the area. Instead, it became a retail tragedy. Apparently, well-heeled shoppers and victims of crack don't mix.

I sipped a pop in Tinseltown's Food Court while trying to erase seeing the destructiveness of VICE from my mind. Since it was around eight pm, the mall was almost empty. Twenty tables to my right sat a raggedy looking man slouched over with his head in his hands trying to rest before being escorted out of the mall into his home.

Three tables to my left sat a couple shovelling down tacos.

I took the last sip of my cola and began to head back to the job site.

The director of this scene called for:

ACTION

I strolled toward the escalator approximately sixty feet from my table. I noticed a man approaching me. He was decked out in a robe. A second man followed closely behind. With each step we took toward each other, the gap between us closed further, and we looked into each other's eyes. The energy in the mall felt strangely electrified. The thought crossed my mind:

I know this man—

Three more steps and my eyes remained in contact with his. Another step and we were only a few feet apart. For some reason unbeknownst to me, in this vast, empty mall, we were being drawn together.

He had a calm and glowing presence. His robe lightly brushed against my shirtsleeve. He looked directly at me and said in the softest of tones: *Hello.*

My heart skipped a beat. I returned the hello. I shivered. A sense of calmness flooded through me.

I dashed back to the job site. Excitedly, I said to Tom, my co-worker: *You won't believe who I just met in the mall's food court. The Dalai Lama!*

Tom is of Indian descent.

He sprang out of his chair and rushed to the mall.

The next morning when I went from Job 1 to Job 2, I opened a copy of the morning issue of 24 Hours VANCOUVER. The Dalai Lama was visiting Vancouver. There was a picture accompanying the article; the picture was of the Dalai Lama. The man I had brushed past ten hours before.

Another chill shot up my spine.

THE "THING" AT THE ELBOW ROOM

DATELINE: 28 September 2006

"The Thing" is a hideously misshapen monster with superhuman strength from the *Fantastic Four* movie franchise.

Little did I know when I woke up on this pleasant September day, I would be sharing a table with him at breakfast.

My friends Greg and Sylvia who were visiting from Germany were with me.

The Thing's days usually consisted of joining his comrades to fight the evil lurking on every corner. He often teamed with the Invisible Woman and the Human Torch to fight Doctor Doom. The Penn Station Carnivorous Gnome often waited in the wings to help if needed.

This A-list team of good-doers were eradicating evil from my spirit, just in case evil was to return: Detective Vic Mackey, Police Commissioner Toni Scali—along with several animated voices including Big Fat Paulie joined my day, virtually guaranteeing safety.

Patrick, a flamboyantly gay man, owns the Elbow Room. Verbal abuse is on the menu. Patrick is known for his sassiness.

Get off your fat lazy ass and get your coffee yourself, bitch.

Teresa our server seated us at a table.

A man approached.

I know this man. I thought.

I wanted to say something. Teresa seated him in the spare seat at our table.

He was a celebrity.

I decided to let him eat in peace, but I couldn't resist saying: *Fifteen years ago I made you laugh on the set of your TV series. Do you remember me?*

He sported a shaved head, roughly my age—including his head. I'm a wee bit slighter—his wallet is more wadded than mine. He asked what I did to make him laugh.

I expressed how making him chuckle had meant something to me. I painted the scene. We were in a hospital in front of a delivery room. We were looking in on a mother with her plastic baby. You bent over for a closer look. I casually stated: *It's amazing how life-like they are.*

The three of us were breaking bread with Michael Chiklis.

For the next hour, we chatted. Michael asked Greg and Silvia if they'd seen his new show, "The Shield". He'd heard it was a big hit in Germany.

I piped in asking him if he enjoyed sharing the podium with Hasselhoff.

He muttered: *Fucker!*

Michael has been with his wife for sixteen years. They have three daughters. He couldn't stand being away from them for too long.

The phone rang. Michael excused himself momentarily. His eyes lit up. His wife was on the phone line.

True love exists.

At that moment, I decided: The Thing could play me in the movie version of my life, not The Thing, but Michael Chiklis.

As we pressed on with our day; all that was left to protect us from evil were The Thing and the Penn Station Carnivorous Gnome, because Mr Chiklis played every other character mentioned above, including the voices.

X-FILES

WAYBACK: 12 September 1994 - Olympic Athletic Club – Vancouver, British Columbia

My legs were trembling. I was gasping for air. I needed to find composure. I sat on a bench in the weight room. Sweat was beading on my face and dripping off of my nose.

I had just finished a set of squats; if I remember correctly: with just the weight of the bar.

I looked up, a man I recognised; was standing in front of me, he asked if I'd like to play ball; two-on-two. They need another player, he said.

I tried to stand; I wobbled. I steadied myself. *No*, was on the tip of my tongue.

Sure, why not?

During warm up, my first three shots, hit nothing but—air.

I said to my new friends: *Yesterday I hit the guns of redemption, my pipes of fading glory; that's why I was struggling to raise my arms.*

Your what—?

The man I recognise asked as if I was speaking a foreign dialect.

My pipes—biceps—

Biff, it's time for the player introductions: From NYC—

David Duchovny, hand outstretched; introduced himself.

I tried to place where I'd heard that name before.

Next, DB Sweeny shook my hand.

And, finally, a nondescript actor said, hello—I just didn't catch his name—sorry nondescript.

My guns began to recoil; The X-Files entered my mind. I thought that's where; Fox Mulder. I'm going to play hoops with Fox Mulder!

Chauncy, quite the lineup here tonight—DB & Lindsay versus Mulder & Nondescript—unless Lindsay's pregame warm up was an act—this could get ugly fast.

Adrenalin kicked in; the guns were ready to fire.

We all shot, sliced, stole, dished; went hard to the hole. The battle for position was fierce. The hammers of pending doom, intimidated; and eventually, allowed me to hit from downtown.

The Hollywood pretty boys took the game seriously; driving the lane with reckless abandon. I floored Mulder with an accidental vicious elbow.

WITH THE SERIES TIED AT ONE GAME APIECE, GAME 3 the decider; was in full swing.

Mulder nailed a shot from the corner narrowing the score to 10–9 for DB and me.

He drove hard again. I stole the ball. From the top of the key, I crossover dribbled. Mulder was on me like white on rice (lazy writing). I dribbled behind my back, with Mulder glued to me. I pivoted, reversed; slashed hard to the basket, elevated, and then dished the rock to DB.

DB calmly dribbled.

I cleared the key and then stood in the corner wanting to collapse from exhaustion.

DB dribbled three times to the left. He stopped. He popped. Nondescript and Mulder waved frantically, whiffing at the perfect arc of the shot. One—two—three revolutions, the ball rose in slow motion and then dropped toward the basket; SWISH. Sweet victory was ours.

The following week Duchovny was on the cover of *Details Magazine*. The X-Files was launching into the TV stratospheres. Duchovny's international star was rising rapidly.

I purchased the magazine. It said Mulder grew up NYC. I extrapolated:

NYC is one of the Largest Cities in the World—The article suggested Mulder was one of the best high school basketball players in NYC—Biff announced: I just beat him = I AM ONE OF THE BEST BASKETBALL PLAYERS, IN THE WORLD.

I glanced to my right; a man was staring at me. I asked him to stop. If he didn't, I would have to bring out the guns of—

He kept staring; a cigarette was dangling from his lips.

I calmly said to him:

Hey, mister, you can't smoke in here.

NOTE: Mulder if you happen to read this—I will grant you: one rematch.

19

WHAT MATTERS

I've shared my story because I've determined we're supposed to bring light into people's lives, not darkness.
We are simply supposed to be kind to each other.
Seed

A meta-memoir

MIRROR, MIRROR ON THE WALL

Discovering inner peace and living in harmony with existence is difficult at best.

Positioned in front of the mirror some mornings startle us into realising the *being* staring back at us with tired eyes has become unrecognisable. It has become worn down, beleaguered and exasperated by life. Ambition has been stripped away by pain. Potential brilliance trounced by troubles.

But just as quickly as the downward spiral brings defeat, a subtle change can reroute destiny at a pace as rapid as the fall. Accepting the struggle and not fighting against what is, introduces the pleasure in life. Life is a wild ride.

If we can accept our new course, the inner turbulence will subside—we will look at ourselves inwardly.

When this happens the ride will become smoother, the bumps and deviations from the road will be fewer and farther between. We live in difficult times. Our reality gets skewed daily by the media. We are bombarded 24/7 with distraction. We are told to care about athletes and celebrities. Finding one's way amid the noise is a formidable task.

But if we listen inwardly the clatter will lead to silence. In the calm of this new found peace we can begin to value people more than stuff.

Now when things get fucked up at times, I pause and look deep into the mirror once more. Sometimes my reflection shines back brightly as a vibrant, beautiful man, still in his prime, not washed up. It tells me I have the tools to take the world by storm. It screams for me to achieve something greater than self, something offering hope to others and moments of laughter.

At other times, I only see sadness and pain. I see heartache chiselled deep in wrinkles replacing smile lines.

I hope that you allow the mirror to become your friend. If you do, you'll see the roadmap of life on your face. Every smile—every tear—and every moment of happiness or despair is traceable. If you allow the mirror to become your friend, then one day, the reflection looking back to you will help you realise you have something wonderful to offer the world:

YOU—and you're beautiful!

THE LAST KEYSTROKES

Life can't begin until reality, is revealed!

Well, friends, we've come to the exit point. This volume of my LIFE STORY is winding down. How can I end a story that keeps retelling itself even as I write this?

I want it to be powerful.

I want it to leave you spent at the end.

As you learned during our journey together through my life to this point, I'm lucky:

I GOT A SECOND CHANCE!

Of course, it's not as simple as that. I had to get knocked around a bit, actually a lot; almost too much. Somehow, I survived and managed to come out a NEW MAN. I believe a better person; more compassionate; and without question, less judgemental.

You probably didn't realise it while you were reading this story that you played a significant role in my transformation. Writing this story for YOU was a vital part of the cleansing process. It helped me to put my heartaches in a place where they're manageable. But most important: The process of writing helped me to realise my story is much LARGER than just me. It made me realise: I have a responsibility to myself, and hopefully to others, to share it.

We need to care for each other. We need to be kind.

When I found out the partial truths about my family, darkness smothered me; I went through a series of emotions; powerful emotions; mostly bad. I was angry.

I hated my ~~sister~~ mother, Bernice.

How could my whole family have participated in a lie which affects my life the most?

I'm the main character, DAMMIT!

With each page I typed, I searched for a way to relieve my anger and tell my truth.

Who do I blame?

What a fantastic question. I came to the realisation that if I BLAME someone—anyone—I will never be okay. I would never find forgiveness.

This epiphany doesn't let my family off the hook. They've failed me. When I needed them the most, they disappeared. They are still invisible to this day. That hurts. I miss them.

You're better off without them.

Maybe I am?

What I do know is they're not bad people. I don't think their life cards were any better than mine. I do know they had to participate in a life-altering lie without the option of—opting out—that must've sucked.

As for Bernice, I can only speculate about what she went through all those years—

Hopefully, in the next volume of MY LIFE I can gain a greater understanding of what happened after I was born. Why didn't Bernice give me away for adoption?

Do I want to be an advocate for adoption?

No, but I do want to share my opinion.

If you choose to adopt a child, give yourself a pat on the back. Many lost children need a second chance in a loving home.

ONE LAST POINT: If you happen to be the parents of adopted children and they don't already know: **TELL THEM**, it is the only way to give them an opportunity to discover greatness.

If you hesitate to reveal the truth, ask yourself, why? Who are you protecting?

If you happen to be the product of an adoption, or worse, and you find out by accident, I want you to know:

IT'S NOT YOUR FAULT

I'm lucky. Not only have I been blessed with a second chance, but I have also found my lost HAPPY!

It's time for me to wrap this VOLUME OF MY LIFE.

DATELINE: 21 October 2006 – 7:33 PM – Vancouver, British Columbia

This day marks my THIRD BIRTHDAY, so to speak. Today marks the third anniversary of discovering the path to the new me.

How do I find the strength to stop typing?

Secrets hide the truth. Square pegs don't fit into round holes.

If truth isn't paramount—living will be missing something vital.

My pegs have started to fit.

Before we flip to next and the last pages of my book—I'd like to share one more thought:

We matter. It is as simple as that!

ACKNOWLEDGEMENTS

To those who love – to those who encourage – to those who bring light!

Who to thank?

THANK YOU, reader, for taking the ride with me. If you're reading this, I guess you care. I'm lucky you cracked open the cover of my book and stepped inside. I'd like to think of this book as a DOOR on the RIGHT!

And, by opening it, you are deciding to go toward happiness.

Thanking Wes is a no-brainer. He set the wheels in motion by raising my hand in the air at the Sell Your Story Forum. If he hadn't have done so, who knows where I'd be today?

Of course, I must thank David, for tagging along with me through Europe. He was a brilliant chaperone, assuring I didn't implode.

Wayne, Fiona, and Greg, and their families, for becoming my family, they've saved me from feeling lost and alone. They have always been there for me when I've needed them the most.

The list is long; however, I've decided to thank one more person here before I take a creative turn in these acknowledgements.

Kendra Langeteig, my Editor/book doctor/literary shrink, deserves a tremendous THANK YOU for cheering for me. Kendra's encouragement of my talent as a writer helped me to accept myself as worthy of being read. She also helped me rearrange and polish up my living room (this book) to make the reading experience better for everyone!

And now for the creative twist...

Of course, I must take a line to thank all the Eds [who helped me to find my voice]. Thank you, Ed!

Here are a few more people/places/things I'd like to thank.

1. My mother and father, and my mother and father. Without them I wouldn't be where; or who, I am today.
2. My siblings, Sadie, Beverly, James, Donald, and Brian. I wish them happiness.
3. I'd need to thank BOOZE (in moderation).
4. I must thank my late Aunt and Uncle, Priscilla and Roy. I genuinely do miss Priscilla's random calls just to say: *I love you.*
5. Sex.
6. Jamaica, Miami, and Panama.
7. Whitey, Corrie & Vern, Barb, Kleo, Flouff, Gord Tank, Lori ~~Tank~~ Olson, Tony Gagnon, Pat K M, Slick, Big Red, Wally, Danielle, ~~Thieving Spike~~, Rhonda, Joanne, Jana, and the whole Ellis and Tank clans; Jeffbo—and on and on and on—
8. Montreal, New York City, ~~London~~, Amsterdam; the Citroen (automobile), Munich, Salzburg, Munich again, Venice, Florence, Monte Carlo, Monaco, Nice, Sitges, Andorra, Brive-la-Gaillarde, Paris; and London—and all the people I met during my journey through these beautiful places.
9. Gail. She deserves a BIG THANK YOU. She also deserves an even BIGGER SORRY, because I didn't accept the end of our relationship.
10. Trish, or as my friend Jay likes to refer to her, Trash. As much as our time together wasn't all peachy – without Trish coming into my life, I may not have accepted who I am.
11. Chewable vitamins.
12. Baylene, the Super Model, for treating Dave and I, like Rock Stars.

13. Maria, Vignette, Marc, and Sven x 3.
14. Condoms.
15. ~~Porn.~~
16. EVERYONE I've met up to this point in my life journey, the good, the bad, and everyone in between. They have all had a hand in filling my life with countless moments to be cherished that have helped me to become the man I am today!

17. TOMORROW

AUTHOR'S NOTE

Dear Reader

Now what?

This can't be the end of us, can it?

Do we ever get to meet Elmer, your father? You might ask.

What about Trish?

One day when you were out with Wayne you ended a conversation with: Wayne, it's about Trish—is it fair to leave us hanging?

OMG, is your ~~sister~~ mother Bernice okay? Do you reunite?

To read more of my continuing saga you will have to stay tuned for the sequel: *PLAY (working title— in revision).*

PLAY addresses many of these unresolved issues, maybe resolving the odd one? By continuing down the delightful paths of life, my life just seems to get richer every step of the way, regardless of the crap thrown at me!

Here's a sneak peak:

I wait in my car in the parking lot at Earl's Restaurant on Fir Street. The rain is pelting down as a windstorm rattled the city, the windows of my car are draped in a dark, thick mist. I hear three taps on the driver's window. I roll it down. A tall, sturdy looking, older man is standing in the unrelenting rain, the wind is howling. He looks at me and smiles; his eyes are peaceful. He calmly says, *Lindsay, are you going to sit in there all day?*

I was meeting my father for the first time.

In PLAY, I step out of my universe when I get involved as a key player in the first Hate Crime in Canadian Legal History—and become a public figure in spite of myself.

I believe the UNIVERSE is talking to us. We just need to pay attention to the signs it sends.

The guidance these messages deliver—help us to find clarity. It's not always easy to read the signs or stay focused on the right kind of path, but I think we must at least try!

Just when you think you have the world figured out, life has a way of knocking you down. If you find the strength to pick yourself up and dust yourself off, you may have an epiphany and realise you don't know squat. And maybe, that's the way it's supposed to be.

Maybe we are not supposed to figure *IT* out?

I think the most important thing is never to quit trying. Trying is necessary for finding out who we are.

It's time to go. I'll leave you with this: The road behind had its share of potholes, poor choices, blind corners, the occasional flat, at times several at once—I survived!

Let us travel the roads ahead with happiness and joy. It's our responsibility to do so if we want to live our lives to the fullest. I implore you to learn to find joy in life—despite the occasional bump.

It sucks when a tire goes flat when you're travelling down life's roads, but nothing beats the satisfaction of yanking the jack out of the trunk, wrestling the lug nuts off the car, throwing on the temporary spare and moving on to what's NEXT!

All the Best,

Lindsay

16 JULY 1960 – 21 OCTOBER 2006 – 7 JULY 2017

→←→

DEDICATION: PART 2

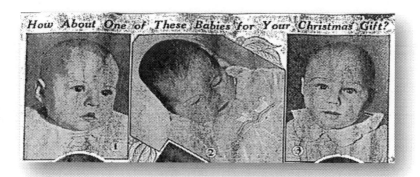

ADVERTISEMENT: EDMONTON JOURNAL (DATE UNKNOWN)

The pensive-looking baby in (1) Leslie, a little Englishmen, born last July 8.

The little laddie taking a nap in (2) is Ernst, a Canadian, born just last month.

Wide-awake, bright as a silver dollar Paul is (3). A Canadian, born last March.

I dedicate this book to my mother, Bernice.

I have no idea of what you had to endure.
I hope you have found peace.

I hope one day ~~you~~ we will find the strength to come together for the first time as mother and son.